LORD, I LOVE YOU!

Volume 2

ADVENT, CHRISTMAS,
MARIAN FEASTS, & SAINTS' DAYS

BENEDICT XVI

LORD, I LOVE YOU!

HOMILIES THROUGH THE LITURGICAL YEAR

Volume 2

ADVENT, CHRISTMAS, MARIAN FEASTS, & SAINTS' DAYS

Edited by Pietro Rossotti

Foreword by Cardinal Seán Patrick O'Malley

THE CATHOLIC UNIVERSITY OF AMERICA PRESS
WASHINGTON, D.C.

The paper used in this publication meets the minimum requirements
of American National Standards for Information Science—
Permanence of Paper for Printed Library Materials, ANSI Z39.48-1992.

Cataloging-in-Publication Data is available at the Library of Congress

ISBN (PAPERBACK): 978-0-8132-3993-4 | ISBN (EBOOK): 978-0-8132-3994-1

The text is set in Dante MT.

CONTENTS

MARIAN SOLEMNITIES AND FEASTS

MARY, MOTHER OF GOD

OUR LADY OF LOURDES

ANNUNCIATION

OUR LADY OF FATIMA

ASSUMPTION

IMMACULATE CONCEPTION

OUR LADY OF GUADALUPE

SAINTS

ST. JOSEPH

STS. PETER AND PAUL

ST. AUGUSTINE

ST. JOHN HENRY NEWMAN

ST. JOHN PAUL II

ALL SAINTS

FOREWORD

Cardinal Seán Patrick O'Malley, OFM, Cap.

Bishops are often invited to preach retreats for religious. In 2004, Mother Shaun Vergauwen, FSE, invited me to give a retreat to their entire community, which would be gathered in Rome for the occasion at the Domus Carmelitana. I was happy to accept; however, I was stunned when she revealed that actually the retreat would have two retreat masters, a sort of Huntley-Brinkley approach, and the other preacher was to be the prefect of the CDF, Cardinal Joseph Ratzinger.

The prospect of having one of the greatest living theologians sitting there listening to my homilies with a red pencil in his hand made me a little nervous. I was trying to get my head around the likely division of labor, namely, that he would give all the good conferences and I would give all the bad conferences. Fortunately, I was saved not by the proverbial bell, but by the white smoke. Before the date of the retreat, Cardinal Joseph Ratzinger was elected pope, taking the name Benedict XVI. In my opening talk to the sisters, I chided the nuns that some people would do anything to get out of preaching their retreat.

St. Francis, in his last Testament, which for the Capuchins is the official commentary on the Rule, urges his friars to honor and venerate all theologians, "those who administer to us the most holy word of God since they administer spirit and life." I like to think that St. Francis had theologians like Ratzinger in mind when he included these instructions for us in his Testament. Like many priests and bishops, I have assiduously read the homilies of Cardinal Ratzinger, later Pope Benedict. From those sermons, I have been able to mine many brilliant insights into the word of God and practical applications of the Gospel to our everyday life. But more than a source of "homily helps," I found inspiration, encouragement to be a better disciple, a better minister of the word, and a better preacher.

When St. Paul VI named him Archbishop of Munich in 1977, the then Father Ratzinger chose as his episcopal motto *Cooperatores Veritatis*; that is, "Coworkers in the Truth." The phrase is taken from the third letter of St. John, where John is congratulating Gaius for welcoming fellow evangelizers. Ratzinger saw his ministry as bishop in terms of welcoming and helping others who work for the truth. It is the motto of a humble, self-effacing man of God.

Cardinal Ratzinger is convinced the truth will make us free, but that the greatest threat to the faith today is the dictatorship of relativism. Responding to some of the excesses of modern exegesis, Cardinal Ratzinger always presents the foundational truth that the Scriptures cannot be adequately understood apart from the Church and its mission and liturgy. He proposes this as an alternative to the exclusive use of the historical critical method, which is often inadequate to explain the religious meaning of the sacred texts. Likewise, this method does not exhibit any capacity to identify the inner unity or inner logic within the Scripture passages. This methodology renders the Bible simply a history book that speaks only of the past rather than the living word of God, which has the power to instill wisdom and change hearts.

It was because of the distortion that Pope Benedict saw in the image of Jesus resulting from an exclusive reliance on historical-critical methods that led Pope Benedict to publish *Jesus of Nazareth*, which is such an important contribution to contemporary theology.

Von Balthasar speaks about *kniende theologie*, "theology on the knees." I believe there is a good description of the theology of Pope Benedict. It is not just the fruit of his inexhaustible intellect or careful study. His theology springs from a deep life of faith and prayer. It is obvious that he has pondered these great truths in his heart before sharing them with others.

The emphasis that Pope Benedict gives to preaching shows the deep pastoral nature of his theological investigations. His writings are to communicate, as St. Francis said, spirit and life.

Father Pietro Rossotti has compiled a masterful collection of Pope Benedict's finest preaching. These reflections are valuable for those who are involved in the preaching ministry, but also for everyone longing to have a deeper encounter with the word of God. Despite his personal brilliance and intellectual prowess, Pope Benedict has the gift of communicating difficult truths in an understandable way. I heard it said that people went to Rome to *see* John Paul II, and they went to Rome to *hear* Pope Benedict XVI. The success of Benedict's writings and preaching is in great part due to his ability to touch people's hearts by the testimony of his faith and love. *Lord, I Love You!* is an apt title for this collection of his sermons.

Benedict is so aware of the power of God's beauty to attract the human heart. His love for music and the liturgy opened up for him a path to experience the source of all beauty and the joy that God's presence instills in the hearts of those who listen to his word and embrace it.

Every Pope brings his own signature contribution to the life of the Church. Benedict gives us a theology that is life-giving, that allows us not just to know about God, but to know God. I have no doubts that in a hundred years, devout Catholics praying the Liturgy of the Hours will find themselves spiritually nourished by reading Benedict's homilies in their breviaries.

INTRODUCTION

Fr. Pietro Rossotti, FSCB

This second volume of *Lord, I love You!* gathers Benedict XVI's main homilies on Advent, Christmas, and various Marian celebrations, as well as a few delivered on specific celebrations in honor of particular saints.[1] There are many common elements throughout the homilies, and each one shows clearly the basic features of Benedict XVI's relationship with the Lord and the Church. In particular there are three facets of Christian faith, so beautifully highlighted by Benedict XVI, that I would like to briefly illustrate as a guide for the reader of this volume.

First and foremost, we can see the centrality of the mystery of the Incarnation in Benedict XVI's exposition of the Christian faith. Benedict XVI strongly re-emphasizes that the Incarnation of the Only Begotten Son is the true turning point in the history of the world. The event of the Incarnation of the Son of God marks the intersection of time and eternity, of past, present, and future time. With the Incarnation, "God's truth has sprung from the earth and justice looks down from heaven, the earth has yielded its fruit."[2] In the Incarnation, "the Son of God wanted to share fully

1. See Benedict XVI, *Lord, I Love You!*, vol. 1 (The Catholic University of America Press, 2025).

2. Benedict XVI, homily, Solemnity of Mary, Mother of God, Saint Peter's Basilica, Sunday, January 1, 2012 (in this volume, p. 91).

in our human condition."[3] In the little child of Bethlehem, whose identity is totally *from* and *for* the Father, we see the fulfillment and realization of what it means for all of us to be children of God.[4] Only when we accept that we are made *from* and *for* Another, called out of Love to love, do we find our fulfillment in imitation of the Eternal Son.

Even more, for Benedict XVI, in the Incarnation "we recognize the origins of the Church."[5] The Child Jesus is the gift of the Father so that through him true communion among people may be established. When we follow Jesus, we "step outside" of ourselves and we "enter the great communal truth, the communion of the one God."[6] The Church begins in the Incarnation, and "every historical realization of the Church and every one of her institutions must be shaped by that primordial wellspring."[7] The Church, as a community of believers, must constantly celebrate the "Emmanuel, God-with-us, through whom the saving will of God the Father has been accomplished."[8] To proceed on the journey of faith means to be children forever, to acknowledge that our origin and destiny are revealed to us in the Incarnate Son whose face we

3. Benedict XVI, homily, First Vespers of the First Sunday of Advent, Saint Peter's Basilica, Saturday, November 29, 2008 (in this volume, p. 9).

4. In my opinion, this is one of the central points of the entire Christological reflection of Joseph Ratzinger (Benedict XVI) so clearly expressed in many of his works. In particular, see Joseph Ratzinger, *Behold the Pierced One* (Ignatius Press, 1986).

5. Benedict XVI, homily, Solemnity of the Annunciation of the Lord, Saint Peter's Square, Saturday, March 25, 2006 (in this volume, p. 121).

6. Benedict XVI, homily, Solemnity of the Nativity of the Lord, Midnight Mass, Saint Peter's Basilica, Thursday, December 24, 2009 (in this volume, p. 28).

7. Benedict XVI, homily, Solemnity of the Annunciation of the Lord, Saint Peter's Square, Saturday, March 25, 2006 (in this volume, p. 121).

8. Benedict XVI, homily, Solemnity of the Annunciation of the Lord, Saint Peter's Square, Saturday, March 25, 2006 (in this volume, p. 121).

must always seek more than anything else. In other words, faith is that fundamental recognition and acknowledgement of Christ as our dominant thought and the center of our existence, just as for Christ the relationship with the Father was the center of His very being. As Benedict XVI so beautifully summarizes: "Jesus is a way that can be travelled, open to everyone."[9] Only in this universal beholding of the Lord is unity among believers possible so that the Church can flourish.

The second fundamental aspect emerging from these homilies is Benedict XVI's constant reference to the foundational Marian dimension of our Catholic faith and tradition.[10] For the German pope, Mary is not just the ideal model and prototype of every Christian's life. In her being both virgin and mother, she sums up the Church's primary vocation of being totally receptive to the action of the Holy Spirit, protector against all heresies and temptations, and fruitful handmaid of the Lord. We as church must put ourselves in the school of the silent Blessed Mother, and with her as guide, must "learn to become attentive and docile disciples of the Lord."[11] Especially in time of trial and persecution, we must learn from "the courageous woman who stood beneath the Cross

9. Benedict XVI, homily, Solemnity of Mary, Mother of God, Saint Peter's Basilica, Sunday, January 1, 2012 (in this volume, p. 91).

10. The reflection upon the Marian dimension of the Christian Faith and tradition is certainly one of the most important aspects of Joseph Ratzinger's (Benedict XVI's) entire theological reflection, and arguably one of his most important contributions to ecclesiology. See, in particular, Ratzinger, *Daughter Zion: Meditations on the Church's Marian Belief* (Ignatius Press, 1983); and H. U. Von Balthasar and Ratzinger, *Mary: The Church at the Source* (Ignatius Press, 2005).

11. Benedict XVI, homily, Solemnity of Mary, Mother of God, Saint Peter's Basilica, Sunday, January 1, 2006 (in this volume, p. 80).

while the disciples fled."[12] Mary is the ever Virgin Mother who carries the Church along "into a living stream in which the faith can rediscover new vigor, in which the Church can be strengthened so as to proclaim the mystery of Christ ever more boldly."[13] Like Mary, "the Church is the mediator of God's blessing for the world: she receives it in receiving Jesus and she transmits it in bearing Jesus."[14] If we forget this foundational Marian dimension of our faith, the Church risks becoming a self-referential institution marred by all sorts of human mistakes, power struggles, and abuses. Our faith in the saving power of the Son, whose body is the Church, can only grow in as much as it is guided by the gentle hands of the Mother.

The third aspect that emerges in these homilies is Benedict XVI's reflection on the meaning of holiness. Following the longstanding tradition of the Church, and in particular the recent magisterial teaching of the Second Vatican Council, Benedict XVI emphasizes that holiness is the fundamental vocation of all the baptized. The Christian reaches holiness only when faith blossoms and envelops the whole of the person: reason and will, thoughts and feeling. The goal of faith is to center one's own existence on Jesus Christ. Indeed, Christian life is "a call to holiness, experienced as the profound desire of the human heart to enter into intimate communion with the Heart of God."[15] The journey of faith is "based on a certainty, on

12. Benedict XVI, homily, Solemnity of the Immaculate Conception of the Blessed Virgin Mary, St. Peter's Basilica, Thursday, December 8, 2005 (in this volume, p. 157).

13. Benedict XVI, homily, Mass on the 150th Anniversary of the Apparitions of the Blessed Virgin Mother at Lourdes, Lourdes, Sunday, September 14, 2008 (in this volume, p. 107).

14. Benedict XVI, homily, Solemnity of Mary, Mother of God, Saint Peter's Basilica, Sunday, January 1, 2012 (in this volume, p. 88).

15. Benedict XVI, homily, Mass with the Beatification of Venerable John Henry Newman, Cofton Park of Rednal, Birmingham, Sunday, September 19, 2010 (in this volume, p. 248–49).

the experience that there is nothing greater than knowing Christ and communicating friendship with him to others; only in this friendship is the enormous potential of the human condition truly revealed, and we can experience what is beautiful and sets us free."[16] The source and summit of holiness is, therefore, friendship with the Lord lived within the communion of the Church. We must seek this friendship even though we are sinners in constant need of conversion, which is "the grace to return to him with [our] whole heart, to belong totally to him."[17] This vocation to holiness, like any friendship, "demands a constant effort"; however, "it is possible for everyone because, rather than a human effort, it is first and foremost a gift of God."[18] For this reason, as a necessity, to grow in holiness, to grow in faith, to become more Christlike, we must enter into the habit of prayer. The example of the saints is a constant reminder that faithful prayer transforms us, and following them encourages us to "experience the joy of those who trust in God."[19]

I hope that the reading of these homilies can help all of us grow in faith and guide many people into a deeper love and knowledge of the Lord following the profound example of faith lived by Benedict XVI.

16. Benedict XVI, homily, Feast of the Baptism of the Lord, Sistine Chapel, Sunday, January 13, 2013 (in this volume, p. 73).

17. Benedict XVI, homily, Feast of the Baptism of the Lord, Sistine Chapel, Sunday, January 13, 2013 (in this volume, p. 71).

18. Benedict XVI, homily, Solemnity of All Saints, Saint Peter's Basilica, Wednesday, November 1, 2006 (in this volume, p. 291).

19. Benedict XVI, homily, Solemnity of All Saints, Saint Peter's Basilica, Wednesday, November 1, 2006 (in this volume, p.291).

The texts in this collection are based on the English texts available on the Vatican website, with only minor modifications to aid the reader. In particular, greetings and concluding blessings in the spoken texts have been omitted. American spellings have been adopted, and citations have been moved to footnotes. The selection, division, titles, and order of texts in the different chapters are mine, as Pope Benedict XVI never intended or set out to produce such a collection. Although I have attempted to avoid repetitions of themes, there is some overlapping.

I dedicate this small effort to the memory of the late Pope Benedict XVI, with immense gratitude for his teaching and preaching as the supreme head of the Catholic Church. I hope that this volume can help all the faithful, and especially bishops, priests, and deacons, to appreciate the importance of homiletics in our Catholic tradition. Moreover, I hope that this volume can be a useful companion on the journey of life for many people who continue to find Benedict XVI's words a bright light of Christian hope in our times.

The Saint Paul Seminary
Saint Paul, MN
February 22, 2025
Feast of the Chair of St. Peter the Apostle

ADVENT

1. *The Coming of the Lord*

From the Homily of His Holiness Pope Benedict XVI
First Vespers of the First Sunday of Advent
Saint Peter's Basilica, Saturday, 26 November 2005

With the celebration of First Vespers of the First Sunday in Advent, we are beginning a new liturgical year. In singing the Psalms together, we have raised our hearts to God, placing ourselves in the spiritual attitude that marks this season of grace: "vigilance in prayer" and "exultation in praise."[1]

Taking as our model Mary Most Holy, who teaches us to live by devoutly listening to the Word of God, let us reflect on the short Bible reading just proclaimed. It consists of two verses contained in the concluding part of the First Letter of St. Paul to the Thessalonians (1 Thes 5:23–24). The first expresses the Apostle's greeting to the community: the second offers, as it were, the guarantee of its fulfilment.

The hope expressed is that each one may be made holy by God and preserved irreproachable in his entire person—"spirit, soul, and body"—for the final coming of the Lord Jesus; the guarantee that this can happen is offered by the faithfulness of God himself, who will not fail to bring to completion the work he has begun in believers.

1. "Preface II of Advent," in *The Roman Missal*, 3rd typical ed. (United States Conference of Catholic Bishops, 2011), sec. 34, 536.

This First Letter to the Thessalonians is the first of all St. Paul's letters, written probably in the year 51. In this first letter we can feel, more than in the others, the Apostle's pulsating heart, his paternal, indeed we can say maternal, love for this new community. And we also feel his anxious concern that the faith of this new Church not die, surrounded as she was by a cultural context in many regards in opposition to the faith. Thus, Paul ends his letter with a hope, or we might almost say with a prayer. The content of the prayer we have heard is that they [the Thessalonians] should be holy and irreproachable to the moment of the Lord's coming. The central word of this prayer is "coming." We should ask ourselves, what does "coming of the Lord" mean? In Greek it is "*Parousia*," in Latin "*adventus*," "advent," "coming." What is this "coming"? Does it involve us or not?

To understand the meaning of this word, hence, of the Apostle's prayer for this community and for communities of all times—also for us—we must look at the person through whom the coming of the Lord was uniquely brought about: the Virgin Mary. Mary belonged to that part of the People of Israel who in Jesus's time were waiting with heartfelt expectation for the Savior's coming. And from the words and acts recounted in the Gospel, we can see how she truly lived steeped in the Prophets' words; she entirely expected the Lord's coming. She could not, however, have imagined how this coming would be brought about. Perhaps she expected a coming in glory. The moment when the Archangel Gabriel entered her house and told her that the Lord, the Savior, wanted to take flesh in her, wanted to bring about his coming through her, must have been all the more surprising to her. We can imagine the Virgin's apprehension. Mary, with a tremendous act of faith and obedience, said "yes": "I am the servant of the Lord." And so it was that she became the "dwelling place" of the Lord, a true "temple" in the world and a "door" through which the Lord entered upon the earth.

We have said that this coming was unique: "the" coming of the Lord. Yet there is not only the final coming at the end of time: in a certain sense the Lord always wants to come through us. And he knocks at the door of our hearts: are you willing to give me your flesh, your time, your life? This is the voice of the Lord who also wants to enter our epoch, he wants to enter human life through us. He also seeks a living dwelling place in our personal lives. This is the coming of the Lord. Let us once again learn this in the season of Advent: The Lord can also come among us.

Therefore we can say that this prayer, this hope, expressed by the Apostle, contains a fundamental truth that he seeks to inculcate in the faithful of the community he founded and that we can sum up as follows: God calls us to communion with him, which will be completely fulfilled in the return of Christ, and he himself strives to ensure that we will arrive prepared for this final and decisive encounter. The future is, so to speak, contained in the present, or better, in the presence of God himself, who in his unfailing love does not leave us on our own or abandon us even for an instant, just as a father and mother never stop caring for their children while they are growing up. Before Christ who comes, men and women are defined in the whole of their being, which the Apostle sums up in the words "spirit, soul, and body," thereby indicating the whole of the human person as a unit with somatic, psychic, and spiritual dimensions. Sanctification is God's gift and his project, but human beings are called to respond with their entire being without excluding any part of themselves.

It is the Holy Spirit himself who formed in the Virgin's womb Jesus, the perfect man, who brings God's marvelous plan to completion in the human person, first of all by transforming the heart and from this center, all the rest. Thus, the entire work of creation and redemption which God, Father and Son and Holy Spirit, continues to bring about, from the beginning to the end of the cosmos and of history, is summed up in every individual person. And since the first coming of Christ is at the center of the history of humanity and at its end, his glorious return, so every personal existence is called to be measured against him—in a mysterious and multiform way—during the earthly pilgrimage, in order to be found "in him" at the moment of his return.

May Mary Most Holy, the faithful Virgin, guide us to make this time of Advent and of the whole new liturgical year a path of genuine sanctification, to the praise and glory of God, Father, Son, and Holy Spirit.

2. *The "Color" of Hope*

From the Homily of His Holiness Pope Benedict XVI
First Vespers of the First Sunday of Advent
Saint Peter's Basilica, Saturday, 29 November 2008

With this evening liturgy, we begin the itinerary of a new liturgical year, entering into the first of its seasons: Advent. In the biblical reading that we have just heard, taken from the First Letter to the Thessalonians, the Apostle Paul uses precisely this word: "coming," which in Greek is *parusia* and *adventus* in Latin (1 Thes 5:23). According to the common tradition of this text, Paul urges the Christians of Thessalonica to keep themselves blameless "*for* the coming" of the Lord. However, in the original text one reads "*in* the coming" (*ἐν τῇ παρουσίᾳ*), almost as if the advent of the Lord were, more so than a future point in time, a spiritual place in which to walk already in the present, while waiting, and in which one is indeed perfectly preserved in every personal dimension. In fact, it is exactly this that we live out in the liturgy. By celebrating the liturgical seasons, we actualize the mystery—in this case, the Lord's coming—as it were "walking in it" towards its full realization at the end of time, but already drawing sanctifying virtue from it, since the last times have already begun with Christ's death and Resurrection.

The word that sums up this particular state, in which one awaits something that is to be manifested but of which one also already has a glimpse and a foretaste, is "hope." Advent is the spiritual season of hope par excellence, and in it the whole Church is called to become hope, for herself and for the world. The whole organism of the Mystical Body acquires, so to speak, the "color" of hope. The whole People of God continue on their journey, attracted by this mystery: that our God is "the God who comes" and calls us to go to meet him. How? In the first place, in that universal form of hope and expectation which is prayer, which is eminently expressed in the Psalms, human words in which God himself has placed and continually places the invocation of his coming on the lips and in the hearts of believers. Let us therefore reflect for a few moments on two of his Psalms which we have just prayed, and which are consecutive in the biblical Book: Psalms 141 and 142, according to the Jewish numbering. "I have called to you, Lord; hasten to help me! / Hear my voice, when I cry to you. / Let my prayer arise before you like incense, / the raising of my hands like an evening oblation" (Ps 141[140]:1–2). Thus begins the first Psalm of the First Vespers for the first week of the Psalter: words which, at the beginning of Advent, acquire a new "color," because the Holy Spirit makes them resound ever anew within us in the Church on her way between the time of God and human times. "Lord, hasten to help me!" It is the cry of someone who feels he is in grave danger, but it is also the cry of the Church amid the many dangers that surround her, that threaten her holiness, that irreproachable integrity of which the Apostle Paul speaks, which must instead be preserved for the coming of the Lord. And in this invocation, the cry of all the just also resounds, of all those who want to resist evil, the seduction of an iniquitous well-being, of pleasures offensive to human dignity and to the condition of the poor. At the beginning of Advent, the Church's liturgy once again makes this cry her own, and raises it to God "like incense" (v. 2). The evening offering of incense is in fact a symbol of prayer, of the outpouring of hearts turned to God, to the Most High, as well as "the raising of . . . hands like an evening oblation" (v. 2). Material sacrifices, as it also took place in the Jewish temple, are no longer offered in the Church, but the spiritual offering of prayer is raised, joined to that of Jesus Christ who is at the same time Sacrifice and Priest of the new and eternal covenant. In the cry of the Mystical Body, we recognize the very voice of the Head: the Son of God who has taken upon himself our trials and our temptations, to give us the grace of his victory.

This identification of Christ with the Psalmist is particularly evident in the second Psalm (142). Here, every word, every invocation, makes one think of Jesus in his passion, and in particular of his prayer to the Father in Gethsemane. In his first coming, with the Incarnation, the Son of God wanted to share fully in our human condition. Of course, he did not share in sin, but for our salvation suffered all its consequences. In praying Psalm 142, the Church relives every time the grace of this compassion, of this "coming" of the Son of God in human anguish so deeply as to plumb its depths. The Advent cry of hope then expresses, from the outset and very powerfully, the full gravity of our state, of our extreme need for salvation. It is as if to say: we await the Lord not in the same way as a beautiful decoration upon a world already saved, but as the only way of liberation from a mortal danger and we know that he himself, the Liberator, had to suffer and die to bring us out of this prison (cf. v. 8).

In short, these two Psalms shelter us from any temptation to escape or flee from reality; they preserve us from a false hope that might desire to enter Advent and move towards Christmas forgetting the tragedy of our personal and collective existence. In fact, a trustworthy hope that is not deceptive can only be a "Paschal" hope, as the canticle of the Letter to the Philippians reminds us every Saturday evening, with which we praise the Incarnate Christ, crucified, risen, and our universal Lord. Let us turn our gaze and our heart to him, in spiritual union with the Virgin Mary, Our Lady of Advent. Let us place our hand in hers and enter joyfully into this new time of grace that God gives as a gift to his Church for the good of all humanity. Like Mary and with her maternal help, let us make ourselves docile to the action of the Holy Spirit, so that the God of peace may sanctify us totally, and the Church become a sign and instrument of hope for all men. Amen.

3. *The Favorable Opportunity*

From the Homily of His Holiness Pope Benedict XVI
First Vespers of the First Sunday of Advent
Saint Peter's Basilica, Saturday, 28 November 2009

With this celebration, we are entering the liturgical season of Advent. In the biblical reading we have just heard, taken from the First Letter to the Thessalonians, the Apostle Paul invites us to prepare for "the coming of our Lord Jesus Christ" (5:23), with God's grace keeping ourselves blameless. The exact word Paul uses is "coming," in Latin *adventus*, from which the term "Advent" derives. Let us reflect briefly on the meaning of this word, which can be rendered as "presence," "arrival," or "coming." In the language of the ancient world, it was a technical term used to indicate the arrival of an official or the visit of the king or emperor to a province. However, it could also mean the coming of the divinity that emerges from concealment to manifest himself forcefully or that was celebrated as being present in worship. Christians used the word "advent" to express their relationship with Jesus Christ: Jesus is the King who entered this poor "province" called "earth" to pay everyone a visit; he makes all those who believe in him participate in his Coming, all who believe in his presence in the liturgical assembly. The essential meaning of the word *adventus* was: God is here, he has not withdrawn from the world, he has not deserted us. Even if we cannot see and touch him as we can tangible realities, he is here and comes to visit us in many ways.

The meaning of the expression "advent" therefore includes that of *visitatio*, which simply and specifically means "visit"; in this case it is a question of a visit from God: he enters my life and wishes to speak to me. In our daily lives we all experience having little time for the Lord and also little time for ourselves. We end by being absorbed in "doing." Is it not true that activities often absorb us and that society with its multiple interests monopolizes our attention? Is it not true that we devote a lot of time to entertainment and to various kinds of amusement? At times we get carried away. Advent, this powerful liturgical season that we are beginning, invites us to pause in silence to understand a presence. It is an invitation to understand that the individual events of the day are hints that God is giving us, signs of the attention he has for each one of us. How often does God give us a glimpse of his love! To keep, as it were, an "interior journal" of this love would be a beautiful and salutary task for our life! Advent invites and stimulates us to contemplate the Lord present. Should not the certainty of his presence help us see the world with different eyes? Should it not help us to consider the whole of our life as a "visit," as a way in which he can come to us and become close to us in every situation?

Another fundamental element of Advent is expectation, an expectation which is at the same time hope. Advent impels us to understand the meaning of time and of history as a *kairós*, as a favorable opportunity for our salvation. Jesus illustrated this mysterious reality in many parables: in the story of the servants sent to await the return of their master; in the parable of the virgins who await the bridegroom; and in those of the sower and of the harvest. In their lives, human beings are constantly waiting: when they are children they want to grow up, as adults they are striving for fulfilment and success and, as they advance in age, they look forward to the rest they deserve. However, the time comes when they find they have hoped too little if, over and above their profession or social position, there is nothing left to hope for. Hope marks humanity's journey, but for Christians it is enlivened by a certainty: the Lord is present in the passage of our lives; he accompanies us and will one day also dry our tears. One day, not far off, everything will find its fulfilment in the Kingdom of God, a kingdom of justice and peace.

However, there are many different ways of waiting. If time is not filled by a present endowed with meaning, expectation risks becoming unbearable; if one expects something but at a given moment there is nothing—in other words, if the present remains empty—every instant that passes appears extremely long and waiting becomes too heavy a burden because the future remains completely uncertain. On the other hand, when time is endowed with meaning and at every instant we perceive something specific and worthwhile, it is then that the joy of expectation makes the present more precious. Dear brothers and sisters, let us experience intensely the present in which we already receive the gifts of the Lord, let us live it focused on the future, a future charged with hope. In this manner, Christian Advent becomes an opportunity to reawaken within ourselves the true meaning of waiting, returning to the heart of our faith which is the mystery of Christ, the Messiah who was expected for long centuries and was born in poverty, in Bethlehem. In coming among us, he brought us and continues to offer us the gift of his love and his salvation. Present among us, he speaks to us in many ways: in Sacred Scripture, in the liturgical year, in the saints, in the events of daily life, in the whole of the creation whose aspect changes according to whether Christ is behind it or whether he is obscured by the fog of an uncertain origin and an uncertain future. We in turn may speak to him, presenting to him the suffering that afflicts us, our impatience, the questions that well up in our hearts. We may be sure that he always listens to us! And if Jesus is present, there is no longer any time that lacks meaning or is empty. If he is present, we may continue to hope, even when others can no longer assure us of any support, even when the present becomes trying.

Dear friends, Advent is the season of the presence and expectation of the eternal. For this very reason, it is in a particular way a period of joy, an interiorized joy that no suffering can diminish. It is joy in the fact that God made himself a Child. This joy, invisibly present within us, encourages us to journey on with confidence. A model and support of this deep joy is the Virgin Mary, through whom we were given the Infant Jesus. May she, a faithful disciple of her Son, obtain for us the grace of living this liturgical season alert and hardworking, while we wait. Amen!

CHRISTMAS SEASON

CHRISTMAS

4. *God's Simplicity*

From the Homily of His Holiness Pope Benedict XVI
Solemnity of the Nativity of the Lord, Midnight Mass
Saint Peter's Basilica, Sunday, 24 December 2006

We have just heard in the Gospel the message given by the angels to the shepherds during that Holy Night, a message which the Church now proclaims to us: "To you is born this day in the city of David a Savior, who is Christ the Lord. And this will be a sign for you: you will find a babe wrapped in swaddling clothes and lying in a manger" (Lk 2:11–12). Nothing miraculous, nothing extraordinary, nothing magnificent is given to the shepherds as a sign. All they will see is a child wrapped in swaddling clothes, one who, like all children, needs a mother's care; a child born in a stable, who therefore lies not in a cradle but in a manger. God's sign is the baby in need of help and in poverty. Only in their hearts will the shepherds be able to see that this baby fulfils the promise of the prophet Isaiah, which we heard in the first reading: "For to us a child is born, to us a son is given; and the government will be upon his shoulder" (Is 9:5). Exactly the same sign has been given to us. We too are invited by the angel of God, through the message of the Gospel, to set out in our hearts to see the child lying in the manger.

God's sign is simplicity. God's sign is the baby. God's sign is that he makes himself small for us. This is how he reigns. He does not come with power and outward splendor. He comes as a baby—defenseless and in need of our help. He does not want to overwhelm us with his strength. He takes away our fear of his greatness. He asks for our love: so he makes himself a child. He wants nothing other from us than our love, through which we spontaneously learn to enter into his feelings, his thoughts and his will—we learn to live with him and to practice with him that humility of renunciation that belongs to the very essence of love. God made himself small so that we could understand him, welcome him, and love him. The Fathers of the Church, in their Greek translation of the Old Testament, found a passage from the prophet Isaiah that Paul also quotes in order to show how God's new ways had already been foretold in the Old Testament. There we read: "God made his Word short, he abbreviated it" (Is 10:23; Rom 9:28). The Fathers interpreted this in two ways. The Son himself is the Word, the Logos; the eternal Word became small—small enough to fit into a manger. He became a child, so that the Word could be grasped by us. In this way God teaches us to love the little ones. In this way he teaches us to love the weak. In this way he teaches us respect for children. The child of Bethlehem directs our gaze towards all children who suffer and are abused in the world, the born and the unborn. Towards children who are placed as soldiers in a violent world; towards children who have to beg; towards children who suffer deprivation and hunger; towards children who are unloved. In all of these it is the Child of Bethlehem who is crying out to us; it is the God who has become small who appeals to us. Let us pray this night that the brightness of God's love may enfold all these children. Let us ask God to help us do our part so that the dignity of children may be respected.

May they all experience the light of love, which mankind needs so much more than the material necessities of life.

And so we come to the second meaning that the Fathers saw in the phrase: "God made his Word short." The Word which God speaks to us in Sacred Scripture had become long in the course of the centuries. It became long and complex, not just for the simple and unlettered, but even more so for those versed in Sacred Scripture, for the experts who evidently became entangled in details and in particular problems, almost to the extent of losing an overall perspective. Jesus "abbreviated" the Word—he showed us once more its deeper simplicity and unity. Everything taught by the Law and the Prophets is summed up—he says—in the command: "You shall love the Lord your God with all your heart, and with all your soul, and with all your mind. . . . You shall love your neighbor as yourself" (Mt 22:37–40). This is everything—the whole faith is contained in this one act of love which embraces God and humanity. Yet now further questions arise: how are we to love God with all our mind, when our intellect can barely reach him? How are we to love him with all our heart and soul, when our heart can only catch a glimpse of him from afar, when there are so many contradictions in the world that would hide his face from us? This is where the two ways in which God has "abbreviated" his Word come together. He is no longer distant. He is no longer unknown. He is no longer beyond the reach of our heart. He has become a child for us, and in so doing he has dispelled all doubt. He has become our neighbor, restoring in this way the image of man, whom we often find so hard to love. For us, God has become a gift. He has given himself. He has entered time for us. He who is the Eternal One, above time, has assumed our time and raised it to himself on high. Christmas has become the Feast of gifts in imitation of God who has given himself to us. Let us allow our heart, our soul, and our mind to be touched by this fact! Among the many gifts that we buy and receive, let us not forget the true gift: to give each other something of ourselves, to give each other something of our time, to open our time to God. In this way anxiety disappears, joy is born, and the feast is created. During the festive meals of these days, let us remember the Lord's words: "When you give a dinner or a banquet, do not invite those who will invite you in return, but invite those whom no one invites and who are not able to invite you" (Lk 14:12–14). This also means: when you give gifts for Christmas, do not give only to those who will give to you in return, but give to those who receive from no one and who cannot give you anything back. This is what God has done: he invites us to his wedding feast, something which we cannot reciprocate, but can only receive with joy. Let us imitate him! Let us love God and, starting from him, let us also love man, so that, starting from man, we can then rediscover God in a new way!

And so, finally, we find yet a third meaning in the saying that the Word became "brief" and "small." The shepherds were told that they would find the child in a manger for animals, who were the rightful occupants of the stable. Reading Isaiah (1:3), the Fathers concluded that beside the manger of Bethlehem there stood an ox and an ass. At the same time, they interpreted the text as symbolizing the Jews and the pagans—and thus all humanity—who each in their own way have need of a Savior: the God who became a child. Man, in order to live, needs bread, the fruit of the earth and of his labor. But he does not live by bread alone. He needs nourishment for his soul: he needs meaning that can fill his life.

Thus, for the Fathers, the manger of the animals became the symbol of the altar, on which lies the Bread which is Christ himself: the true food for our hearts.

Once again we see how he became small: in the humble appearance of the host, in a small piece of bread, he gives us himself. All this is conveyed by the sign that was given to the shepherds and is given also to us: the child born for us, the child in whom God became small for us. Let us ask the Lord to grant us the grace of looking upon the crib this night with the simplicity of the shepherds, so as to receive the joy with which they returned home (Lk 2:20). Let us ask him to give us the humility and the faith with which Saint Joseph looked upon the child that Mary had conceived by the Holy Spirit. Let us ask the Lord to let us look upon him with that same love with which Mary saw him. And let us pray that in this way the light that the shepherds saw will shine upon us too, and that what the angels sang that night will be accomplished throughout the world: "Glory to God in the highest, and on earth peace among men with whom he is pleased." Amen!

5. *God's Ways*

From the Homily of His Holiness Pope Benedict XVI
Solemnity of the Nativity of the Lord, Midnight Mass
Saint Peter's Basilica, Tuesday, 25 December 2007

"The time came for Mary to be delivered. And she gave birth to her first-born son and wrapped him in swaddling clothes, and laid him in a manger, because there was no room for them in the inn" (Lk 2:6f.). These words touch our hearts every time we hear them.

This was the moment that the angel had foretold at Nazareth: "you will bear a son, and you shall call his name Jesus. He will be great and will be called the Son of the Most High" (Lk 1:31). This was the moment that Israel had been awaiting for centuries, through many dark hours—the moment that all mankind was somehow awaiting, in terms as yet ill-defined: when God would take care of us, when he would step outside his concealment, when the world would be saved and God would renew all things. We can imagine the kind of interior preparation, the kind of love with which Mary approached that hour. The brief phrase "She wrapped him in swaddling clothes" allows us to glimpse something of the holy joy and the silent zeal of that preparation. The swaddling clothes were ready, so that the child could be given a fitting welcome. Yet there is no room at the inn. In some way, mankind is awaiting God, waiting for him to draw near. But when the moment comes, there is no room for him. Man is so preoccupied with himself, he has such urgent need of all the space and all the time for his own things, that nothing remains for others—for his neighbor, for the poor, for God. And the richer men become, the more they fill up all the space by themselves. And the less room there is for others.

Saint John, in his Gospel, went to the heart of the matter, giving added depth to Saint Luke's brief account of the situation in Bethlehem: "He came to his own home, and his own people received him not" (Jn 1:11). This refers first and foremost to Bethlehem: The Son of David comes to his own city, but has to be born in a stable, because there is no room for him at the inn. Then it refers to Israel: the one who is sent comes among his own, but they do not want him. And truly, it refers to all mankind: he through whom the world was made, the primordial Creator-Word, enters into the world, but he is not listened to, he is not received.

These words refer ultimately to us, to each individual and to society as a whole. Do we have time for our neighbor who is in need of a word from us, from me, or in need of my affection? For the sufferer who is in need of help? For the fugitive or the refugee who is seeking asylum? Do we have time and space for God? Can he enter into our lives? Does he find room in us, or have we occupied all the available space in our thoughts, our actions, our lives for ourselves?

Thank God, this negative detail is not the only one, nor the last one that we find in the Gospel. Just as in Luke we encounter the maternal love of Mary and the fidelity of Saint Joseph, the vigilance of the shepherds and their great joy, just as in Matthew we encounter the visit of the wise men, come from afar, so too John says to us: "To all who received him, he gave power to become children of God" (Jn 1:12). There are those who receive him, and thus, beginning with the stable, with the outside, there grows silently the new house, the new city, the new world. The message of Christmas makes us recognize the darkness of a closed world, and thereby no doubt illustrates a reality that we see daily. Yet it also tells us that God does not allow himself to be shut out. He finds a space, even if it means entering through the stable; there are people who see his light and pass it on. Through the word of the Gospel, the angel also speaks to us, and in the sacred liturgy the light of the Redeemer enters our lives. Whether we are shepherds or "wise men"—the light and its message call us to set out, to leave the narrow circle of our desires and interests, to go out to meet the Lord and worship him. We worship him by opening the world to truth, to good, to Christ, to the service of those who are marginalized and in whom he awaits us.

In some Christmas scenes from the late Middle Ages and the early modern period, the stable is depicted as a crumbling palace. It is still possible to recognize its former splendor, but now it has become a ruin, the walls are falling down—in fact, it has become a stable. Although it lacks any historical basis, this metaphorical interpretation nevertheless expresses something of the truth that is hidden in the mystery of Christmas. David's throne, which had been promised to last forever, stands empty. Others rule over the Holy Land. Joseph, the descendant of David, is a simple artisan; the palace, in fact, has become a hovel. David himself had begun life as a shepherd. When Samuel sought him out in order to anoint him, it seemed impossible and absurd that a shepherd-boy such as he could become the bearer of the promise of Israel. In the stable of Bethlehem, the very town where it had all begun, the Davidic kingship started again in a new way—in that child wrapped in swaddling clothes and laid in a manger. The new throne from which this David will draw the world to himself is the Cross. The new throne—the Cross—corresponds to the new beginning in the stable. Yet this is exactly how the true Davidic palace, the true kingship, is being built. This new palace is so different from what people imagine a palace and royal power ought to be like. It is the community of those who allow themselves to be drawn by Christ's love and so become one body with him, a new humanity. The power that comes from the Cross, the power of self-giving goodness—this is the true kingship. The stable becomes a palace—and setting out from this starting point, Jesus builds the great new community, whose keyword the angels sing at the hour of his birth:

"Glory to God in the highest, and peace on earth to those whom he loves"—those who place their will in his, in this way becoming men of God, new men, a new world.

Gregory of Nyssa, in his Christmas homilies, developed the same vision setting out from the Christmas message in the Gospel of John: "He pitched his tent among us" (Jn 1:14). Gregory applies this passage about the tent to the tent of our body, which has become worn out and weak, exposed everywhere to pain and suffering. And he applies it to the whole universe, torn and disfigured by sin. What would he say if he could see the state of the world today, through the abuse of energy and its selfish and reckless exploitation? Anselm of Canterbury, in an almost prophetic way, once described a vision of what we witness today in a polluted world whose future is at risk: "Everything was as if dead, and had lost its dignity, having been made for the service of those who praise God. The elements of the world were oppressed, they had lost their splendor because of the abuse of those who enslaved them for their idols, for whom they had not been created."[1] Thus, according to Gregory's vision, the stable in the Christmas message represents the ill-treated world. What Christ rebuilds is no ordinary palace. He came to restore beauty and dignity to creation, to the universe: this is what began at Christmas and makes the angels rejoice. The Earth is restored to good order by virtue of the fact that it is opened up to God, it obtains its true light anew, and in the harmony between human will and divine will, in the unification of height and depth, it regains its beauty and dignity. Thus, Christmas is a feast of restored creation. It is in this context that the Fathers interpret the song of the angels

1. Anselm of Canterbury, *Orationes*, *Patrologiae Cursus Completus*, Patrologia Latina (PL), ed. Jacques P. Migne (Paris: 1844–1864), 158:955f.

on that holy night: it is an expression of joy over the fact that the height and the depth, Heaven and Earth, are once more united; that man is again united to God. According to the Fathers, part of the angels' Christmas song is the fact that now angels and men can sing together and in this way the beauty of the universe is expressed in the beauty of the song of praise. Liturgical song—still according to the Fathers—possesses its own peculiar dignity through the fact that it is sung together with the celestial choirs. It is the encounter with Jesus Christ that makes us capable of hearing the song of the angels, thus creating the real music that fades away when we lose this singing-with and hearing-with.

In the stable at Bethlehem, Heaven and Earth meet. Heaven has come down to Earth. For this reason, a light shines from the stable for all times; for this reason, joy is enkindled there; for this reason, singing is born there. At the end of our Christmas meditation, I should like to quote a remarkable passage from Saint Augustine. Interpreting the invocation in the Lord's Prayer: "Our Father who art in Heaven," he asks: what is this—Heaven? And where is Heaven? Then comes a surprising response: ". . . who art in Heaven—that means: in the saints and in the just. Yes, the heavens are the highest bodies in the universe, but they are still bodies, which cannot exist except in a given location. Yet if we believe that God is located in the heavens, meaning in the highest parts of the world, then the birds would be more fortunate than we, since they would live closer to God. Yet it is not written: 'The Lord is close to those who dwell on the heights or on the mountains,' but rather: 'the Lord is close to the brokenhearted' (Ps 34:18[33:19]), an expression which refers to humility. Just as the sinner is called 'Earth,' so by contrast the just man can be called 'Heaven.'"[2] Heaven does not belong to the geography of space, but to the geography of the heart. And the heart of God, during the Holy Night, stooped down to the stable: the humility of God is Heaven. And if we approach this humility, then we touch Heaven. Then the Earth too is made new. With the humility of the shepherds, let us set out, during this Holy Night, towards the Child in the stable! Let us touch God's humility, God's heart! Then his joy will touch us and will make the world more radiant. Amen.

6. *The Lord is Here*

From the Homily of His Holiness Pope Benedict XVI
Solemnity of the Nativity of the Lord, Midnight Mass
Saint Peter's Basilica, Thursday, 24 December 2009

"A child is born for us, a son is given to us" (Is 9:5). What Isaiah prophesied as he gazed into the future from afar, consoling Israel amid its trials and its darkness, is now proclaimed to the shepherds as a present reality by the Angel, from whom a cloud of light streams forth: "To you is born this day in the city of David a Savior, who is Christ the Lord" (Lk 2:11). The Lord is here. From this moment, God is truly "God with us." No longer is he the distant God who can in some way be perceived from afar, in creation and in our own consciousness. He has entered the world. He is close to us. The words of the risen Christ to his followers are addressed also to us: "Lo, I am with you always, to the close of the age" (Mt 28:20). For you the Savior is born: through the Gospel and those who

2. Augustine, *De Sermone Domini in Monte, Patrologiae Cursus Completus*, PL 2:5, 17.

proclaim it, God now reminds us of the message that the Angel announced to the shepherds. It is a message that cannot leave us indifferent. If it is true, it changes everything. If it is true, it also affects me. Like the shepherds, then, I too must say: Come on, I want to go to Bethlehem to see the Word that has occurred there. The story of the shepherds is included in the Gospel for a reason. They show us the right way to respond to the message that we too have received. What is it that these first witnesses of God's incarnation have to tell us?

The first thing we are told about the shepherds is that they were on the watch—they could hear the message precisely because they were awake. We must be awake, so that we can hear the message. We must become truly vigilant people. What does this mean? The principal difference between someone dreaming and someone awake is that the dreamer is in a world of his own. His "self" is locked into this dreamworld that is his alone and does not connect him with others. To wake up means to leave that private world of one's own and to enter the common reality, the truth that alone can unite all people. Conflict and lack of reconciliation in the world stem from the fact that we are locked into our own interests and opinions, into our own little private world. Selfishness, both individual and collective, makes us prisoners of our interests and our desires that stand against the truth and separate us from one another. Awake, the Gospel tells us. Step outside, so as to enter the great communal truth, the communion of the one God. To awake, then, means to develop a receptivity for God: for the silent promptings with which he chooses to guide us; for the many indications of his presence. There are people who describe themselves as "religiously tone deaf." The gift of a capacity to perceive God seems as if it is withheld from some. And indeed—our way of thinking and acting, the mentality of today's world, the whole range of our experience is inclined to deaden our receptivity for God, to make us "tone deaf" towards him. And yet in every soul, the desire for God, the capacity to encounter him, is present, whether in a hidden way or overtly. In order to arrive at this vigilance, this awakening to what is essential, we should pray for ourselves and for others, for those who appear "tone deaf" and yet in whom there is a keen desire for God to manifest himself. The great theologian Origen said this: if I had the grace to see as Paul saw, I could even now (during the Liturgy) contemplate a great host of angels.[3] And indeed, in the sacred liturgy, we are surrounded by the angels of God and the saints. The Lord himself is present in our midst. Lord, open the eyes of our hearts, so that we may become vigilant and clear-sighted, in this way bringing you close to others as well!

Let us return to the Christmas Gospel. It tells us that after listening to the Angel's message, the shepherds said one to another: "'Let us go over to Bethlehem' . . . they went at once" (Lk 2:15f.). "They made haste" is literally what the Greek text says. What had been announced to them was so important that they had to go immediately. In fact, what had been said to them was utterly out of the ordinary. It changed the world. The Savior is born. The long-awaited Son of David has come into the world in his own city. What could be more important? No doubt they were partly driven by curiosity, but first and foremost it was their excitement at the wonderful news that had been conveyed to them, of all people, to the little ones, to the seemingly unimportant. They made

3. Cf. Origen, *Homilies on Luke*, trans. Joseph T. Lienhard, The Fathers of the Church 94 (The Catholic University of America Press, 2009), 23:9.

haste—they went at once. In our daily life, it is not like that. For most people, the things of God are not given priority, they do not impose themselves on us directly. And so the great majority of us tend to postpone them. First, we do what seems urgent here and now. In the list of priorities, God is often more or less at the end. We can always deal with that later, we tend to think. The Gospel tells us: God is the highest priority. If anything in our life deserves haste without delay, then, it is God's work alone. The Rule of Saint Benedict contains this teaching: "Place nothing at all before the work of God (i.e., the divine office)."[4] For monks, the Liturgy is the first priority. Everything else comes later. In its essence, though, this saying applies to everyone. God is important, by far the most important thing in our lives. The shepherds teach us this priority. From them we should learn not to be crushed by all the pressing matters in our daily lives. From them we should learn the inner freedom to put other tasks in second place—however important they may be—so as to make our way towards God, to allow him into our lives and into our time. Time given to God and, in his name, to our neighbor is never time lost. It is the time when we are most truly alive, when we live our humanity to the full.

Some commentators point out that the shepherds, the simple souls, were the first to come to Jesus in the manger and to encounter the Redeemer of the world. The wise men from the East, representing those with social standing and fame, arrived much later. The commentators go on to say: this is quite natural. The shepherds lived nearby. They only needed to "come over" (Lk 2:15), as we do when we go to visit our neighbors. The wise men, however,

4. *Rule of St. Benedict*, Ch. 43.

lived far away. They had to undertake a long and arduous journey in order to arrive in Bethlehem. And they needed guidance and direction. Today too there are simple and lowly souls who live very close to the Lord. They are, so to speak, his neighbors and they can easily go to see him. But most of us in the world today live far from Jesus Christ, the incarnate God who came to dwell amongst us. We live our lives by philosophies, amid worldly affairs and occupations that totally absorb us and are a great distance from the manger. In all kinds of ways, God has to prod us and reach out to us again and again, so that we can manage to escape from the muddle of our thoughts and activities and discover the way that leads to him. But a path exists for all of us. The Lord provides everyone with tailor-made signals. He calls each one of us, so that we too can say: Come on, "let us go over" to Bethlehem—to the God who has come to meet us. Yes indeed, God has set out towards us. Left to ourselves we could not reach him. The path is too much for our strength. But God has come down. He comes towards us. He has travelled the longer part of the journey. Now he invites us: come and see how much I love you. Come and see that I am here. *Transeamus usque* Bethlehem, the Latin Bible says. Let us go there! Let us surpass ourselves! Let us journey towards God in all sorts of ways: along our interior path towards him, but also along very concrete paths—the Liturgy of the Church, the service of our neighbor, in whom Christ awaits us.

Let us once again listen directly to the Gospel. The shepherds tell one another the reason why they are setting off: "Let us see this thing that has happened." Literally the Greek text says: "Let us see this Word that has occurred there." Yes indeed, such is the radical newness of this night: the Word can be seen. For it has become flesh. The God of whom no image may be made—because any image would only diminish or rather distort him—this God has himself become visible in the One who is his true image, as Saint Paul puts it (2 Cor 4:4; Col 1:15). In the figure of Jesus Christ, in the whole of his life and ministry, in his dying and rising, we can see the Word of God and hence the mystery of the living God himself. This is what God is like. The Angel had said to the shepherds: "This will be a sign for you: you will find a babe wrapped in swaddling clothes and lying in a manger" (Lk 2:12; cf. 2:16). God's sign, the sign given to the shepherds and to us, is not an astonishing miracle. God's sign is his humility. God's sign is that he makes himself small; he becomes a child; he lets us touch him and he asks for our love. How we would prefer a different sign, an imposing, irresistible sign of God's power and greatness! But his sign summons us to faith and love, and thus it gives us hope: This is what God is like. He has power, he is Goodness itself. He invites us to become like him. Yes indeed, we become like God if we allow ourselves to be shaped by this sign; if we ourselves learn humility and hence true greatness; if we renounce violence and use only the weapons of truth and love. Origen, taking up one of John the Baptist's sayings, saw the essence of paganism expressed in the symbol of stones: paganism is a lack of feeling, it means a heart of stone that is incapable of loving and perceiving God's love. Origen says of the pagans: "Lacking feeling and reason, they are transformed into stones and wood."[5] Christ, though, wishes to give us a heart of flesh. When we see him, the God who became a child, our hearts are opened. In the Liturgy of the holy night,

5. Cf. Origen, *Homilies on Luke*, 22:9.

God comes to us as man, so that we might become truly human. Let us listen once again to Origen: "Indeed, what use would it be to you that Christ once came in the flesh if he did not enter your soul? Let us pray that he may come to us each day, that we may be able to say: I live, yet it is no longer I that live, but Christ lives in me (Gal 2:20)."[6]

Yes, indeed, that is what we should pray for on this Holy Night. Lord Jesus Christ, born in Bethlehem, come to us! Enter within me, within my soul. Transform me. Renew me. Change me, change us all from stone and wood into living people, in whom your love is made present and the world is transformed. Amen.

7. *God's Glory*

From the Homily of His Holiness Pope Benedict XVI
Solemnity of the Nativity of the Lord, Midnight Mass
Saint Peter's Basilica, Monday, 24 December 2012

Again and again the beauty of this Gospel touches our hearts: a beauty that is the splendor of truth. Again and again, it astonishes us that God makes himself a child so that we may love him, so that we may dare to love him, and as a child trustingly lets himself be taken into our arms. It is as if God were saying: I know that my glory frightens you, and that you are trying to assert yourself in the face of my grandeur. So now I am coming to you as a child, so that you can accept me and love me.

I am also repeatedly struck by the Gospel writer's almost casual remark that there was no room for them at the inn. Inevitably

6. Origen, *Homilies on Luke*, 22:3.

the question arises, what would happen if Mary and Joseph were to knock at my door? Would there be room for them? And then it occurs to us that Saint John takes up this seemingly chance comment about the lack of room at the inn, which drove the Holy Family into the stable; he explores it more deeply and arrives at the heart of the matter when he writes: "he came to his own home, and his own people received him not" (Jn 1:11). The great moral question of our attitude towards the homeless, towards refugees and migrants, takes on a deeper dimension: do we really have room for God when he seeks to enter under our roof? Do we have time and space for him? Do we not actually turn away God himself? We begin to do so when we have no time for God. The faster we can move, the more efficient our time-saving appliances become, the less time we have. And God? The question of God never seems urgent. Our time is already completely full. But matters go deeper still. Does God actually have a place in our thinking? Our process of thinking is structured in such a way that he simply ought not to exist. Even if he seems to knock at the door of our thinking, he has to be explained away. If thinking is to be taken seriously, it must be structured in such a way that the "God hypothesis" becomes superfluous. There is no room for him. Not even in our feelings and desires is there any room for him. We want ourselves. We want what we can seize hold of, we want happiness that is within our reach, we want our plans and purposes to succeed. We are so "full" of ourselves that there is no room left for God. And that means there is no room for others either, for children, for the poor, for the stranger. By reflecting on that one simple saying about the lack of room at the inn, we have come to see how much we need to listen to Saint Paul's exhortation: "Be transformed by the renewal of your mind" (Rom 12:2). Paul speaks of renewal, the opening up of our intellect (*nous*), of the whole way we view the world and ourselves. The conversion that we need must truly reach into the depths of our relationship with reality. Let us ask the Lord that we may become vigilant for his presence, that we may hear how softly yet insistently he knocks at the door of our being and willing. Let us ask that we may make room for him within ourselves, that we may recognize him also in those through whom he speaks to us: children, the suffering, the abandoned, those who are excluded and the poor of this world.

There is another verse from the Christmas story on which I should like to reflect with you—the angels' hymn of praise, which they sing out following the announcement of the new-born Savior: "Glory to God in the highest and on earth peace among men with whom he is pleased." God is glorious. God is pure light, the radiance of truth and love. He is good. He is true goodness, goodness par excellence. The angels surrounding him begin by simply proclaiming the joy of seeing God's glory. Their song radiates the joy that fills them. In their words, it is as if we were hearing the sounds of heaven. There is no question of attempting to understand the meaning of it all, but simply the overflowing happiness of seeing the pure splendor of God's truth and love. We want to let this joy reach out and touch us: truth exists, pure goodness exists, pure light exists. God is good, and he is the supreme power above all powers. All this should simply make us joyful tonight, together with the angels and the shepherds.

Linked to God's glory on high is peace on earth among men. Where God is not glorified, where he is forgotten or even denied, there is no peace either. Nowadays, though, widespread currents of thought assert the exact opposite: they say that religions, especially monotheism, are the cause of the violence and the wars in the world. If there is to be peace, humanity must first be liberated from them. Monotheism, belief in one God, is said to be arrogance, a cause of intolerance, because by its nature, with its claim to possess the sole truth, it seeks to impose itself on everyone. Now it is true that in the course of history, monotheism has served as a pretext for intolerance and violence. It is true that religion can become corrupted and hence opposed to its deepest essence, when people think they have to take God's cause into their own hands, making God into their private property. We must be on the lookout for these distortions of the sacred. While there is no denying a certain misuse of religion in history, yet it is not true that denial of God would lead to peace. If God's light is extinguished, man's divine dignity is also extinguished. Then the human creature would cease to be God's image, to which we must pay honor in every person, in the weak, in the stranger, in the poor. Then we would no longer all be brothers and sisters, children of the one Father, who belong to one another on account of that one Father. The kind of arrogant violence that then arises, the way man then despises and tramples upon man: we saw this in all its cruelty in the last century. Only if God's light shines over man and within him, only if every single person is desired, known, and loved by God is his dignity inviolable, however wretched his situation may be. On this Holy Night, God himself became man; as Isaiah prophesied, the child born here is "Emmanuel," God with us (Is 7:14). And down the centuries, while there has been misuse of religion, it is also true that forces of reconciliation and goodness have constantly sprung up from faith in the God who became man. Into the darkness of sin and violence, this faith has shone a bright ray of peace and goodness, which continues to shine.

So, Christ is our peace, and he proclaimed peace to those far away and to those near at hand (Eph 2:14, 17). How could we now do other than pray to him: Yes, Lord, proclaim peace today to us too, whether we are far away or near at hand. Grant also to us today that swords may be turned into ploughshares (Is 2:4), that instead of weapons for warfare, practical aid may be given to the suffering. Enlighten those who think they have to practice violence in your name, so that they may see the senselessness of violence and learn to recognize your true face. Help us to become people "with whom you are pleased"—people according to your image and thus people of peace.

Once the angels departed, the shepherds said to one another: Let us go over to Bethlehem and see this thing that has happened for us (Lk 2:15). The shepherds went with haste to Bethlehem, the Evangelist tells us (2:16). A holy curiosity impelled them to see this child in a manger, who the angel had said was the Savior, Christ the Lord. The great joy of which the angel spoke had touched their hearts and given them wings.

Let us go over to Bethlehem, says the Church's liturgy to us today. *Trans-eamus* is what the Latin Bible says: let us go "across," daring to step beyond, to make the "transition" by which we step outside our habits of thought and habits of life, across the purely material world into the real one, across to the God who in his turn has come across to us. Let us ask the Lord to grant that we may overcome our limits, our world, to help us to encounter him, especially at the moment when he places himself into our hands and into our heart in the Holy Eucharist.

Let us go over to Bethlehem: as we say these words to one another, along with the shepherds, we should not only think of the great "crossing over" to the living God, but also of the actual town of Bethlehem and all those places where the Lord lived, ministered, and suffered. Let us pray at this time for the people who live and suffer there today. Let us pray that there may be peace in that land. Let us pray that Israelis and Palestinians may be able to live their lives in the peace of the one God and in freedom. Let us also pray for the countries of the region, for Lebanon, Syria, Iraq, and their neighbors: that there may be peace there, that Christians in those lands where our faith was born may be able to continue living there, that Christians and Muslims may build up their countries side by side in God's peace.

The shepherds made haste. Holy curiosity and holy joy impelled them. In our case, it is probably not very often that we make haste for the things of God. God does not feature among the things that require haste. The things of God can wait, we think and we say. And yet he is the most important thing, ultimately the one truly important thing. Why should we not also be moved by curiosity to see more closely and to know what God has said to us? At this hour, let us ask him to touch our hearts with the holy curiosity and the holy joy of the shepherds, and thus let us go over joyfully to Bethlehem, to the Lord who today once more comes to meet us. Amen.

CHRISTMAS SEASON

EPIPHANY OF THE LORD

8. *The Law of Love*

From the Homily of His Holiness Pope Benedict XVI
Solemnity of the Epiphany of the Lord
Saint Peter's Basilica, Tuesday, 6 January 2009

Epiphany, the "manifestation" of Our Lord Jesus Christ, is a many-facetted mystery. The Latin tradition identifies it with the visit of the Magi to the Infant Jesus in Bethlehem and thus interprets it above all as a revelation of the Messiah of Israel to the Gentiles. The Eastern tradition, on the other hand, gives priority to the moment of Jesus's Baptism in the River Jordan, when he manifested himself as the Only-Begotten Son of the heavenly Father, consecrated by the Holy Spirit. John's Gospel, however, also invites us to consider as an "epiphany" the Wedding at Cana, during which, by changing the water into wine, Jesus "manifested his glory; and his disciples believed in him" (Jn 2:11). And what should we say, dear brothers and sisters, especially we priests of the New Covenant who are every day witnesses and ministers of the "epiphany" of Jesus Christ in the Holy Eucharist? The Church celebrates all the mysteries of the Lord in this most holy and most humble Sacrament, in which he both reveals and conceals his glory. *"Adoro te devote, latens Deitas"*; in adoration, thus we pray along with St. Thomas Aquinas.[1]

In this year 2009, which has been dedicated in a special way to astronomy to mark the fourth centenary of Galileo Galilei's first

1. Cf. St. Thomas Aquinas, *Adoro te Devote*, ca. 1264.

observations with the telescope, we cannot fail to pay particular attention to the symbol of the star that is so important in the Gospel account of the Magi (Mt 2:1–12). In all likelihood, the Wise Men were astronomers. From their observation point, situated in the East compared to Palestine, perhaps in Mesopotamia, they had noticed the appearance of a new star and had interpreted this celestial phenomenon as the announcement of the birth of a king, specifically that in accordance with the Sacred Scriptures of the King of the Jews (Nm 24:17). The Fathers of the Church also saw this unique episode recounted by St. Matthew as a sort of cosmic "revolution" caused by the Son of God's entry into the world. For example, St. John Chrysostom writes: "The star, when it stood over the young Child, stayed its course again: which thing itself was of a greater power than belongs to a star, now to hide itself, now to appear, and having appeared to stand still."[2] St. Gregory of Nazianzen states that the birth of Christ gave the stars new orbits.[3] This is clearly to be understood in a symbolic and theological sense. In effect, while pagan theology divinized the elements and forces of the cosmos, the Christian faith, in bringing the biblical Revelation to fulfilment, contemplates only one God, Creator and Lord of the whole universe.

The divine and universal law of creation is divine love, incarnate in Christ. However, this should not be understood in a poetic but in a real sense. Moreover, this is what Dante himself meant when, in the sublime verse that concludes the *Paradiso* and the entire *Divina*

2. St. John Chrysostom, *Homilies of the Gospel of Matthew*, Library of the Fathers of the Holy Catholic Church 7 (J.G. & F. Rivington, 1841), 3.

3. Cf. St. Gregory of Nazianzen, *Dogmatic Poems*, v, 53–64, Patrologia Graeca (PG), 37, 428–29.

Commedia, he describes God as "the Love which moves the sun and the other stars."[4] This means that the stars, planets and the whole universe are not governed by a blind force, they do not obey the dynamics of matter alone. Therefore, it is not the cosmic elements that should be divinized. Indeed, on the contrary, within everything and at the same time above everything there is a personal will, the Spirit of God, who in Christ has revealed himself as Love.[5] If this is the case, then as St. Paul wrote to the Colossians, people are not slaves of the "elemental spirits of the universe" (Col 2:8) but are free, that is, capable of relating to the creative freedom of God. God is at the origin of all things and governs all things, not as a cold and anonymous engine but rather as Father, Husband, Friend, Brother, and as the Logos, "Word-Reason" who was united with our mortal flesh once and for all and fully shared our condition, showing the superabundant power of his grace. Thus, there is a special concept of the cosmos in Christianity which found its loftiest expression in medieval philosophy and theology. In our day too, it shows interesting signs of a new flourishing, thanks to the enthusiasm and faith of many scientists who, following in Galileo's footsteps, renounce neither reason nor faith; instead, they develop both in their reciprocal fruitfulness.

Christian thought compares the cosmos to a "book"—the same Galileo said this as well—considering it as the work of an Author who expresses himself in the "symphony" of the Creation. In this symphony is found, at a certain point, what might be called in musical terminology a "solo," a theme given to a single instrument or voice; and it is so important that the significance of the entire

4. Dante, *Paradiso*, xxxiii, 145.

5. Cf. Pope Benedict XVI, Encyclical Letter *Spe Salvi* (November 30, 2007), no. 5.

work depends on it. This "solo" is Jesus, who is accompanied by a royal sign: the appearance of a new star in the firmament. Jesus is compared by ancient Christian writers to a new sun. According to current astrophysical knowledge, we should compare it with a star that is even more central, not only for the solar system but also for the entire known universe. Within this mysterious design, simultaneously physical and metaphysical, which led to the appearance of the human being as the crowning of Creation's elements, Jesus came into the world: "born of woman" (Gal 4:4), as St. Paul writes. The Son of man himself epitomizes the earth and Heaven, the Creation and the Creator, the flesh and the Spirit. He is the center of the cosmos and of history, for in him the Author and his work are united without being confused with each other.

In the earthly Jesus the culmination of Creation and of history is found, but in the Risen Christ this is surpassed: the passage through death to eternal life anticipates the point of the "recapitulation" of all things in Christ (cf. Eph 1:10). Indeed "all things," the Apostle wrote, "were created through him and for him" (Col 1:16). And it is precisely with the resurrection of the dead that he became "preeminent in all things" (Col 1:18). Jesus himself affirms this, appearing to his disciples after the Resurrection: "all authority in Heaven and on earth has been given to me" (Mt 28:18). This awareness supports the way of the Church, Body of Christ, on the paths of history. There is no shadow, however dark, that can obscure Christ's light. This is why believers in Christ never lack hope, even today, in the face of the great social and financial crisis that is tormenting humanity, in the face of the destructive hatred and violence that have not ceased to stain many of the earth's regions with blood, in the face of the selfishness and pretension of the human being in establishing himself as his own God, which sometimes leads to dangerous distortions of the divine plan concerning life and the dignity of the human being, the family, and the harmony of the Creation. Our efforts to free human life and the world from the forms of poison and contamination that could destroy the present and the future retain their value and meaning, as I noted in the Encyclical *Spe Salvi* mentioned above, even if we apparently fail or seem powerless when hostile forces appear to gain the upper hand, because "it is the great hope based upon God's promises that gives us courage and directs our action in good times and bad."[6]

Christ's universal lordship is exercised in a special way on the Church. We read in the Letter to the Ephesians that God "has put all things under [Christ's] feet and has made him the head over all things for the Church, which is his body, the fullness of him who fills all in all" (Eph 1:22–23). The Epiphany is the manifestation of the Lord and, as a reflection, it is the manifestation of the Church, since the Body is inseparable from the Head. Today's first reading, from "Third Isaiah," gives us the precise perspective for understanding the reality of the Church as a mystery of reflected light: "Arise, shine," the Prophet says, addressing Jerusalem, "for your light has come, / and the glory of the Lord has risen upon you" (Is 60:1). The Church is humanity illuminated, "baptized" in the glory of God—that is, in his love, in his beauty, in his dignity. The Church knows that her own humanity, with its limitations and wretchedness, serves especially to highlight the work of the Holy Spirit. She can boast of nothing, save in her Lord. It is not from her that light comes; the glory is not hers. But this is precisely her joy,

6. Pope Benedict XVI, *Spe Salvi*, no. 35.

which no one can take from her: to be a "sign and instrument" of the One who is *lumen gentium*, the light of humanity.[7]

Dear friends, in this Pauline Year, the Feast of the Epiphany invites the Church, and in her, every community and every individual member of the faithful, to imitate, as did the Apostle to the Gentiles, the service that the star rendered to the Magi from the East, guiding them to Jesus.[8] What was Paul's life after his conversion other than a "race" to bring the light of Christ to the peoples, and vice versa, to lead the peoples to Christ? God's grace made Paul a "star" for the Gentiles. His ministry is an example and an incentive for the Church to rediscover herself as essentially missionary and to renew the commitment to proclaim the Gospel, especially to those who do not yet know it. Yet, in looking at St. Paul, we cannot forget that his preaching was completely nourished by the Sacred Scriptures. Therefore, it should be powerfully reaffirmed in the perspective of the recent Assembly of the Synod of Bishops that the Church and individual Christians can be a light that leads to Christ only if they are diligently and intimately nourished by the Word of God. It is the Word, certainly not us, that illumines, purifies, and converts. We are merely servants of the Word of life. This is how Paul saw himself and his ministry: as a service to the Gospel. "I do it all for the sake of the Gospel," he wrote (1 Cor 9:23). The Church, every ecclesial community, every Bishop, and every priest ought also to be able to say this: "I do it all for the sake of the Gospel." Dear brothers and sisters, pray for us, Pastors of the Church, that by assimilating the Word of God

7. Cf. Second Vatican Council, Dogmatic Constitution *Lumen Gentium* (November 21, 1964), no. 1.

8. Cf. St. Leo the Great, *Disc. 3 for Epiphany*, 5: PL 54, 244.

daily we may pass it on faithfully to our brethren. Yet we too pray for you, all the faithful, because every Christian is called through Baptism and Confirmation to proclaim Christ, the light of the world, in word and in the witness of his life. May the Virgin Mary, Star of Evangelization, help us to bring this mission to completion together, and may St. Paul, the Apostle to the Gentiles, intercede for us from Heaven. Amen.

9. *Follow the Star*

From the Homily of His Holiness Pope Benedict XVI
Solemnity of the Epiphany of the Lord
Saint Peter's Basilica, Friday, 6 January 2012

The Epiphany is a feast of light. "Arise, shine; for your light has come, and the glory of the Lord has risen upon you" (Is 60:1). With these words of the prophet Isaiah, the Church describes the content of the feast. He who is the true light, and by whom we too are made to be light, has indeed come into the world. He gives us the power to become children of God (cf. Jn 1:9,12). The journey of the wise men from the East is, for the liturgy, just the beginning of a great procession that continues throughout history. With the Magi, humanity's pilgrimage to Jesus Christ begins—to the God who was born in a stable, who died on the Cross and who, having risen from the dead, remains with us always, until the consummation of the world (Mt 28:20). The Church reads this account from Matthew's Gospel alongside the vision of the prophet Isaiah that we heard in the first reading: the journey of these men is just the beginning. Before them came the shepherds—simple souls, who dwelt closer to the God who became a child, and could more easily "go over" to him (Lk 2:15) and recognize him as Lord. But now the wise of this world are also coming. Great and small, kings and slaves, men of all cultures and all peoples are coming. The men from the East are the first, followed by many more throughout the centuries. After the great vision of Isaiah, the reading from the Letter to the Ephesians expresses the same idea in sober and simple terms: the Gentiles share the same heritage (cf. Eph 3:6). Psalm 2 puts it like this: "I shall bequeath you the nations, put the ends of the earth in your possession" (v. 8).

The wise men from the East lead the way. They open up the path of the Gentiles to Christ. During this holy Mass, I will ordain two priests to the episcopate, I will consecrate them as shepherds of God's people. According to the words of Jesus, part of a shepherd's task is to go ahead of the flock (cf. Jn 10:4). So, allowing for all the differences in vocation and mission, we may well look to these figures, the first Gentiles, to find the pathway to Christ, for indications concerning the task of bishops. What kind of people were they? The experts tell us that they belonged to the great astronomical tradition that had developed in Mesopotamia over the centuries and continued to flourish. But this information alone is not enough. No doubt there were many astronomers in ancient Babylon, but only these few set off to follow the star that they recognized as the star of the promise, pointing them along the path towards the true King and Savior. They were, as we might say, men of science, but not simply in the sense that they were searching for a wide range of knowledge: they wanted something more. They wanted to understand what being human is all about. They had doubtless heard of the prophecy of the Gentile prophet

Balaam: "A star shall come forth out of Jacob and a scepter shall rise out of Israel" (Num 24:17). They explored this promise. They were men with restless hearts, not satisfied with the superficial and the ordinary. They were men in search of the promise, in search of God. And they were watchful men, capable of reading God's signs, his soft and penetrating language. But they were also courageous, yet humble: we can imagine them having to endure a certain amount of mockery for setting off to find the King of the Jews, at the cost of so much effort. For them it mattered little what this or that person, what even influential and clever people, thought and said about them. For them it was a question of truth itself, not human opinion. Hence, they took upon themselves the sacrifices and the effort of a long and uncertain journey. Their humble courage was what enabled them to bend down before the child of poor people and to recognize in him the promised King, the one they had set out, on both their outward and their inward journey, to seek and to know.

Dear friends, how can we not see in all this some essential traits of the episcopal ministry? The bishop too must be a man of restless heart, not satisfied with the ordinary things of this world, but inwardly driven by his heart's unrest to draw ever closer to God, to seek his face, to recognize him more and more, to be able to love him more and more. The bishop too must be a man of watchful heart, who recognizes the gentle language of God and understands how to distinguish truth from mere appearance. The bishop too must be filled with the courage of humility, not asking what prevailing opinion says about him, but following the criterion of God's truth and taking his stand accordingly: "opportune—importune." He must be able to go ahead and mark out the path. He must go ahead, in the footsteps of him who went ahead of us all because he is the true shepherd, the true star of the promise: Jesus Christ. And he must have the humility to bend down before the God who made himself so tangible and so simple that he contradicts our foolish pride in its reluctance to see God so close and so small. He must devote his life to adoration of the incarnate Son of God, which constantly points him towards the path.

The liturgy of episcopal ordination interprets the essential features of this ministry in eight questions addressed to the candidates, each beginning with the word "*Vultis?*"—"Do you want?" These questions direct the will and mark out the path to be followed. Here I shall briefly cite just a few of the most important words of this presentation, where we find explicit mention of the elements we have just considered in connection with the wise men of today's feast. The bishops' task is *praedicare Evangelium Christi*, it is *custodire et dirigere*, it is *pauperibus se misericordes praebere*, it is *indesinenter orare*. Preaching the Gospel of Jesus Christ, going ahead and leading, guarding the sacred heritage of our faith, showing mercy and charity to the needy and the poor, thus mirroring God's merciful love for us, and finally, praying without ceasing: these are the fundamental features of the episcopal ministry. Praying without ceasing means: never losing contact with God, letting ourselves be constantly touched by him in the depths of our hearts and, in this way, being penetrated by his light. Only someone who actually knows God can lead others to God. Only someone who leads people to God leads them along the path of life.

The restless heart of which we spoke earlier, echoing Saint Augustine, is the heart that is ultimately satisfied with nothing less than God, and in this way becomes a loving heart. Our heart is restless for God and remains so, even if every effort is made today, by means of most effective anaesthetizing methods, to deliver people from this unrest. But not only are we restless for God: God's heart is restless for us. God is waiting for us. He is looking for us. He knows no rest either, until he finds us. God's heart is restless, and that is why he set out on the path towards us—to Bethlehem, to Calvary, from Jerusalem to Galilee and on to the very ends of the earth. God is restless for us, he looks out for people willing to "catch" his unrest, his passion for us, people who carry within them the searching of their own hearts and at the same time open themselves to be touched by God's search for us. Dear friends, this was the task of the Apostles: to receive God's unrest for man and then to bring God himself to man. And this is your task as successors of the Apostles: let yourselves be touched by God's unrest, so that God's longing for man may be fulfilled.

The wise men followed the star. Through the language of creation, they discovered the God of history. To be sure—the language of creation alone is not enough. Only God's word, which we encounter in sacred Scripture, was able to mark out their path definitively. Creation and Scripture, reason and faith, must come together, so as to lead us forward to the living God. There has been much discussion over what kind of star it was that the wise men were following. Some suggest a planetary constellation, or a supernova—that is to say, one of those stars that is initially quite weak, in which an inner explosion releases a brilliant light for a certain time, or a comet, etc. This debate we may leave to the experts. The great star, the true supernova that leads us on, is Christ himself. He is as it were the explosion of God's love, which causes the great white light of his heart to shine upon the world. And we may add: the wise men from the East, who feature in today's Gospel, like all the saints, have themselves gradually become constellations of God that mark out the path. In all these people, being touched by God's word has, as it were, released an explosion of light, through which God's radiance shines upon our world and shows us the path. The saints are stars of God, by whom we let ourselves be led to him for whom our whole being longs. Dear friends: you followed the star Jesus Christ when you said "yes" to the priesthood and to the episcopacy. And no doubt smaller stars have enlightened and helped you not to lose your way. In the litany of saints we call upon all these stars of God, that they may continue to shine upon you and show you the path. As you are ordained bishops, you too are called to be stars of God for men, leading them along the path towards the true light, towards Christ. So let us pray to all the saints at this hour, asking them that you may always live up to this mission you have received, to show God's light to mankind.

10. *In Contact with God*

From the Homily of His Holiness Pope Benedict XVI
Solemnity of the Epiphany of the Lord
Saint Peter's Basilica, Sunday, 6 January 2013

For the Church which believes and prays, the Wise Men from the East who, guided by the star, made their way to the manger of Bethlehem, are only the beginning of a great procession which winds throughout history. Thus, the liturgy includes the Gospel which relates the journey of the Wise Men, together with the magnificent prophetic visions of the sixtieth chapter of the Book of Isaiah and Psalm 71, which depict in bold imagery the pilgrimage of the peoples to Jerusalem. Like the shepherds, who as the first visitors to the newborn Child in the manger, embodied the poor of Israel and more generally those humble souls who live in deep interior closeness to Jesus, so the men from the East embody the peoples of the world, the church of the Gentiles—the men and women who in every age set out on the way which leads to the Child of Bethlehem, to offer him homage as the Son of God and to bow down before him. The Church calls this feast "Epiphany"—the appearance of the Godhead. If we consider the fact that from the very beginning men and women of every place, of every continent, of all the different cultures, mentalities and lifestyles, have been on the way to Christ, then we can truly say that this pilgrimage and this encounter with God in the form of a Child is an epiphany of God's goodness and loving kindness for humanity (cf. Tit 3:4).

Following a tradition begun by Pope John Paul II, we celebrate the feast of the Epiphany of the Lord also as the day when episcopal ordination will be conferred on four priests who will now cooperate in different ways in the ministry of the Pope for the unity of the one Church of Jesus Christ in the multiplicity of the particular churches. The connection between this episcopal ordination and the theme of the pilgrimage of the peoples to Jesus Christ is evident. It is the task of the Bishop in this pilgrimage not merely to walk beside the others, but to go before them, showing the way. But in this liturgy, I would like to reflect with you on a more concrete question. Based on the account of Matthew, we can gain a certain idea of what sort of men these were, who followed the sign of the star and set off to find that King who would establish not only for

Israel but for all mankind a new kind of kingship. What kind of men were they? And we can also ask whether, despite the difference of times and tasks, we can glimpse in them something of what a Bishop is and how he is to carry out his task.

These men who set out towards the unknown were, in any event, men with a restless heart. Men driven by a restless quest for God and the salvation of the world. They were filled with expectation, not satisfied with their secure income and their respectable place in society. They were looking for something greater. They were no doubt learned men, quite knowledgeable about the heavens and probably possessed of a fine philosophical formation. But they desired more than simply knowledge about things. They wanted above all else to know what is essential. They wanted to know how we succeed in being human. And, therefore, they wanted to know if God exists, and where and how he exists. Whether he is concerned about us and how we can encounter him. Nor did they want just to know. They wanted to understand the truth about ourselves and about God and the world. Their outward pilgrimage was an expression of their inward journey, the inner pilgrimage of their hearts. They were men who sought God and were ultimately on the way towards him. They were seekers after God.

Here we come to the question: What sort of man must he be, upon whom hands are laid in episcopal ordination in the Church of Jesus Christ? We can say that he must above all be a man concerned for God, for only then will he also be truly concerned about men. Inversely, we could also say that a Bishop must be a man concerned for others, one who is concerned about what happens to them. He must be a man for others. But he can only truly be so if he is a man seized by God, if concern for God has also become for him concern for God's creature who is man. Like the Wise Men from the East, a Bishop must not be someone who merely does his job and is content with that. No, he must be gripped by God's concern for men and women. He must in some way think and feel with God. Human beings have an innate restlessness for God, but this restlessness is a participation in God's own restlessness for us. Since God is concerned about us, he follows us even to the crib, even to the Cross. "Thou with weary steps hast sought me, crucified hast dearly bought me, may thy pains not be in vain," the Church prays in the *Dies Irae*. The restlessness of men for God and hence the restlessness of God for men must unsettle the Bishop. This is what we mean when we say that, above all else, the Bishop must be a man of faith. For faith is nothing less than being interiorly seized by God, something which guides us along the pathways of life. Faith draws us into a state of being seized by the restlessness of God and it makes us pilgrims who are on an inner journey towards the true King of the world and his promise of justice, truth, and love. On this pilgrimage the Bishop must go ahead, he must be the guide pointing out to men and women the way to faith, hope, and love.

Faith's inner pilgrimage towards God occurs above all in prayer. Saint Augustine once said that prayer is ultimately nothing more than the realization and radicalization of our yearning for God. Instead of "yearning," we could also translate the word as "restlessness" and say that prayer would detach us from our false security, from our being enclosed within material and visible realities, and would give us a restlessness for God and thus an openness to and concern for one another. The Bishop, as a pilgrim of God, must be above all a man of prayer. He must be in constant inner contact with God; his soul must be open wide to God. He must bring before God his own needs and the needs of others, as well as his joys and the joys of others, and thus in his own way establish contact between God and the world in communion with Christ, so that Christ's light can shine in the world.

Let us return to the Wise Men from the East. These were also, and above all, men of courage, the courage and humility born of faith. Courage was needed to grasp the meaning of the star as a sign to set out, to go forth—towards the unknown, the uncertain, on paths filled with hidden dangers. We can imagine that their decision was met with derision: the scorn of those realists who could only mock the reveries of such men. Anyone who took off on the basis of such uncertain promises, risking everything, could only appear ridiculous. But for these men, inwardly seized by God, the way which he pointed out was more important than what other people thought. For them, seeking the truth meant more than the taunts of the world, so apparently clever.

How can we not think, in this context, of the task of a Bishop in our own time? The humility of faith, of sharing the faith of the Church of every age, will constantly be in conflict with the prevailing wisdom of those who cling to what seems certain. Anyone who lives and proclaims the faith of the Church is on many points out of step with the prevalent way of thinking, even in our own day. Today's regnant agnosticism has its own dogmas and is extremely intolerant regarding anything that would question it and the criteria it employs. Therefore, the courage to contradict the prevailing mindset is particularly urgent for a Bishop today. He must be courageous. And this courage or forcefulness does not consist in striking out or in acting aggressively, but rather in allowing oneself to be struck and to be steadfast before the principles of the prevalent way of thinking. The courage to stand firm in the truth is unavoidably demanded of those whom the Lord sends like sheep among wolves. "Those who fear the Lord will not be timid," says the Book of Sirach (34:16). The fear of God frees us from the fear of men. It liberates.

Here I am reminded of an episode at the very beginning of Christianity which Saint Luke recounts in the Acts of the Apostles. After the speech of Gamaliel, who advised against violence in dealing with the earliest community of believers in Jesus, the Sanhedrin summoned the Apostles and had them flogged. It then forbade them from preaching in the name of Jesus and set them free. Saint Luke continues: "As they left the council, they rejoiced that they were considered worthy to suffer dishonor for the name of Jesus. And every day . . . they did not cease to teach and proclaim Jesus as the Messiah" (Acts 5:40ff.). The successors of the Apostles must also expect to be repeatedly beaten, by contemporary methods, if they continue to proclaim the Gospel of Jesus Christ in a way that can be heard and understood. Then they can rejoice that they have been considered worthy of suffering for him. Like the Apostles, we naturally want to convince people and, in this sense, to obtain their approval. Naturally, we are not provocative; on the contrary we invite all to enter into the joy of that truth which shows us the way. The approval of the prevailing wisdom, however, is not the criterion to which we submit. Our criterion is the Lord himself. If we defend his cause, we will, thank God, win people over again and again to the path of the Gospel. But inevitably we will also be beaten by those who live lives opposed to the Gospel, and then we can be grateful for having been judged worthy to share in the passion of Christ.

The Wise Men followed the star, and thus came to Jesus, to the great Light which enlightens everyone coming into this world (cf. Jn 1:9). As pilgrims of faith, the Wise Men themselves became stars shining in the firmament of history and they show us the way. The saints are God's true constellations, which light up the nights of this world, serving as our guides. Saint Paul, in his Letter to the Philippians, told his faithful that they must shine like stars in the world (2:15).

Dear friends, this holds true for us too. It holds true above all for you who are now to be ordained Bishops of the Church of Jesus Christ. If you live with Christ, bound to him anew in this sacrament, then you too will become wise men. Then you will become stars which go before men and women, pointing out to them the right path in life. All of us here are now praying for you, that the Lord may fill you with the light of faith and love. That that restlessness of God for man may seize you, so that all may experience his closeness and receive the gift of his joy. We are praying for you, that the Lord may always grant you the courage and humility of faith. We ask Mary, who showed to the Wise Men the new King of the world (Mt 2:11), as a loving mother, to show Jesus Christ also to you and to help you to be guides along the way which leads to him. Amen.

CHRISTMAS SEASON

BAPTISM OF THE LORD

11. *Immersed in Communion*

From the Homily of His Holiness Pope Benedict XVI
Feast of the Baptism of the Lord
Sistine Chapel, Sunday, 9 January 2011

I am glad to offer a cordial welcome, especially to you, the parents and godparents of the 21 infants to whom, in a little while, I shall have the joy of administrating the sacrament of Baptism. Now a tradition, this year too the rite is taking place during the Holy Eucharistic Celebration with which we celebrate the Baptism of the Lord. It is the Feast which, on the first Sunday after the Epiphany, concludes the Christmas Season with the Lord's manifestation at the River Jordan. According to the account of the Evangelist Matthew (3:13–17), Jesus came from Galilee to the River Jordan to be baptized by John; indeed, people were flocking from all over Palestine to hear the preaching of this great Prophet and the proclamation of the coming of the Kingdom of God and to receive Baptism, that is, to submit to that sign of penance which calls for conversion from sin.

Although it was called "Baptism," it did not have the sacramental value of the rite we are celebrating today; as you well know, it was actually with his death and Resurrection that Jesus instituted the sacraments and caused the Church to be born. What John administered was a penitential act, a gesture of humility to God that invited a new beginning: by immersing themselves in the water, penitents recognized that they had sinned, begged God for purification from their sins and were asked to change wrong behavior, dying in the water, as it were, and rising from it to new life. For this reason, when John the Baptist saw Jesus who had come to be baptized queuing with sinners he was amazed; recognizing him as the Messiah, the Holy One of God, the One who is without sin, John expressed his consternation: he, the Baptist, would himself have liked to be baptized by Jesus. But Jesus urged him not to put up any resistance, to agree to do this act, to do what is fitting "to fulfil all righteousness." With these words Jesus showed that he had come into the world to do the will of the One who had sent him, to carry out all that the Father would ask of him. It was in order to obey the Father that he accepted to be made man. This act reveals, first of all, who Jesus is: he is the Son of God, true God as the Father; he is the One who "humbled himself" to make himself one of us, the One who was made man and who accepted to humble himself unto death on a cross (cf. Phil 2:7).

The Baptism of Jesus, which we are commemorating today, fits into this logic of humility and solidarity: it is the action of the One who wanted to make himself one of us in everything and who truly joined the line of sinners; he, who knew no sin, let himself be treated as a sinner (cf. 2 Cor 5:21), to take upon his shoulders the burden of the sin of all humanity, including our own sin. He is the "servant" of Yahweh of whom the Prophet Isaiah spoke in the first reading (42:1). His humility is dictated by the desire to establish full communion with humanity, by the desire to bring about true solidarity with man and with his human condition. Jesus's action anticipates the Cross, his acceptance of death for man's sins. This act of abasement, by which Jesus wanted to comply totally with the loving plan of the Father and to conform himself with us, expresses the full harmony of will and intentions that exists between the Persons of the Most Holy Trinity. For this act of love, the Spirit of God revealed himself and descended to alight upon Jesus as a dove, and at that moment the love which unites Jesus to the Father was witnessed to all who were present at the Baptism by a voice from Heaven that everyone heard.

The Father reveals openly to human beings, to us, the profound communion that binds him to the Son: the voice that resounds from on high testifies that Jesus is obedient to the Father in all things and that this obedience is an expression of the love that unites them to each other. Therefore, the Father delights in Jesus, for he recognizes in the Son's behavior the wish to obey his will in all things: "This is my beloved Son, with whom I am well pleased" (Mt 3:17). And these words of the Father also allude, in advance, to the victory of the Resurrection and tell us how we must live in order to please the Father, by behaving like Jesus.

Dear parents, the Baptism, that you are asking for your children today, inserts them into this exchange of reciprocal love that is in God between the Father, the Son, and the Holy Spirit; through this act that I am about to carry out, God's love is poured out upon them, showering them with his gifts. Your children, cleansed by the water, are inserted into the very life of Jesus who died on the Cross to free us from sin and in rising, conquered death. Therefore, spiritually immersed in his death and Resurrection, they are set free from original sin and the life of grace is born within them, which is the very life of the Risen Jesus. He "gave himself for us," St. Paul says, "to redeem us from all iniquity and to purify for himself a people of his own who are zealous for good deeds"

(Tit 2:14). Dear friends, in giving us faith, the Lord has given us what is most precious in life, that is, the truest and most beautiful reason for living: it is through grace that we have believed in God, that we have known his love with which he wants to save us and to deliver us from evil. Faith is the great gift with which he also gives us eternal life, true life. Now, dear parents and godparents, you are asking the Church to receive these children within her, to give them Baptism; and you are making this request by virtue of the gift of faith that you yourselves, in turn, have received.

Together with the Prophet Isaiah, every Christian can say: "The Lord . . . formed me from the womb to be his servant" (49:5); thus, dear parents, your children are a precious gift of the Lord, who has kept their hearts for himself in order to fill them with his love. Today, through the sacrament of Baptism, he consecrates them and calls them to follow Jesus, through the realization of their personal vocation in accordance with that particular plan of love that the Father has in mind for each one of them; the destination of this earthly pilgrimage will be full communion with him in eternal happiness. In receiving Baptism, these children obtain as a gift an indelible spiritual seal, the "character" that inwardly marks their belonging to the Lord forever and makes them living members of his Mystical Body, which is the Church. While they become part of the People of God, today a journey begins for these children which must be a journey of holiness and of conformation to Jesus, a reality that is placed within them like the seed of a splendid tree whose growth must be nurtured.

Therefore, understanding the greatness of this gift, from the earliest centuries care has been taken to give Baptism to newborn infants. Of course, later there will be the need for a free and conscious adherence to this life of faith and love. For this reason, after Baptism they must be educated in the faith, instructed in accordance with the wisdom of Sacred Scripture and the teachings of the Church so that this seed of faith that they are receiving today may grow within them and that they may attain full Christian maturity. The Church, which welcomes them among her children, must take charge of them, together with their parents and godparents, to accompany them on this journey of growth. Collaboration between the Christian community and the family is especially necessary in the contemporary social context in which the family institution is threatened on many sides and finds itself having to face numerous difficulties in its role of raising children in the faith. The lack of stable cultural references and the rapid transformation to which society is constantly subjected truly make the commitment to bring them up arduous. Parishes must therefore do their utmost increasingly to sustain families, small domestic churches, in their task of passing on the faith.

Dear parents, together with you I thank the Lord for the gift of the Baptism of your little sons and daughters; in raising our prayers for them, let us invoke in abundance the gift of the Holy Spirit, who today consecrates them in the image of Christ the Priest, King, and Prophet. As I entrust them to the motherly intercession of Mary Most Holy, let us ask for life and health for them, so that they may grow and mature in the faith and with their lives bear fruits of holiness and of love. Amen!

12. *The Springs of Salvation*

From the Homily of His Holiness Pope Benedict XVI
Feast of the Baptism of the Lord
Sistine Chapel, Sunday, 8 January 2012

It is always a joy to celebrate this Holy Mass with the baptism of children on the Feast of the Baptism of the Lord. I greet you all with affection, dear parents, godparents, and all of you, relatives, and friends! You have come here—you said so aloud—so that your newborn babies may receive the gift of God's grace, the seed of eternal life. You, parents, have desired this. You thought of Baptism even before your child was born. Your duty as Christian parents made you think immediately of the sacrament that marks entry into divine life and into the community of the Church. We can say that this was your first educational decision as witnesses of the faith to your children: it is a fundamental decision! The parents' task, helped by the godfather and godmother, is to raise their son or daughter. Raising children is very demanding and at times taxes our human capability, which is always limited. However, educating becomes a marvelous mission if it is carried out in collaboration with God who is the first and true educator of every human being.

In the first reading, we heard from the Book of the Prophet Isaiah; God addresses his people precisely as a teacher. He puts the Israelites on their guard against the danger of quenching their thirst and appeasing their hunger at the wrong sources: "Why," he says, "do you spend your money for that which is not bread, and your labor for that which does not satisfy?" (Is 55:2). God wants to give us good things to drink and to eat, things that do us good; whereas at times we use our resources mistakenly, we use them for things that are useless, indeed, even harmful. Above all, God wants to give us himself and his Word. He knows that in distancing ourselves from him we will soon run into difficulty—like the Prodigal Son of the parable—and, especially, that we will lose our human dignity. And for this reason, he assures us that he is infinite mercy, that his thoughts and ways are unlike ours—fortunately!—and that we can always return to him, to the Father's house. Thereafter he assures us that if we receive his Word it will bear good fruits in our life, like the rain that waters the earth (cf. Is 55:10–11).

We responded to these words which the Lord has addressed to us through the Prophet Isaiah with the refrain of the Psalm: We will "draw water joyfully from the springs of salvation." As adults, we have striven to draw from the good springs for our own good and for the good of those entrusted to our responsibility, and you in particular, dear parents and godparents, for the good of these children. And what are "the springs of salvation"? They are the Word of God and the sacraments. Adults are the first who should nourish themselves at these sources, so as to be able to guide those who are younger in their development. Parents must give much, but in order to give they need in turn to receive, otherwise they are drained, they dry up. Parents are not the spring, just as we priests are not the spring. Rather, we are like channels through which the life-giving sap of God's love must flow. If we cut ourselves off from his spring, we ourselves are the first to feel the negative effects and are no longer able to educate others. For this reason, we have committed ourselves by saying: We will "draw water joyfully from the springs of salvation."

And we now come to the second reading and to the Gospel. They say that the first and principal education takes place through testimony. The Gospel speaks of John the Baptist. John was a great educator of his disciples, because he led them to the encounter with Jesus to whom he bore witness. He did not exalt himself, he did not wish to keep his disciples bound to him. Yet John was a great prophet, his fame was very great. When Jesus arrived, John drew back and pointed to him: "After me comes he who is mightier than I. . . . I have baptized you with water; but he will baptize you with the Holy Spirit" (Mk 1:7–8). The true teacher does not bind people to himself, he is not possessive. He wants his son or daughter, or disciple, to learn to know the truth and to establish a personal relationship with it. The educator carries out his duty to the fullest, and does not fail to provide his attentive and faithful presence; however, his goal is for the student to listen to the voice of truth speaking to his heart and follow it on a personal path.

Let us return once again to the witness. In the second reading, the Apostle John writes: "And the Spirit is the witness" (1 Jn 5:7). He is referring to the Holy Spirit, the Spirit of God, who bears witness to Jesus, testifying that he is the Christ, the Son of God. This is also apparent in the scene of the Baptism in the River Jordan: the Holy Spirit descends upon Jesus as a dove to reveal that he is the Only-Begotten Son of the eternal Father (cf. Mk 1:10). In his Gospel, too, John underlines this aspect where Jesus says to the disciples: "When the Counselor comes, whom I shall send to you from the Father, even the Spirit of truth, who proceeds from the Father, he will bear witness to me; and you also are witnesses, because you have been with me from the beginning" (Jn 15:26–27). This is a great comfort to us in the work of educating in faith, because we know that we are not alone and that our witness is sustained by the Holy Spirit.

It is very important for you, parents, and also for the godparents, to believe strongly in the presence and in the action of the Holy Spirit, to invoke him and to welcome him within you, through prayer and through the sacraments. It is he, in fact, who illumines the mind and warms the heart of the educator so that he or she can pass on the knowledge and love of Jesus. Prayer is the first condition for teaching, because by praying we prepare ourselves to leave the initiative to God, to entrust children to him, who knows them before and better than we, and who knows perfectly what their true good is. And at the same time, when we pray, we listen to God's inspiration in order to do our part well, which in any case is our duty and which we are bound to do. The sacraments, especially the Eucharist and Penance, enable us to carry out our educational action in union with Christ, in communion with him and continuously renewed by his forgiveness. Prayer and the sacraments obtain for us that light of truth thanks to which we are able to be at once tender and strong, gentle and firm, silent and communicative at the right time, admonishing and correcting in the right way.

Dear friends, let us therefore all invoke the Holy Spirit together so that he may come down upon these children in abundance, consecrate them in the image of Jesus Christ and always go with them on their journey through life. Let us entrust them to the motherly guidance of Mary Most Holy, so that they may grow in age, wisdom, and grace and become true Christians, faithful and joyful witnesses of God's love. Amen.

13. *United with Jesus*

From the Homily of His Holiness Pope Benedict XVI
Feast of the Baptism of the Lord
Sistine Chapel, Sunday, 13 January 2013

The joy that flowed from the celebration of holy Christmas is fulfilled today in the Feast of the Baptism of the Lord. A further reason for jubilation comes to us who are gathered here: indeed, in the sacrament of Baptism that I shall shortly administer to these newborn babies is expressed the living and active presence of the Holy Spirit who, enriching the Church with new children, vitalizes and develops her, and we cannot but rejoice in this. I would like to address a special greeting to you, dear parents and godparents who are witnessing to your faith today by asking for baptism for these children, so that they may be born to new life in Christ and become part of the community of believers.

The Gospel account of the baptism of Jesus which we heard in St. Luke's version shows the life of meekness and humility that the Son of God chose freely, complying with the Father's plan to be obedient to his desire for love for man in all things, even to his sacrifice on the Cross. Having reached adulthood, Jesus began his public ministry by going to the River Jordan to receive from John a baptism of penance and conversion. What might seem paradoxical in our eyes actually happened. Did Jesus need penance and conversion? Of course not. Yet the One who is without sin put himself among sinners to have himself baptized, to make this act of penance. The Holy One of God joined those who recognized they were in need of forgiveness and asked God for the gift of conversion, that is, the grace to return to him with their whole heart, to belong totally to him. Jesus chose to join the ranks of sinners, to be in solidarity with them, expressing God's closeness.

Jesus shows his solidarity with us, with our efforts to convert and to be rid of our selfishness, to break away from our sins in order to tell us that if we accept him in our life he can uplift us and lead us to the heights of God the Father. And Jesus's solidarity is not, as it were, a mere exercise of mind and will. Jesus truly immersed himself in our human condition, lived it to the end, in all things save sin, and was able to understand our weakness and frailty. For this reason, he was moved to compassion, he chose to "suffer with" men and women, to become a penitent with us. This is God's work which Jesus wanted to carry out: the divine mission to heal those who are wounded and give medicine to the sick, to take upon himself the sin of the world. What happened at the moment when Jesus had himself baptized by John? In the face of this act of humble love by the Son of God, the heavens opened and the Holy Spirit showed himself in the form of a dove, while a voice from on high expressed the pleasure of the Father who acknowledged his Only-Begotten, his beloved Son. This was a real manifestation of the Blessed Trinity, that bears witness to the divinity of Jesus, of his being the promised Messiah, the One whom God sent to set his People free in order to save them (cf. Is 40:2). In this way the prophecy of Isaiah that we heard in the first reading came true: the Lord God comes with might to destroy the work of sin and his arm rules in order to disarm the Evil One. However, let us bear in mind that this arm is the arm stretched out on the Cross and that Christ's power is the power of the One who suffered for us; this is the power of God, different from the power of the world; thus God comes with power to destroy sin.

Indeed, Jesus acted as the Good Shepherd who tended his sheep and gathered his flock, so that none might stray (cf. Is 40:10–11), and laid down his life so that it might have life. It is through his redeeming death that man is liberated from the dominion of sin and reconciled with the Father; it is through his resurrection that man is saved from eternal death and enabled to triumph over the Evil One. Dear brothers and sisters, what happens in the baptism that I shall shortly be administering to your children? Exactly this: they will be deeply united with Jesus forever, immersed in the mystery of his power, of his might, namely, in the mystery of his death which is a source of life so as to share in his resurrection, to be reborn to new life. This is the miracle that is repeated today, also for your children: in receiving baptism they are reborn as children of God who share in the filial relationship that Jesus has with the Father, in other words, who can address God, calling him with full confidence and trust: "Abba, Father." The heavens are also opened above your children and God says: these are my children, children in whom I am well pleased. Inserted into this relationship and liberated from original sin, they become living members of the one body that is the Church and are enabled to live their vocation to holiness in fullness, so as to be able to inherit eternal life, obtained for us by Jesus's Resurrection.

Dear parents, in asking for Baptism for your children you express and witness to your faith, to the joy of being Christian and of belonging to the Church. It is the joy that comes from knowing you have received a great gift from God, faith itself, a gift which not one of us has been able to deserve but which was freely given to us and to which we responded with our "yes." It is the joy of recognizing that we are children of God, of discovering that we have been entrusted to his hands, of feeling welcomed in a loving embrace in the same way that a mother holds and embraces her child. This joy, which guides every Christian's journey, is based on a personal relationship with Jesus, a relationship that directs the whole of human existence. Indeed, it is he who is the meaning of our life, the One on whom it is worth keeping our eyes fixed so as to be illuminated by his Truth and to be able to live to the full. The journey of faith that begins for these infants today is therefore based on a certainty, on the experience that there is nothing greater than knowing Christ and communicating friendship with him to others; only in this friendship is the enormous potential of the human condition truly revealed and we can experience what is beautiful and sets us free.[1] Whoever has had this experience is not prepared to give up his faith for anything in the world. Dear godparents, it is your important duty to sustain and help the parents in their educational task, supporting them in the transmission of the truths of the faith and in their witness to the Gospel values and bringing up these children in an ever-deeper friendship with the Lord. May you always be able to offer them your good example, through the practice of the Christian virtues. It is not easy to express what one believes in, openly and without compromises. This is especially true in the context in which we live, in the face of a society that all too often considers those who live by faith in Jesus as out of fashion and out of time.

1. Cf. Pope Benedict XVI, *Homily at Holy Mass for the Inauguration of the Pontificate*, April 24, 2005.

On the crest of this mentality, Christians too can risk seeing the relationship with Jesus as restrictive, something that humiliates one's fulfilment; "God is constantly regarded as a limitation placed on our freedom, that must be set aside if man is ever to be completely himself."[2] But this is not how it is! This vision shows that it has not understood the relationship with God at all, for as we gradually proceed on our journey of faith, we realize that Jesus exercises on us the liberating action of God's love which brings us out of our selfishness, our withdrawal into ourselves, to lead us to a full life in communion with God and open to others. "'God is love, and he who abides in love abides in God, and God abides in him' (1 Jn 4:16). These words from the First Letter of John express with remarkable clarity the heart of the Christian faith: the Christian image of God and the resulting image of mankind and its destiny."[3] The water which will sign these children in the name of the Father and of the Son and of the Holy Spirit will immerse them in that "fount" of life which is God himself and will make them his own true sons. And the seed of the theological virtues, faith, hope, and charity, sown by God, seeds that are planted in their hearts today through the power of the Holy Spirit, must always be nourished by the word of God and by the sacraments so that these Christian virtues may grow and attain full maturity, until they make each one of them a true witness of the Lord. As we invoke upon these little ones the outpouring of the Holy Spirit, let us entrust them to the protection of the Blessed Virgin; may she always preserve them with her motherly presence and accompany them at every moment of their lives. Amen.

2. Pope Benedict XVI, *Jesus of Nazareth: The Infancy Narratives* (Ignatius Press, 2013), 86.

3. Pope Benedict XVI, Encyclical Letter *Deus Caritas Est* (December 25, 2005), no. 1.

MARIAN SOLEMNITIES AND FEASTS

MARY, MOTHER OF GOD

14. *Attentive Disciples of the Lord*

From the Homily of His Holiness Pope Benedict XVI
Solemnity of Mary Mother of God
Saint Peter's Basilica, Sunday, 1 January 2006

In today's liturgy our gaze continues to be turned to the great mystery of the Incarnation of the Son of God, while with particular emphasis we contemplate the Motherhood of the Virgin Mary. In the Pauline passage we have heard (Gal 4:4), the Apostle very discreetly points to the one through whom the Son of God enters the world: Mary of Nazareth, Mother of God, *Theotokos*. At the beginning of a new year, we are invited, as it were, to attend her school, the school of the faithful disciple of the Lord, in order to learn from her to accept in faith and prayer the salvation God desires to pour out upon those who trust in his merciful love. Salvation is a gift of God; in the first reading, it was presented as a blessing: "The Lord bless you and keep you! . . . The Lord look upon you kindly and give you peace!" (Nm 6:24,26). This is the blessing that priests used to invoke upon the people at the end of the great liturgical feasts, particularly the feast of the New Year. We are in the presence of a text packed with meaning, punctuated by the Name of the Lord which is repeated at the beginning of every verse. This text is not limited to the mere enunciation of principles but strives to realize what it says. Indeed, as is widely known, in Semitic thought the blessing of the Lord produces well-being and salvation through its own power, just as cursing procures disgrace and ruin. The effectiveness of blessing is later more specifically brought about by God, who protects us (Nm 6:24), favors us (Nm 6:25), and gives us peace, which is to say, in other words, he offers us an abundance of happiness. By having us listen once again to this ancient blessing at the beginning of a new solar year, the liturgy, as it were, encourages us in turn to invoke the Lord's blessing upon the New Year that is just beginning, so that it may be a year of prosperity and peace for us all. It is precisely this wish that I would like to address to the distinguished Ambassadors of the Diplomatic Corps accredited to the Holy See who are taking part in today's liturgical celebration.

I greet Cardinal Angelo Sodano, my Secretary of State. With him, I greet Cardinal Renato Raffaele Martino and all the members of the Pontifical Council for Justice and Peace. I am particularly grateful to them for their commitment to disseminating the annual Message for the World Day of Peace, addressed to Christians and to all men and women of good will. I also offer a cordial greeting to the many choirboys who with their singing add to the solemnity of this Holy Mass, during which we ask God for the gift of peace for the whole world. By choosing the theme "In truth, peace" as the Message for the World Day of Peace, I wanted to express the conviction that "whenever men and women are enlightened by the splendor of truth, they naturally set out on the path of peace."[1] How can we not see in this an effective and appropriate realization of the Gospel just proclaimed, in which we contemplated the scene of the shepherds on their way to Bethlehem to adore the

1. Pope Benedict XVI, *Message for the Celebration of the World Day of Peace*, January 1, 2006, no. 3.

Child? (cf. Lk 2:16). Are not those shepherds, whom the Evangelist Luke describes to us in their poverty and simplicity, obedient to the Angel's order and docile to God's will, perhaps the image most easily accessible to each one of us of the person who allows himself to be enlightened by the truth and is thereby enabled to build a world of peace?

Peace! This great, heartfelt aspiration of every man and every woman is built day after day by the contribution of all and by treasuring the wonderful heritage passed down to us by the Second Vatican Council with the Pastoral Constitution *Gaudium et Spes*, which says, among other things, that humanity will not succeed in "the establishment of a truly human world for all men over the entire earth, unless everyone devotes himself to the cause of true peace with renewed vigor."[2] The time in history when the Constitution *Gaudium et Spes* was promulgated, 7 December 1965, was not very different from our time. Then, as unfortunately also in our day and age, tensions of various kinds were looming on the world horizon. In the face of the lasting situations of injustice and violence that continue to oppress various parts of the earth, in the face of those that are emerging as new and more insidious threats to peace—terrorism, nihilism, and fanatical fundamentalism—it is becoming more necessary than ever to work together for peace! A "start" of courage and trust in God and man is necessary if we are to choose the path of peace. And it must be on the part of all: individuals and peoples, international organizations and world powers. In the Message for today's event, I wanted in particular to call the United Nations Organization to a renewed awareness of its

2. Second Vatican Council, Pastoral Constitution *Gaudium et Spes*, no. 77.

responsibilities in encouraging the values of justice, solidarity, and peace in a world that is ever more marked by the vast phenomenon of globalization. If peace is the aspiration of every person of good will, for Christ's disciples it is a permanent mandate that involves all; it is a demanding mission that impels them to announce and witness to "the Gospel of Peace," proclaiming that recognition of God's full truth is an indispensable pre-condition for the consolidation of the truth of peace. May this awareness continue to grow so that every Christian community becomes the "leaven" of a humanity renewed by love.

"And Mary kept all these things, reflecting on them in her heart" (Lk 2:19). The first day of the year is placed under the sign of a woman, Mary. The Evangelist Luke describes her as the silent Virgin who listens constantly to the eternal Word, who lives in the Word of God. Mary treasures in her heart the words that come from God and, piecing them together as in a mosaic, learns to understand them. Let us too, at her school, learn to become attentive and docile disciples of the Lord. With her motherly help, let us commit ourselves to working enthusiastically in the "workshop" of peace, following Christ, the Prince of Peace. After the example of the Blessed Virgin, may we let ourselves be guided always and only by Jesus Christ, who is the same yesterday, today, and forever! (Heb 13:8). Amen.

15. *Mother of Peace*

From the Homily of His Holiness Pope Benedict XVI
Solemnity of Mary Mother of God
Saint Peter's Basilica, Tuesday, 1 January 2008

Today, we are beginning a new year and Christian hope takes us by the hand; let us begin it by invoking divine Blessings upon it and imploring, through the intercession of Mary, Mother of God, the gift of peace: for our families, for our cities, for the whole world. With this hope, I greet all of you present here, starting with the distinguished Ambassadors of the Diplomatic Corps accredited to the Holy See who have gathered at this celebration on the occasion of the World Day of Peace. I greet Cardinal Tarcisio Bertone, my Secretary of State, and Cardinal Renato Raffaele Martino and all members of the Pontifical Council for Justice and Peace. I am particularly grateful to them for their commitment to spread the Message for the World Day of Peace whose theme this year is: "The human family, a community of peace."

Peace: in the first reading, from the Book of Numbers, we heard the invocation: "The Lord . . . give you peace" (Nm 6:26); may the Lord grant peace to each one of you, to your families and to the whole world. We all aspire to live in peace but true peace, the peace proclaimed by the Angels on Christmas night, is not merely a human triumph or the fruit of political agreements; it is first and foremost a divine gift to be ceaselessly implored, and at the same time a commitment to be carried forward patiently, always remaining docile to the Lord's commands. This year, in my Message for today's World Day of Peace, I wanted to highlight the close relationship that exists between the family and building peace in the world. The natural family, founded on the marriage of a man and a woman, is a "cradle of life and love" and "the first and indispensable teacher of peace." For this very reason the family is "the primary 'agency' of peace," and "the denial or even the restriction of the rights of the family, by obscuring the truth about man, threatens the very foundations of peace."[3] Since humanity is a "great family," if it wants to live in peace it cannot fail to draw inspiration from those values on which the family community is based and stands. The providential coincidence of various recurrences spurs us this year to make an even greater effort to achieve peace in the world. Sixty years ago, in 1948, the General Assembly of the United Nations published the "Universal Declaration of Human Rights"; 40 years ago, my venerable Predecessor Paul VI celebrated the first World Day of Peace; this year, in addition, we will be commemorating the 25th anniversary of the Holy See's adoption of the "Charter of the Rights of the Family." "In the light of these significant anniversaries"—I am repeating here what I wrote precisely at the end of the Message—"I invite every man and woman to have a more lively sense of belonging to the one human family, and to strive to make human coexistence increasingly reflect this conviction, which is essential for the establishment of true and lasting peace."[4]

Our thoughts now turn spontaneously to Our Lady, whom we invoke today as the Mother of God. It was Pope Paul VI who moved to January 1st the Feast of the Divine Motherhood of Mary,

3. Pope Benedict XVI, *Message for the Celebration of the World Day of Peace*, January 1, 2008, nos. 1–5.

4. Pope Benedict XVI, *Message for the Celebration of the World Day of Peace*, no. 15.

which was formerly celebrated on the 11th of October. Indeed, even before the liturgical reform that followed the Second Vatican Council, the memorial of the circumcision of Jesus on the eighth day after his birth—as a sign of submission to the law, his official inclusion in the Chosen People—used to be celebrated on the first day of the year and the Feast of the Name of Jesus was celebrated the following Sunday. We perceive a few traces of these celebrations in the Gospel passage that has just been proclaimed, in which St. Luke says that eight days after his birth the Child was circumcised and was given the name "Jesus," "the name given by the Angel before he was conceived in his Mother's womb" (Lk 2:21). Today's feast, therefore, as well as being a particularly significant Marian feast, also preserves a strongly Christological content because, we might say, before the Mother, it concerns the Son, Jesus, true God and true Man.

The Apostle Paul refers to the mystery of the divine motherhood of Mary, the *Theotokos*, in his Letter to the Galatians. "When the time had fully come," he writes, "God sent forth his Son, born of woman, born under the law" (Gal 4:4). We find the mystery of the Incarnation of the Divine Word and the Divine Motherhood of Mary summed up in a few words: the Virgin's great privilege is precisely to be Mother of the Son who is God. The most logical and proper place for this Marian feast is therefore eight days after Christmas. Indeed, in the night of Bethlehem, when "she gave birth to her first-born son" (Lk 2:7), the prophesies concerning the Messiah were fulfilled. "The virgin shall be with child and bear a son," Isaiah had foretold (7:14); "Behold, you will conceive in your womb and bear a son," the Angel Gabriel said to Mary (Lk 1:31); and again, an Angel of the Lord, the Evangelist Matthew recounts, appeared to Joseph in a dream to reassure him and said: "Do not fear to take Mary for your wife, for that which is conceived in her is of the Holy Spirit; she will bear a son" (Mt 1:20–21).

The title "Mother of God," together with the title "Blessed Virgin," is the oldest, on which all the other titles with which Our Lady was venerated are based, and it continues to be invoked from generation to generation in the East and in the West. A multitude of hymns and a wealth of prayers of the Christian tradition refer to the mystery of her divine motherhood, such as, for example, a Marian antiphon of the Christmas season, *Alma Redemptoris Mater*, with which we pray in these words: *Tu quae genuisti, natura mirante, tuum sanctum Genitorem, Virgo prius ac posterius*—"You, in the wonder of all creation, have brought forth your Creator, Mother ever virgin."[5] Dear brothers and sisters, let us today contemplate Mary, ever-virgin Mother of the Only-Begotten Son of the Father; let us learn from her to welcome the Child who was born for us in Bethlehem. If we recognize in the Child born of her the Eternal Son of God and accept him as our one Savior, we can be called and we really are children of God: sons in the Son. The Apostle writes: "God sent forth his Son, born of woman, born under the law, to redeem those who were under the law, so that we might receive adoption as sons" (Gal 4:4).

The Evangelist Luke repeats several times that Our Lady meditated silently on these extraordinary events in which God had involved her. We also heard this in the short Gospel passage that the Liturgy presents to us today. "Mary kept all these things, pondering them in her heart" (Lk 2:19). The Greek verb used, *sumbállousa*,

5. Hermannus Contractus, *Alma Redemptoris Mater*.

literally means "piecing together" and makes us think of a great mystery to be discovered little by little. Although the Child lying in a manger looks like all children in the world, at the same time he is totally different: he is the Son of God, he is God, true God and true man. This mystery—the Incarnation of the Word and the divine Motherhood of Mary—is great and certainly far from easy to understand with the human mind alone.

Yet, by learning from Mary, we can understand with our hearts what our eyes and minds do not manage to perceive or contain on their own. Indeed, this is such a great gift that only through faith are we granted to accept it, while not entirely understanding it. And it is precisely on this journey of faith that Mary comes to meet us as our support and guide. She is mother because she brought forth Jesus in the flesh; she is mother because she adhered totally to the Father's will. St. Augustine wrote: "The divine motherhood would have been of no value to her had Christ not borne her in his heart, with a destiny more fortunate than the moment when she conceived him in the flesh."[6] And in her heart Mary continued to treasure, to "piece together" the subsequent events of which she was to be a witness and protagonist, even to the death on the Cross and the Resurrection of her Son Jesus.

Dear brothers and sisters, it is only by pondering in the heart, in other words, by piecing together and finding unity in all we experience, that, following Mary, we can penetrate the mystery of a God who was made man out of love and who calls us to follow him on the path of love; a love to be expressed daily by generous service to the brethren. May the new year which we are confidently

6. St. Augustine, *De Sancta Virginitate*, 3.

beginning today be a time in which to advance in that knowledge of the heart, which is the wisdom of saints. Let us pray, as we heard in the first reading, that the Lord may "make his face to shine" upon us, "and be gracious" to us (Nm 6:24–27) and bless us. We may be certain of it: if we never tire of seeking his Face, if we never give in to the temptation of discouragement and doubt, if also among the many difficulties we encounter we always remain anchored to him, we will experience the power of his love and his mercy. May the fragile Child who today the Virgin shows to the world make us peacemakers, witnesses of him, the Prince of Peace. Amen!

16. *Mary and Education*

From the Homily of His Holiness Pope Benedict XVI
Solemnity of Mary Mother of God
Saint Peter's Basilica, Sunday, 1 January 2012

On the first day of the year, the liturgy resounds in the Church throughout the world with the ancient priestly blessing that we heard during today's first reading: "The Lord bless you and keep you; the Lord make his face to shine upon you, and be gracious to you; the Lord lift up his countenance upon you and give you peace" (Nm 6:24–26). This blessing was entrusted by God, through Moses, to Aaron and his sons, that is, to the priests of the people of Israel. It is a triple blessing filled with light, radiating from the repetition of the name of God, the Lord, and from the image of his face. In fact, in order to be blessed, we have to stand in God's presence, take his Name upon us and remain in the cone of light that issues from his Face, in a space lit up by his gaze, diffusing grace and peace.

This was the very experience that the shepherds of Bethlehem had, who reappear in today's Gospel. They had the experience of standing in God's presence, they received his blessing not in the hall of a majestic palace, in the presence of a great sovereign, but in a stable, before a "babe lying in a manger" (Lk 2:16). From this child, a new light issues forth, shining in the darkness of the night, as we can see in so many paintings depicting Christ's Nativity. Henceforth, it is from him that blessing comes, from his name—Jesus, meaning "God saves"—and from his human face, in which God, the almighty Lord of heaven and earth, chose to become incarnate, concealing his glory under the veil of our flesh, so as to reveal fully to us his goodness (cf. Tit 3:4).

The first to be swept up by this blessing was Mary the virgin, the spouse of Joseph, chosen by God from the first moment of her existence to be the mother of his incarnate Son. She is the "blessed among women" (Lk 1:42)—in the words of Saint Elizabeth's greeting. Her whole life was spent in the light of the Lord, within the radius of his name and of the face of God incarnate in Jesus, the "blessed fruit of her womb." This is how Luke's Gospel presents her to us: fully intent upon guarding and meditating in her heart upon everything concerning her son Jesus (cf. Lk 2:19, 51). The mystery of her divine motherhood that we celebrate today contains in superabundant measure the gift of grace that all human motherhood bears within it, so much so that the fruitfulness of the womb has always been associated with God's blessing. The Mother of God is the first of the blessed, and it is she who bears the blessing; she is the woman who received Jesus into herself and brought him forth for the whole human family. In the words of the liturgy: "without losing the glory of virginity, she brought forth into the world the eternal light, Jesus Christ our Lord."[7]

Mary is the mother and model of the Church, who receives the divine Word in faith and offers herself to God as the "good soil" in which he can continue to accomplish his mystery of salvation. The Church also participates in the mystery of divine motherhood, through preaching, which sows the seed of the Gospel throughout the world, and through the sacraments, which communicate grace and divine life to men. The Church exercises her motherhood especially in the sacrament of Baptism, when she generates God's children from water and the Holy Spirit, who cries out in each of them: "Abba, Father!" (Gal 4:6). Like Mary, the Church is the mediator of God's blessing for the world: she receives it in receiving Jesus and she transmits it in bearing Jesus. He is the mercy and the peace that the world, of itself, cannot give, and which it needs always, at least as much as bread.

Dear friends, peace, in the fullest and highest sense, is the sum and synthesis of all blessings. So when two friends meet, they greet one another, wishing each other peace. The Church, too, on the first day of the year, invokes this supreme good in a special way; she does so, like the Virgin Mary, by revealing Jesus to all, for as Saint Paul says, "He is our peace" (Eph 2:14), and at the same time the "way" by which individuals and peoples can reach this goal to which we all aspire. With this deep desire in my heart, I am glad to welcome and greet all of you who have come to Saint Peter's Basilica on this 45th World Day of Peace: Cardinals, Ambassadors

7. "Preface I of the Blessed Virgin Mary," in *The Roman Missal*, sec. 62, 590.

from so many friendly countries, who more than ever on this happy occasion share with me and with the Holy See the desire for renewed commitment to the promotion of peace in the world; the President of the Pontifical Council for Justice and Peace, who with the Secretary and the officials of the Dicastery work in a particular way towards this goal; the other Bishops and Authorities present; the representatives of ecclesial associations and movements and all of you, brothers and sisters, especially those among you who work in the field of educating the young. Indeed—as you know—the role of education is what I highlighted in my Message for this year.

"Educating Young People in Justice and Peace" is a task for every generation, and thanks be to God, after the tragedies of the two great world wars, the human family has shown increasing awareness of it, as we can witness, on the one hand, from international statements and initiatives, and on the other, from the emergence among young people themselves, in recent decades, of many different forms of social commitment in this field. For the ecclesial community, educating men and women in peace is part of the mission received from Christ, it is an integral part of evangelization, because the Gospel of Christ is also the Gospel of justice and peace. But the Church, in recent times, has articulated a demand that affects everyone with a sensitive and responsible conscience regarding humanity's future; the demand to respond to a decisive challenge that consists precisely in education. Why is this a "challenge"? For at least two reasons: in the first place, because in the present age, so strongly marked by a technological mentality, the desire to educate and not merely to instruct cannot be taken for granted, it is a choice; in the second place, because the culture of relativism raises a radical question: does it still make sense to educate? And then, to educate for what?

Naturally, now is not the time to address these fundamental questions, which I have tried to answer on other occasions. Instead, I would like to underline the fact that, in the face of the shadows that obscure the horizon of today's world, to assume responsibility for educating young people in knowledge of the truth, in fundamental values and virtues, is to look to the future with hope. And in this commitment to a holistic education, formation in justice and peace has a place. Boys and girls today are growing up in a world that has, so to speak, become smaller, where contacts between different cultures and traditions, even if not always direct, are constant. For them, now more than ever, it is indispensable to learn the importance and the art of peaceful coexistence, mutual respect, dialogue, and understanding. Young people by their nature are open to these attitudes, but the social reality in which they grow up can lead them to think and act in the opposite way, even to be intolerant and violent. Only a solid education of their consciences can protect them from these risks and make them capable of carrying on the fight, depending always and solely on the power of truth and good. This education begins in the family and is developed at school and in other formative experiences. It is essentially about helping infants, children, and adolescents to develop a personality that combines a profound sense of justice with respect for their neighbor, with a capacity to address conflicts without arrogance, with the inner strength to bear witness to good, even when it involves sacrifice, with forgiveness and reconciliation.

Thus, they will be able to become people of peace and builders of peace. In this task of educating young generations, a particular responsibility lies with religious communities. Every pathway of authentic religious formation guides the person, from the most tender age, to know God, to love him, and to do his will. God is love, he is just and peaceable, and anyone wishing to honor him must first of all act like a child following his father's example. One of the Psalms says: "The Lord does deeds of justice, gives judgment for all who are oppressed. . . . The Lord is compassion and love, slow to anger and rich in mercy" (Ps 102:6,8). In God, justice and mercy come together perfectly, as Jesus showed us through the testimony of his life. In Jesus, "love and truth" have met, "justice and peace" have embraced (cf. Ps 84:11). In these days, the Church is celebrating the great mystery of the Incarnation: God's truth has sprung from the earth and justice looks down from heaven, the earth has yielded its fruit (cf. Ps 84:12,13). God has spoken to us in his Son Jesus. Let us hear what God has to say: "a voice that speaks of peace" (Ps 84:9). Jesus is a way that can be travelled, open to everyone. He is the path of peace. Today the Virgin Mary points him out to us, she shows us the Way: let us walk in it! And you, Holy Mother of God, accompany us with your protection. Amen.

17. *The Gift of Peace*

From the Homily of His Holiness Pope Benedict XVI
Solemnity of Mary Mother of God
Saint Peter's Basilica, Tuesday, 1 January 2013

"May God bless us and make his face to shine upon us." We proclaimed these words from Psalm 66 after hearing in the first reading the ancient priestly blessing upon the people of the covenant.

It is especially significant that at the start of every new year God sheds upon us, his people, the light of his Holy Name, the Name pronounced three times in the solemn form of biblical blessing. Nor is it less significant that to the Word of God—who "became flesh and dwelt among us" (Jn 1:14) as "the true light that enlightens every man" (Jn 1:9)—is given, as today's Gospel tells us, the Name of Jesus eight days after his birth (Lk 2:21).

It is in this Name that we are gathered here today. I cordially greet all present, beginning with the Ambassadors of the Diplomatic Corps accredited to the Holy See. I greet with affection Cardinal Bertone, my Secretary of State, and Cardinal Turkson, with all the officials of the Pontifical Council for Justice and Peace; I am particularly grateful to them for their effort to spread the Message for the World Day of Peace, which this year has as its theme "Blessed are the Peacemakers."

Although the world is sadly marked by "hotbeds of tension and conflict caused by growing instances of inequality between rich and poor, by the prevalence of a selfish and individualistic mindset which also finds expression in an unregulated financial capitalism," as well as by various forms of terrorism and crime, I am convinced that "the many different efforts at peacemaking which abound in our world testify to mankind's innate vocation to peace. In every person the desire for peace is an essential aspiration which coincides in a certain way with the desire for a full, happy, and successful human life. In other words, the desire for peace corresponds to a fundamental moral principle, namely, the duty and right to an integral social and communitarian development, which is part of God's plan for mankind. Man is made for the peace which is God's gift. All of this led me to draw inspiration for this Message from the words of Jesus Christ: 'Blessed are the peacemakers, for they will be called children of God' (Mt 5:9)."[8] This beatitude "tells us that peace is both a messianic gift and the fruit of human effort. . . . It is peace with God through a life lived according to his will. It is interior peace with oneself, and exterior peace with our neighbors and all creation."[9] Indeed, peace is the supreme good to ask as a gift from God and, at the same time, that which is to be built with our every effort.

We may ask ourselves: what is the basis, the origin, the root of peace? How can we experience that peace within ourselves, in spite of problems, darkness, and anxieties? The reply is given to us by the readings of today's liturgy. The biblical texts, especially the one just read from the Gospel of Luke, ask us to contemplate the interior peace of Mary, the Mother of Jesus. During the days in which "she gave birth to her first-born son" (Lk 2:7), many unexpected things occurred: not only the birth of the Son but, even before, the tiring journey from Nazareth to Bethlehem, not finding room at the inn, the search for a chance place to stay for the night; then the song of the angels and the unexpected visit of the shepherds. In all this, however, Mary remains even-tempered, she does not get agitated, she is not overcome by events greater than herself; in silence she considers what happens, keeping it in her mind and heart, and pondering it calmly and serenely. This is the interior peace which we ought to have amid the sometimes tumultuous and confusing events of history, events whose meaning we often do not grasp and which disconcert us.

8. Pope Benedict XVI, *Message for the Celebration of the World Day of Peace*, January 1, 2013, no. 1.

9. Pope Benedict XVI, *Message for the Celebration of the World Day of Peace*, nos. 2, 3.

The Gospel passage finishes with a mention of the circumcision of Jesus. According to the Law of Moses, eight days after birth, baby boys were to be circumcised and then given their name. Through his messenger, God himself had said to Mary—as well as to Joseph—that the Name to be given to the child was "Jesus" (Mt 1:21; Lk 1:31); and so it came to be. The Name which God had already chosen, even before the child had been conceived, is now officially conferred upon him at the moment of circumcision. This also changes Mary's identity once and for all: she becomes "the mother of Jesus," that is, the mother of the Savior, of Christ, of the Lord. Jesus is not a man like any other, but the Word of God, one of the Divine Persons, the Son of God: therefore, the Church has given Mary the title *Theotokos* or Mother of God.

The first reading reminds us that peace is a gift from God and is linked to the splendor of the face of God, according to the text from the Book of Numbers, which hands down the blessing used by the priests of the People of Israel in their liturgical assemblies. This blessing repeats three times the Holy Name of God, a Name not to be spoken, and each time it is linked to two words indicating an action in favor of man: "The Lord bless you and keep you: the Lord make his face to shine upon you: the Lord lift up his countenance upon you, and give you peace" (Nm 6:24–26). So, peace is the summit of these six actions of God in our favor, in which he turns towards us the splendor of his face.

For sacred Scripture, contemplating the face of God is the greatest happiness: "You gladden him with the joy of your face" (Ps 21:7). From the contemplation of the face of God are born joy, security, and peace. But what does it mean concretely to contemplate the face of the Lord, as understood in the New Testament? It means knowing him directly, insofar as is possible in this life, through Jesus Christ in whom he is revealed. To rejoice in the splendor of God's face means penetrating the mystery of his Name made known to us in Jesus, understanding something of his interior life and of his will, so that we can live according to his plan of love for humanity. In the second reading, taken from the Letter to the Galatians (4:4–7), Saint Paul says as much, as he describes the Spirit who, in our inmost hearts, cries: "Abba! Father!" It is the cry that rises from the contemplation of the true face of God, from the revelation of the mystery of his Name. Jesus declares, "I have manifested thy name to men" (Jn 17:6). God's Son made man has let us know the Father, he has let us know the hidden face of the Father through his visible human face; by the gift of the Holy Spirit poured into our hearts, he has led us to understand that, in him, we too are children of God, as Saint Paul says in the passage we have just heard: "The proof that you are sons is that God has sent the Spirit of his Son into our hearts: the Spirit that cries, 'Abba, Father'" (Gal 4:6).

Here, dear brothers and sisters, is the foundation of our peace: the certainty of contemplating in Jesus Christ the splendor of the face of God the Father, of being sons in the Son, and thus of having, on life's journey, the same security that a child feels in the arms of a loving and all-powerful Father. The splendor of the face of God, shining upon us and granting us peace, is the manifestation of his fatherhood: the Lord turns his face to us, he reveals himself as our Father and grants us peace. Here is the principle of that profound peace—"peace with God"—which is firmly linked to faith and grace, as Saint Paul tells the Christians of Rome (Rom 5:2). Nothing can take this peace from believers, not even the difficulties and sufferings of life. Indeed, sufferings, trials, and darkness do not undermine but build up our hope, a hope which does not deceive because "God's love has been poured into our hearts through the Holy Spirit which has been given to us" (Rom 5:5).

May the Virgin Mary, whom today we venerate with the title of Mother of God, help us to contemplate the face of Jesus, the Prince of Peace. May she sustain us and accompany us in this New Year: and may she obtain for us and for the whole world the gift of peace. Amen!

MARIAN SOLEMNITIES AND FEASTS

OUR LADY OF LOURDES

18. *I Am the Immaculate Conception*

From the Homily of His Holiness Pope Benedict XVI
Mass on the 150th Anniversary of the Apparitions of the Blessed Virgin Mother at Lourdes, Lourdes, Saturday, 13 September 2008

One hundred and fifty years ago, on 11 February 1858, in this place known as the Grotto of Massabielle, away from the town, a simple young girl from Lourdes, Bernadette Soubirous, saw a light, and in this light she saw a young lady who was "beautiful, more beautiful than any other." This woman addressed her with kindness and gentleness, with respect and trust: "She said *vous* to me," Bernadette recounted, "Would you do me the kindness of coming here for a fortnight?" she asked her. "She was looking at me as one person who speaks to another." It was in this conversation, in this dialogue marked by such delicacy, that the Lady instructed her to deliver certain very simple messages on prayer, penance, and conversion. It is hardly surprising that Mary should be beautiful, given that—during the apparition of 25 March 1858—she reveals her name in this way: "I am the Immaculate Conception."

Let us now look at this "woman clothed with the sun" (Rev 12:1) as she is described for us in Scripture. The Most Holy Virgin Mary, the glorious woman of the Apocalypse, wears on her head a crown of twelve stars which represent the twelve tribes of Israel, the entire people of God, the whole communion of saints, while at her feet is the moon, image of death and mortality. Mary left death behind her; she is entirely re-clothed with life, the life of her Son, the risen Christ. She is thus the sign of the victory of love, of good, and of God, giving our world the hope that it needs. This evening, let us turn our gaze towards Mary, so glorious and so human, allowing her to lead us towards God who is the victor.

Countless people have borne witness to this: when they encountered Bernadette's radiant face, it left a deep impression on their hearts and minds. Whether it was during the apparitions themselves or while she was recounting them, her face was simply shining. Bernadette from that time on had the light of Massabielle dwelling within her. The daily life of the Soubirous family was nevertheless a tale of deprivation and sadness, sickness and incomprehension, rejection and poverty. Even if there was no lack of love and warmth in family relationships, life at the *cachot* was hard. Nevertheless, the shadows of the earth did not prevent the light of heaven from shining. "The light shines in the darkness . . ." (Jn 1:5).

Lourdes is one of the places chosen by God for his beauty to be reflected with particular brightness, hence the importance here of the symbol of light. From the fourth apparition onwards, on arriving at the grotto, Bernadette would light a votive candle each morning and hold it in her left hand for as long as the Virgin was visible to her. Soon, people would give Bernadette a candle to plant in the ground inside the grotto. Very soon, too, people would place their own candles in this place of light and peace. The Mother of God herself let it be known that she liked the touching homage of these thousands of torches, which since that time have continued to shine upon the rock of the apparition and give her glory. From that day, before the grotto, night and day, summer and winter, a burning bush shines out, aflame with the prayers of pilgrims and the sick, who bring their concerns and their needs, but above all their faith and their hope.

By coming here to Lourdes on pilgrimage, we wish to enter, following in Bernadette's footsteps, into this extraordinary closeness between heaven and earth, which never fails and never ceases to grow. In the course of the apparitions, it is notable that Bernadette prays the Rosary under the gaze of Mary, who unites herself to her at the moment of the doxology. This fact confirms the profoundly theocentric character of the prayer of the Rosary. When we pray it, Mary offers us her heart and her gaze in order to contemplate the life of her Son, Jesus Christ. My venerable Predecessor, Pope John Paul II, came here to Lourdes on two occasions. In his life and ministry, we know how much his prayer relied upon the Virgin Mary's intercession. Like many of his predecessors in the Chair of Peter, he also keenly encouraged the prayer of the Rosary; one of the particular ways in which he did so was by enriching the Holy Rosary with the meditation of the Mysteries of Light. These are now represented on the facade of the Basilica in the new mosaics inaugurated last year. As with all the events in the life of Christ, "which she preserved and pondered in her heart" (Lk 2:19), Mary helps us to understand all the stages in his public ministry as integral to the revelation of God's glory. May Lourdes, the land of light, continue to be a school for learning to pray the Rosary, which introduces the disciples of Jesus, under the gaze of his Mother, into an authentic and cordial dialogue with his Master!

On Bernadette's lips we hear the Virgin Mary asking us to come here in procession so as to pray with simplicity and fervor. The torchlight procession expresses the mystery of prayer in a form that our eyes of flesh can grasp: in the communion of the

Church, which unites the elect in heaven with pilgrims on earth, the light of dialogue between man and his Lord blazes forth and a luminous path opens up in human history, even in its darkest moments. This procession is a time of great ecclesial joy, but also a time of seriousness: the intentions we bring emphasize our profound communion with all those who suffer. We think of innocent victims who suffer from violence, war, terrorism, and famine; those who bear the consequences of injustices, scourges and disasters, hatred and oppression; of attacks on their human dignity and fundamental rights; on their freedom to act and think. We also think of those undergoing family problems or suffering caused by unemployment, illness, infirmity, loneliness, or their situation as immigrants. Nor must we forget those who suffer for the name of Christ and die for him.

Mary teaches us to pray, to make of our prayer an act of love for God and an act of fraternal charity. By praying with Mary, our heart welcomes those who suffer. How can our life not be transformed by this? Why should our whole life and being not become places of hospitality for our neighbors? Lourdes is a place of light because it is a place of communion, hope, and conversion.

As night falls, Jesus says to us: "keep your lamps burning" (Lk 12:35); the lamp of faith, the lamp of prayer, the lamp of hope and love! This act of walking through the night, carrying the light, speaks powerfully to the depths of ourselves, touches our heart, and says much more than any other word uttered or heard. This gesture itself summarizes our condition as Christians on a journey: we need light, and at the same time are called to be light. Sin makes us blind; it prevents us from putting ourselves forward as guides for our brothers and sisters, and it makes us unwilling to trust them to guide us. We need to be enlightened, and we repeat the prayer of blind Bartimaeus: "Master, let me receive my sight!" (Mk 10:51). Let me see my sin which holds me back, but above all, Lord, let me see your glory! We know that our prayer has already been granted and we give thanks because, as Saint Paul says in the Letter to the Ephesians, "Christ shall give you light" (Eph 5:14), and Saint Peter adds, "he called you out of darkness into his marvelous light" (1 Pet 2:9).

To us who are not the light, Christ can now say: "You are the light of the world" (Mt 5:14), entrusting us with the responsibility to cause the light of charity to shine. As the Apostle Saint John writes, "He who loves his brother abides in the light, and in him there is no cause for stumbling" (1 Jn 2:10). To live Christian love, means at the same time to introduce God's light into the world and to point out its true source. Saint Leo the Great writes: "Whoever, in fact, lives a holy and chaste life in the Church, whoever sets his mind on things that are above, not on things that are on earth (cf. Col 3:2), in a certain way resembles heavenly light; as long as he himself observes the brilliance of a holy life, he shows to many, like a star, the path that leads to God."[1] In this shrine at Lourdes, to which the Christians of the whole world have turned their gaze since the Virgin Mary caused hope and love to shine here by giving pride of place to the sick, the poor, and the little ones, we are invited to discover the simplicity of our vocation: it is enough to love.

Tomorrow, the celebration of the exaltation of the Holy Cross brings us into the very heart of this mystery. At this vigil, our gaze is already turned towards the sign of the new covenant on which

1. St. Leo the Great, *Sermon* III:5.

the whole life of Jesus converges. The Cross is the supreme and perfect act of the love of Jesus, who lays down his life for his friends. "So must the Son of man be lifted up, that whoever believes in him may have eternal life" (Jn 3:14–15). As proclaimed in the songs of the Suffering Servant, the death of Jesus is a death which becomes a light for the nations; it is a death which, in intimate association with the liturgy of atonement, brings reconciliation, it is a death which marks the end of death. From that day onwards, the Cross is a sign of hope, Jesus's victory standard, "because God so loved the world that he gave his only Son, that whoever believes in him should not perish but have eternal life" (Jn 3:16). Through the Cross, our whole life gains light, strength, and hope. The Cross reveals the whole depth of love contained in the original design of the Creator; through the Cross, all is healed and brought to completion. That is why life lived with faith in Christ dead and risen becomes light.

The apparitions were bathed in light and God chose to ignite in Bernadette's gaze a flame which converted countless hearts. How many come here to see it with the hope—secretly perhaps—of receiving some miracle; then, on the return journey, having had a spiritual experience of life in the Church, they change their outlook upon God, upon others, and upon themselves. A small flame called hope, compassion, and tenderness now dwells within them. A quiet encounter with Bernadette and the Virgin Mary can change a person's life, for they are here, in Massabielle, to lead us to Christ who is our life, our strength, and our light. May the Virgin Mary and Saint Bernadette help you to live as children of light in order to testify, every day of your lives, that Christ is our light, our hope, and our life!

19. *Mary and the Cross*

From the Homily of His Holiness Pope Benedict XVI, Mass on the 150th Anniversary of the Apparitions of the Blessed Virgin Mother at Lourdes
Lourdes, Sunday, 14 September 2008

"Go and tell the priests that people should come here in procession, and that a chapel should be built here." This is the message Bernadette received from the "beautiful lady" in the apparition of 2 March 1858. For 150 years, pilgrims have never ceased to come to the grotto of Massabielle to hear the message of conversion and hope which is addressed to them. And we have done the same; here we are this morning at the feet of Mary, the Immaculate Virgin, eager to learn from her alongside little Bernadette. I would like to thank especially Bishop Jacques Perrier of Tarbes and Lourdes for the warm welcome he has given me, and for the kind words he has addressed to me. I greet the Cardinals, the Bishops, the priests, the deacons, the men and women religious, and all of you, dear Lourdes pilgrims, especially the sick. You have come in large numbers to make this Jubilee pilgrimage with me and to entrust your families, your relatives and friends, and all your intentions to Our Lady. My thanks go also to the civil and military authorities who are here with us at this Eucharistic celebration.

"What a great thing it is to possess the Cross! He who possesses it possesses a treasure."[2] On this day when the Church's liturgy celebrates the feast of the Exaltation of the Holy Cross, the Gospel you have just heard reminds us of the meaning of this great

2. St. Andrew of Crete, *Homily X on the Exaltation of the Cross*, PG, 97, 1020.

mystery: God so loved the world that he gave his only Son, so that men might be saved (Jn 3:16). The Son of God became vulnerable, assuming the condition of a slave, obedient even to death, death on a cross (Phil 2:8). By his Cross we are saved. The instrument of torture which, on Good Friday, manifested God's judgement on the world, has become a source of life, pardon, mercy, a sign of reconciliation and peace. "In order to be healed from sin, gaze upon Christ crucified!" said Saint Augustine.[3] By raising our eyes towards the Crucified one, we adore him who came to take upon himself the sin of the world and to give us eternal life. And the Church invites us proudly to lift up this glorious Cross so that the world can see the full extent of the love of the Crucified one for mankind, for every man and woman. She invites us to give thanks to God because from a tree which brought death, life has burst out anew. On this wood, Jesus reveals to us his sovereign majesty, he reveals to us that he is exalted in glory. Yes, "Come, let us adore him!" In our midst is he who loved us even to giving his life for us, he who invites every human being to draw near to him with trust.

This is the great mystery that Mary also entrusts to us this morning, inviting us to turn towards her Son. In fact, it is significant that, during the first apparition to Bernadette, Mary begins the encounter with the sign of the Cross. More than a simple sign, it is an initiation into the mysteries of the faith that Bernadette receives from Mary. The sign of the Cross is a kind of synthesis of our faith, for it tells how much God loves us; it tells us that there is a love in this world that is stronger than death, stronger than our weaknesses and sins. The power of love is stronger than the evil

3. St. Augustine, *Treatise on the Gospel of John*, XII, 11.

which threatens us. It is this mystery of the universality of God's love for men that Mary came to reveal here, in Lourdes. She invites all people of good will, all those who suffer in heart or body, to raise their eyes towards the Cross of Jesus, so as to discover there the source of life, the source of salvation.

The Church has received the mission of showing all people this loving face of God, manifested in Jesus Christ. Are we able to understand that in the Crucified One of Golgotha, our dignity as children of God, tarnished by sin, is restored to us? Let us turn our gaze towards Christ. It is he who will make us free to love as he loves us, and to build a reconciled world. For on this Cross, Jesus took upon himself the weight of all the sufferings and injustices of our humanity. He bore the humiliation and the discrimination, the torture suffered in many parts of the world by so many of our brothers and sisters for love of Christ. We entrust all this to Mary, mother of Jesus and our mother, present at the foot of the Cross.

In order to welcome into our lives this glorious Cross, the celebration of the Jubilee of Our Lady's apparitions in Lourdes urges us to embark upon a journey of faith and conversion. Today, Mary comes to meet us, so as to show us the way towards a renewal of life for our communities and for each one of us. By welcoming her Son, whom she presents to us, we are plunged into a living stream in which the faith can rediscover new vigor, in which the Church can be strengthened so as to proclaim the mystery of Christ ever more boldly. Jesus, born of Mary, is the Son of God, the sole Savior of all people, living and acting in his Church and in the world. The Church is sent everywhere in the world to proclaim this unique message and to invite people to receive it through an authentic conversion of heart. This mission, entrusted by Jesus to his disciples, receives here, on the occasion of this Jubilee, a breath of new life. After the example of the great evangelizers from your country, may the missionary spirit which animated so many men and women from France over the centuries, continue to be your pride and your commitment!

When we follow the Jubilee Way in the footsteps of Bernadette, we are reminded of the heart of the message of Lourdes. Bernadette is the eldest daughter of a very poor family, with neither knowledge nor power, and in poor health. Mary chose her to transmit her message of conversion, prayer, and penance, which fully accords with words of Jesus: "What you have hidden from the wise and understanding, you have revealed to babes" (Mt 11:25). On their spiritual journey, Christians too are called to render fruitful the grace of their Baptism, to nourish themselves with the Eucharist, to draw strength from prayer so as to bear witness and to express solidarity with all their fellow human beings.[4] It is therefore a genuine catechesis that is being proposed to us in this way, under Mary's gaze. Let us allow her to instruct us too, and to guide us along the path that leads to the Kingdom of her Son!

In the course of her catechesis, the "beautiful lady" reveals her name to Bernadette: "I am the Immaculate Conception." Mary thereby discloses the extraordinary grace that she has received from God, that of having been conceived without sin, for "he has looked on his servant in her lowliness" (Lk 1:48). Mary is the woman from this earth who gave herself totally to God, and who received the privilege of giving human life to his eternal Son. "Behold the handmaid of the Lord; let what you have said be done to me" (Lk

4. Pope Benedict XVI, Address *Act of Veneration to the Immaculate Virgin Mary*, Piazza di Spagna (Rome) (December 8, 2007).

1:38). She is beauty transfigured, the image of the new humanity. By presenting herself in this way, in utter dependence upon God, Mary expresses in reality an attitude of total freedom, based upon the full recognition of her true dignity. This privilege concerns us, too, for it discloses to us our own dignity as men and women, admittedly marked by sin, but saved in hope, a hope which allows us to face our daily life. This is the path which Mary opens up for man. To give oneself fully to God is to find the path of true freedom. For by turning towards God, man becomes himself. He rediscovers his original vocation as a person created in his image and likeness.

Dear brothers and sisters, the primary purpose of the shrine at Lourdes is to be a place of encounter with God in prayer and a place of service to our brothers and sisters, notably through the welcome given to the sick, the poor, and all who suffer. In this place, Mary comes to us as a mother, always open to the needs of her children. Through the light which streams from her face, God's mercy is made manifest. Let us allow ourselves to be touched by her gaze, which tells us that we are all loved by God and never abandoned by him! Mary comes to remind us that prayer which is humble and intense, trusting and persevering, must have a central place in our Christian lives. Prayer is indispensable if we are to receive Christ's power. "People who pray are not wasting their time, even though the situation appears desperate and seems to call for action alone."[5] To allow oneself to become absorbed by activity runs the risk of depriving prayer of its specifically Christian character and its true efficacy. The prayer of the Rosary, so dear to Bernadette and to Lourdes pilgrims, concentrates within itself the depths

5. Pope Benedict XVI, *Deus Caritas Est*, no. 36.

of the Gospel message. It introduces us to contemplation of the face of Christ. From this prayer of the humble, we can draw an abundance of graces.

The presence of young people at Lourdes is also an important element. Dear friends, gathered this morning around the World Youth Day Cross: when Mary received the angel's visit, she was a young girl from Nazareth leading the simple and courageous life typical of the women of her village. And if God's gaze focused particularly upon her, trusting in her, Mary wants to tell you once more that not one of you is indifferent in God's eyes. He directs his loving gaze upon each one of you and he calls you to a life that is happy and full of meaning. Do not allow yourselves to be discouraged by difficulties! Mary was disturbed by the message of the angel who came to tell her that she would become the Mother of the Savior. She was conscious of her frailty in the face of God's omnipotence. Nevertheless, she said "yes," without hesitating. And thanks to her yes, salvation came into the world, thereby changing the history of mankind. For your part, dear young people, do not be afraid to say yes to the Lord's summons when he invites you to walk in his footsteps. Respond generously to the Lord! Only he can fulfil the deepest aspirations of your heart. You have come to Lourdes in great numbers for attentive and generous service to the sick and to the other pilgrims, setting out in this way to follow Christ the servant. Serving our brothers and sisters opens our hearts and makes us available. In the silence of prayer, be prepared to confide in Mary, who spoke to Bernadette in a spirit of respect and trust towards her. May Mary help those who are called to marriage to discover the beauty of a genuine and profound love, lived as a reciprocal and faithful gift! To those among you whom he calls to follow him in the priesthood or the religious life, I would like to reiterate all the joy that is to be had through giving one's life totally for the service of God and others. May Christian families and communities be places where solid vocations can come to birth and grow, for the service of the Church and the world!

Mary's message is a message of hope for all men and women of our day, whatever their country of origin. I like to invoke Mary as the star of hope.[6] On the paths of our lives, so often shrouded in darkness, she is a beacon of hope who enlightens us and gives direction to our journey. Through her "yes," through the generous gift of herself, she has opened up to God the gates of our world and our history. And she invites us to live like her in invincible hope, refusing to believe those who claim that we are trapped in the fatal power of destiny. She accompanies us with her maternal presence amid the events of our personal lives, our family lives, and our national lives. Happy are those men and women who place their trust in him who, at the very moment when he was offering his life for our salvation, gave us his Mother to be our own!

Dear brothers and sisters, in this land of France, the Mother of the Lord is venerated in countless shrines which thereby manifest the faith handed down from generation to generation. Celebrated in her Assumption, she is your country's beloved patroness. May she always be honored fervently in each of your families, in your religious communities, and in your parishes! May Mary watch over all the inhabitants of your beautiful country and over the pilgrims who have come in such numbers from other countries to celebrate this Jubilee! May she be for all people the Mother who surrounds

6. Cf. Pope Benedict XVI, *Spe Salvi*, no. 50.

her children in their joys and their trials! Holy Mary, Mother of God, our Mother, teach us to believe, to hope, and to love with you. Show us the way towards the kingdom of your Son Jesus! Star of the sea, shine upon us and lead us on our way![7] Amen.

20. *The Beautiful Lady*

From the Homily of His Holiness Pope Benedict XVI
Mass on the 150th Anniversary of the Apparitions of the Blessed Virgin Mother at Lourdes, Lourdes, Monday, 15 September 2008

Yesterday we celebrated the Cross of Christ, the instrument of our salvation, which reveals the mercy of our God in all its fullness. The Cross is truly the place where God's compassion for our world is perfectly manifested. Today, as we celebrate the memorial of Our Lady of Sorrows, we contemplate Mary sharing her Son's compassion for sinners. As Saint Bernard declares, the Mother of Christ entered into the Passion of her Son through her compassion.[8] At the foot of the Cross, the prophecy of Simeon is fulfilled: her mother's heart is pierced through (cf. Lk 2:35) by the torment inflicted on the Innocent One born of her flesh. Just as Jesus cried (Jn 11:35), so too Mary certainly cried over the tortured body of her Son. Her self-restraint, however, prevents us from plumbing the depths of her grief; the full extent of her suffering is merely suggested by the traditional symbol of the seven swords. As in the case of her Son Jesus, one might say that she too was led

7. Cf. Pope Benedict XVI, *Spe Salvi*, no. 50.

8. St. Bernard of Clairvaux, *Sermon on the Sunday in the Octave of the Assumption*, PL 183, 437–38.

to perfection through this suffering (cf. Heb 2:10), so as to make her capable of receiving the new spiritual mission that her Son entrusts to her immediately before "giving up his spirit" (Jn 19:30): that of becoming the mother of Christ in his members. In that hour, through the figure of the beloved disciple, Jesus presents each of his disciples to his Mother when he says to her: Behold your son (Jn 19:26–27).

Today Mary dwells in the joy and the glory of the Resurrection. The tears shed at the foot of the Cross have been transformed into a smile which nothing can wipe away, even as her maternal compassion towards us remains unchanged. The intervention of the Virgin Mary in offering succor throughout history testifies to this, and does not cease to call forth, in the people of God, an unshakable confidence in her: the *Memorare* prayer expresses this sentiment very well. Mary loves each of her children, giving particular attention to those who, like her Son at the hour of his Passion, are prey to suffering; she loves them quite simply because they are her children, according to the will of Christ on the Cross.

The psalmist, seeing from afar this maternal bond which unites the Mother of Christ with the people of faith, prophesies regarding the Virgin Mary that "the richest of the people . . . will seek your smile" (Ps 44:13). In this way, prompted by the inspired word of Scripture, Christians have always sought the smile of Our Lady, that smile that artists, in the Middle Ages, were able to so prodigiously represent and enhance. This smile of Mary is for all; but it is directed quite particularly to those who suffer, so that they can find comfort and solace therein. To seek Mary's smile is not an act of devotional or outmoded sentimentality, but rather the proper expression of the living and profoundly human relationship which binds us to her whom Christ gave us as our Mother.

To wish to contemplate this smile of the Virgin does not mean letting oneself be led by an uncontrolled imagination. Scripture itself discloses it to us through the lips of Mary when she sings the Magnificat: "My soul glorifies the Lord, my spirit exults in God my Savior" (Lk 1:46–47). When the Virgin Mary gives thanks to the Lord, she takes us as her witnesses. Mary shares, as if by anticipation, with us, her future children, the joy that dwells in her heart, so that it can become ours. Every time we recite the Magnificat, we become witnesses of her smile. Here in Lourdes, in the course of the apparition of Wednesday, 3 March 1858, Bernadette contemplated this smile of Mary in a most particular way. It was the first response that the "beautiful lady" gave to the young seer who wanted to know who she was. Before introducing herself, some days later, as "the Immaculate Conception," Mary first taught Bernadette to know her smile, this being the most appropriate point of entry into the revelation of her mystery.

In the smile of the most eminent of all creatures, looking down on us, is reflected our dignity as children of God, that dignity which never abandons the sick person. This smile, a true reflection of God's tenderness, is the source of an invincible hope. Unfortunately, we know only too well: the endurance of suffering can upset life's most stable equilibrium; it can shake the firmest foundations of confidence, and sometimes even leads people to despair of the meaning and value of life. There are struggles that we cannot sustain alone, without the help of divine grace. When speech can no longer find the right words, the need arises for a loving presence: we seek then the closeness not only of those who share the same blood or are linked to us by friendship, but also the closeness of those who are intimately bound to us by faith. Who could be more intimate to us than Christ and his holy Mother, the Immaculate One? More than any others, they are capable of understanding us and grasping how hard we have to fight against evil and suffering. The Letter to the Hebrews says of Christ that he "is not unable to sympathize with our weaknesses; for in every respect he has been tempted as we are" (Heb 4:15). I would like to say, humbly, to those who suffer and to those who struggle and are tempted to turn their backs on life: turn towards Mary! Within the smile of the Virgin lies mysteriously hidden the strength to fight against sickness and for life. With her, equally, is found the grace to accept without fear or bitterness to leave this world at the hour chosen by God.

How true was the insight of that great French spiritual writer, Dom Jean-Baptiste Chautard, who in *L'âme de tout apostolat*, proposed to the devout Christian to gaze frequently "into the eyes of the Virgin Mary"! Yes, to seek the smile of the Virgin Mary is not a pious infantilism, it is the aspiration, as Psalm 44 says, of those who are "the richest of the people" (Ps 44:13). "The richest," that is to say, in the order of faith, those who have attained the highest degree of spiritual maturity and know precisely how to acknowledge their weakness and their poverty before God. In the very simple manifestation of tenderness that we call a smile, we grasp that our sole wealth is the love God bears us, which passes through the heart of her who became our Mother. To seek this smile, is first of all to have grasped the gratuitousness of love; it is also to be able to elicit this smile through our efforts to live according to the word of her Beloved Son, just as a child seeks to elicit its mother's smile by doing what pleases her. And we know what pleases Mary, thanks to the words she spoke to the servants at Cana: "Do whatever he tells you" (Jn 2:5).

Mary's smile is a spring of living water. "He who believes in me," says Jesus, "out of his heart shall flow rivers of living water" (Jn 7:38). Mary is the one who believed and, from her womb, rivers of living water have flowed forth to irrigate human history. The spring that Mary pointed out to Bernadette here in Lourdes is the humble sign of this spiritual reality. From her believing heart, from her maternal heart, flows living water which purifies and heals. By immersing themselves in the baths at Lourdes, so many people have discovered and experienced the gentle maternal love of the Virgin Mary, becoming attached to her in order to bind themselves more closely to the Lord! In the liturgical sequence of this feast of Our Lady of Sorrows, Mary is honored with the title of *Fons amoris*, "fount of love." From Mary's heart, there springs up a gratuitous love which calls forth a response of filial love, called to ever greater refinement. Like every mother, and better than every mother, Mary is the teacher of love. That is why so many sick people come here to Lourdes, to quench their thirst at the "spring of love" and to let themselves be led to the sole source of salvation, her son Jesus the Savior.

Christ imparts his salvation by means of the sacraments, and especially in the case of those suffering from sickness or disability, by means of the grace of the sacrament of the sick. For each individual, suffering is always something alien. It can never be tamed. That is why it is hard to bear, and harder still—as certain great witnesses of Christ's holiness have done—to welcome it as a significant element in our vocation, or to accept, as Bernadette expressed it, to "suffer everything in silence in order to please Jesus."

To be able to say that, it is necessary to have travelled a long way already in union with Jesus. Here and now, though, it is possible to entrust oneself to God's mercy, as manifested through the grace of the sacrament of the sick. Bernadette herself, in the course of a life that was often marked by sickness, received this sacrament four times. The grace of this sacrament consists in welcoming Christ the healer into ourselves. However, Christ is not a healer in the manner of the world. In order to heal us, he does not remain outside the suffering that is experienced; he eases it by coming to dwell within the one stricken by illness, to bear it and live it with him. Christ's presence comes to break the isolation which pain induces. Man no longer bears his burden alone: as a suffering member of Christ, he is conformed to Christ in his self-offering to the Father, and he participates, in him, in the coming to birth of the new creation.

Without the Lord's help, the yoke of sickness and suffering weighs down on us cruelly. By receiving the sacrament of the sick, we seek to carry no other yoke that that of Christ, strengthened through his promise to us that his yoke will be easy to carry and his burden light (cf. Mt 11:30). I invite those who are to receive the sacrament of the sick during this Mass to enter into a hope of this kind.

The Second Vatican Council presented Mary as the figure in whom the entire mystery of the Church is typified.[9] Her personal journey outlines the profile of the Church, which is called to be just as attentive to those who suffer as she herself was. I extend an affectionate greeting to those working in the areas of public health

9. Second Vatican Council, *Lumen Gentium*, nos. 63–65.

and nursing, as well as those who, in different ways, in hospitals and other institutions, are contributing to the care of the sick with competence and generosity. Equally, I should like to say to all the *hospitaliers*, the *brancardiers*, and the carers who come from every diocese in France and from further afield, and who throughout the year attend the sick who come on pilgrimage to Lourdes, how much their service is appreciated. They are the arms of the servant Church. Finally, I wish to encourage those who, in the name of their faith, receive and visit the sick, especially in hospital infirmaries, in parishes or, as here, at shrines. May you always sense in this important and delicate mission the effective and fraternal support of your communities! In this regard, I particularly greet and thank my brothers in the Episcopate, the French Bishops, Bishops and priests from afar, and all who serve the sick and suffering throughout the world. Thank you for your ministry close to our suffering Lord. The service of charity that you offer is a Marian service. Mary entrusts her smile to you, so that you yourselves may become, in faithfulness to her son, springs of living water. Whatever you do, you do in the name of the Church, of which Mary is the purest image. May you carry her smile to everyone!

To conclude, I wish to join in the prayer of the pilgrims and the sick, and to pray with you a passage from the prayer to Mary that has been proposed for this Jubilee celebration: "Because you are the smile of God, the reflection of the light of Christ, the dwelling place of the Holy Spirit, because you chose Bernadette in her lowliness, because you are the morning star, the gate of heaven and the first creature to experience the resurrection, Our Lady of Lourdes, with our brothers and sisters whose hearts and bodies are in pain, we pray to you!"

MARIAN SOLEMNITIES AND FEASTS

ANNUNCIATION

21. *Full of Grace*

From the Homily of His Holiness Pope Benedict XVI
Solemnity of the Annunciation of the Lord , Ordinary Public Consistory for the Creation of New Cardinals, Saint Peter's Square, Saturday, 25 March 2006

For me it is a source of great joy to preside at this concelebration with the new Cardinals after yesterday's Consistory, and I consider it providential that it should take place on the liturgical Solemnity of the Annunciation of the Lord and under the sunshine that the Lord gives us. In the Incarnation of the Son of God, in fact, we recognize the origins of the Church. Everything began from there. Every historical realization of the Church and every one of her institutions must be shaped by that primordial wellspring. They must be shaped by Christ, the incarnate Word of God. It is he that we are constantly celebrating: Emmanuel, God-with-us, through whom the saving will of God the Father has been accomplished. And yet—today of all days we contemplate this aspect of the Mystery—the divine wellspring flows through a privileged channel: the Virgin Mary.

St. Bernard speaks of this using the eloquent image of *aquaeductus*.[1] In celebrating the Incarnation of the Son, therefore, we cannot fail to honor his Mother. The Angel's proclamation was addressed to her; she accepted it, and when she responded from the depths of her heart: "Here I am . . . let it be done to me according

1. Cf. St. Bernard of Clairvaux, *Sermo in Nativitate B.V. Mariae*, PL 183, 437–48.

to your word" (Lk 1:38), at that moment the eternal Word began to exist as a human being in time. From generation to generation, the wonder evoked by this ineffable mystery never ceases. St. Augustine imagines a dialogue between himself and the Angel of the Annunciation, in which he asks: "Tell me, O Angel, why did this happen in Mary?" The answer, says the Messenger, is contained in the very words of the greeting: "Hail, full of grace."[2] In fact, the Angel, "appearing to her," does not call her by her earthly name, Mary, but by her divine name, as she has always been seen and characterized by God: "Full of grace"—*gratia plena*, which in the original Greek is *kecharitomene*, "full of grace," and the grace is none other than the love of God; thus, in the end, we can translate this word: "beloved" of God (cf. Lk 1:28). Origen observes that no such title had ever been given to a human being, and that it is unparalleled in all of Sacred Scripture.[3]

It is a title expressed in passive form, but this "passivity" of Mary, who has always been and is forever "loved" by the Lord, implies her free consent, her personal and original response: in being loved, in receiving the gift of God, Mary is fully active, because she accepts with personal generosity the wave of God's love poured out upon her. In this, too, she is the perfect disciple of her Son, who realizes the fullness of his freedom and thus exercises the freedom through obedience to the Father.

In the second reading, we heard the wonderful passage in which the author of the Letter to the Hebrews interprets Psalm 39 in the light of Christ's Incarnation: "When Christ came into the world, he said: . . . 'Here I am, I have come to do your will, O God'" (Heb

2. Cf. St. Augustine, *Sermo* 291:6.
3. Origen, *Homilies on Luke*, 6:7.

10:5–7). Before the mystery of these two "Here I am" statements, the "Here I am" of the Son and the "Here I am" of the Mother, each of which is reflected in the other, forming a single Amen to God's loving will, we are filled with wonder and thanksgiving, and we bow down in adoration. What a great gift, dear brothers, to be able to conduct this evocative celebration on the Solemnity of the Lord's Annunciation! What an abundance of light we can draw from this mystery for our lives as ministers of the Church!

You above all, dear new Cardinals, what great sustenance you can receive for your mission as the eminent "Senate" of Peter's Successor! This providential circumstance helps us to consider today's event, which emphasizes the Petrine principle of the Church, in the light of the other principle, the Marian one, which is even more fundamental. The importance of the Marian principle in the Church was particularly highlighted, after the Council, by my beloved Predecessor Pope John Paul II in harmony with his motto *Totus tuus*. In his spirituality and in his tireless ministry, the presence of Mary as Mother and Queen of the Church was made manifest to the eyes of all. More than ever, he adverted to her maternal presence in the assassination attempt of 13 May 1981 here in St. Peter's Square. In memory of that tragic event, he had a mosaic of the Virgin placed high up in the Apostolic Palace looking down over St. Peter's Square, so as to accompany the key moments and the daily unfolding of his long reign. It is just one year since his Pontificate entered its final phase, full of suffering and yet triumphant and truly paschal.

The icon of the Annunciation, more than any other, helps us to see clearly how everything in the Church goes back to that mystery of Mary's acceptance of the divine Word, by which, through the action of the Holy Spirit, the Covenant between God and humanity was perfectly sealed. Everything in the Church, every institution and ministry, including that of Peter and his Successors, is "included" under the Virgin's mantle, within the grace-filled horizon of her "yes" to God's will. This link with Mary naturally evokes a strong affective resonance in all of us, but first of all it has an objective value. Between Mary and the Church there is indeed a connatural relationship that was strongly emphasized by the Second Vatican Council in its felicitous decision to place the treatment of the Blessed Virgin at the conclusion of the Constitution on the Church, *Lumen Gentium*.[4]

The theme of the relationship between the Petrine principle and the Marian principle is also found in the symbol of the ring which I am about to consign to you. The ring is always a nuptial sign. Almost all of you have already received one, on the day of your episcopal ordination, as an expression of your fidelity and your commitment to watch over the holy Church, the bride of Christ.[5] The ring which I confer upon you today, proper to the cardinal dignity, is intended to confirm and strengthen that commitment, arising once more from a nuptial gift, a reminder to you that first and foremost you are intimately united with Christ so as to accomplish your mission as bridegrooms of the Church. May your acceptance of the ring be for you a renewal of your "yes," your "here I am," addressed both to the Lord Jesus who chose you and constituted you, and to his holy Church, which you are called to serve with the love of a spouse. So the two dimensions of the Church, Marian and Petrine, come together in the supreme

4. Second Vatican Council, Dogmatic Constitution *Lumen Gentium*, nos. 52–69.

5. Cf. *Rite of Ordination of Bishops*.

value of charity, which constitutes the fulfilment of each. As St. Paul says, charity is the "greatest" charism, the "most excellent way" (1 Cor 12:31; 13:13). Everything in this world will pass away. In eternity only Love will remain. For this reason, my brothers, taking the opportunity offered by this favorable time of Lent, let us commit ourselves to ensure that everything in our personal lives and in the ecclesial activity in which we are engaged is inspired by charity and leads to charity. In this respect, too, we are enlightened by the mystery that we are celebrating today.

Indeed, the first thing that Mary did after receiving the Angel's message was to go "in haste" to the house of her cousin Elizabeth in order to be of service to her (Lk 1:39). The Virgin's initiative was one of genuine charity; it was humble and courageous, motivated by faith in God's Word and the inner promptings of the Holy Spirit. Those who love forget about themselves and place themselves at the service of their neighbor. Here we have the image and model of the Church! Every ecclesial community, like the Mother of Christ, is called to accept with total generosity the mystery of God who comes to dwell within her and guides her steps in the ways of love. This is the path along which I chose to launch my Pontificate, inviting everyone, with my first Encyclical, to build up the Church in charity as a "community of love."[6]

In pursuing this objective, venerable brother Cardinals, your spiritual closeness and active assistance is a great support and comfort to me. For this I thank you, and at the same time I invite all of you, priests, deacons, Religious, and lay faithful, to join together in invoking the Holy Spirit, praying that the College of

6. Pope Benedict XVI, *Deus Caritas Est*, Part II.

Cardinals may be ever more ardent in pastoral charity, so as to help the whole Church to radiate Christ's love in the world, to the praise and glory of the Most Holy Trinity. Amen!

MARIAN SOLEMNITIES AND FEASTS

OUR LADY OF FATIMA

22. *The Lord Is with Us*

From the Homily of His Holiness Pope Benedict XVI
On the 10th Anniversary of the Beatification of Jacinta and Francisco
Esplanade of the Shrine of Our Lady of Fátima, Thursday, 13 May 2010

"Their descendants shall be renowned among the nations [. . .], they are a people whom the Lord has blessed" (Is 61:9). Thus, the first reading of this Eucharist began, and its words are wonderfully fulfilled in this assembly devoutly gathered at the feet of Our Lady of Fátima. Dearly beloved brothers and sisters, I too have come as a pilgrim to Fátima, to this "home" from which Mary chose to speak to us in modern times. I have come to Fátima to rejoice in Mary's presence and maternal protection. I have come to Fátima, because today the pilgrim Church, willed by her Son as the instrument of evangelization and the sacrament of salvation, converges upon this place. I have come to Fátima to pray, in union with Mary and so many pilgrims, for our human family, afflicted as it is by various illnesses and sufferings. Finally, I have come to Fátima with the same sentiments as those of Blessed Francisco and Jacinta[1], and the Servant of God Lúcia, in order to entrust to Our Lady the intimate confession that "I love" Jesus, that the Church and priests "love" him and desire to keep their gaze fixed upon him as this Year for

1. Francisco and Jacinta Marto, brother and sister, together with their cousin Lucia dos Santos, were the three children to whom the Blessed Virgin appeared at Fatima, Portugal in 1917. Lucia dos Santos is more commonly known as Lucia, Servant of God.

Priests comes to its end, and in order to entrust to Mary's maternal protection priests, consecrated men and women, missionaries, and all those who by their good works make the House of God a place of welcome and charitable outreach.

These are the "people whom the Lord has blessed." The people whom the Lord has blessed are you, the beloved Diocese of Leiria-Fátima, with your Pastor, Bishop Antonio Marto. I thank him for his words of greeting at the beginning of Mass, and for the gracious hospitality shown particularly by his collaborators at this Shrine. I greet the President of the Republic and the other authorities who serve this glorious Nation. I spiritually embrace all the dioceses of Portugal, represented here by their Bishops, and I entrust to Heaven all the nations and peoples of the earth. In God I embrace all their sons and daughters, particularly the afflicted or outcast, with the desire of bringing them that great hope which burns in my own heart, and which here, in Fátima, can be palpably felt. May our great hope sink roots in the lives of each of you, dear pilgrims, and of all those who join us through the communications media.

Yes! The Lord, our great hope, is with us. In his merciful love, he offers a future to his people: a future of communion with himself. After experiencing the mercy and consolation of God who did not forsake them along their wearisome return from the Babylonian Exile, the people of God cried out: "I greatly rejoice in the Lord, my whole being exults in my God" (Is 61:10). The resplendent daughter of this people is the Virgin Mary of Nazareth who, clothed with grace and sweetly marveling at God's presence in her womb, made this joy and hope her own in the canticle of the Magnificat: "My spirit rejoices in God my Savior." She did not view herself as a fortunate individual in the midst of a barren people, but prophesied for them the sweet joys of a wondrous maternity of God, for "his mercy is for those who fear him from generation to generation" (Lk 1:47, 50).

This holy place is the proof of it. In seven years you will return here to celebrate the centenary of the first visit made by the Lady "come from heaven," the Teacher who introduced the little seers to a deep knowledge of the love of the Blessed Trinity and led them to savor God himself as the most beautiful reality of human existence. This experience of grace made them fall in love with God in Jesus, so much so that Jacinta could cry out: "How much I delight in telling Jesus that I love him! When I tell him this often, I feel as if I have a fire in my breast, yet it does not burn me." And Francisco could say: "What I liked most of all was seeing Our Lord in that light which Our Mother put into our hearts. I love God so much!"[2]

Brothers and sisters, in listening to these innocent and profound mystical confidences of the shepherd children, one might look at them with a touch of envy for what they were able to see, or with the disappointed resignation of someone who was not so fortunate, yet still demands to see. To such persons, the Pope says, as does Jesus: "Is not this the reason you are wrong, that you know neither the Scriptures nor the power of God?" (Mk 12:24). The Scriptures invite us to believe: "Blessed are those who have not seen and yet have come to believe" (Jn 20:29), but God—who is more deeply

2. Sister Lucia, *Fatima in Lucia's Own Words: Memoirs of Sister Lúcia*, ed. Fr. Louis Kondor, trans. Dominican Nuns of Perpetual Rosary, I (Secretariado Dos Pastorinhos, 2000), 42 and 126.

present to me than I am to myself[3]—has the power to come to us, particularly through our inner senses, so that the soul can receive the gentle touch of a reality which is beyond the senses and which enables us to reach what is not accessible or visible to the senses. For this to happen, we must cultivate an interior watchfulness of the heart which, for most of the time, we do not possess on account of the powerful pressure exerted by outside realities and the images and concerns which fill our soul.[4] Yes! God can come to us, and show himself to the eyes of our heart.

Moreover, that Light deep within the shepherd children, which comes from the future of God, is the same Light which was manifested in the fullness of time and came for us all: the Son of God made man. He has the power to inflame the coldest and saddest of hearts, as we see in the case of the disciples on the way to Emmaus (cf. Lk 24:32). Henceforth our hope has a real foundation, it is based on an event which belongs to history and at the same time transcends history: Jesus of Nazareth. The enthusiasm roused by his wisdom and his saving power among the people of that time was such that a woman in the midst of the crowd—as we heard in the Gospel—cried out: "Blessed is the womb that bore you, and the breasts that nursed you!" And Jesus said: "Blessed rather are those who hear the word of God and obey it!" (Lk 11:27–28). But who finds time to hear God's word and to let themselves be attracted by his love? Who keeps watch, in the night of doubt and uncertainty, with a heart vigilant in prayer? Who awaits the dawn of the new day, fanning the flame of faith? Faith in God opens before

3. Cf. St. Augustine, *Confessions*, 3, 6, 11.

4. Cf. Congregation for the Doctrine of the Faith, *Theological Commentary on The Message of Fatima*, 2000.

us the horizon of a sure hope, one which does not disappoint; it indicates a solid foundation on which to base one's life without fear; it demands a faith-filled surrender into the hands of the Love which sustains the world.

"Their descendants shall be known among the nations, [. . .] they are a people whom the Lord has blessed" (Is 61:9) with an unshakable hope which bears fruit in a love which sacrifices for others, yet does not sacrifice others. Rather, as we heard in the second reading, this love "bears all things, believes all things, hopes all things, endures all things" (1 Cor 13:7). An example and encouragement are to be found in the shepherd children, who offered their whole lives to God and shared them fully with others for love of God. Our Lady helped them to open their hearts to universal love. Blessed Jacinta, in particular, proved tireless in sharing with the needy and in making sacrifices for the conversion of sinners. Only with this fraternal and generous love will we succeed in building the civilization of love and peace.

We would be mistaken to think that Fátima's prophetic mission is complete. Here there takes on new life the plan of God which asks humanity from the beginning: "Where is your brother Abel? [. . .] Your brother's blood is crying out to me from the ground!" (Gen 4:9). Mankind has succeeded in unleashing a cycle of death and terror, but failed in bringing it to an end. . . . In sacred Scripture we often find that God seeks righteous men and women in order to save the city of man and he does the same here, in Fátima, when Our Lady asks: "Do you want to offer yourselves to God, to endure all the sufferings which he will send you, in an act of reparation for the sins by which he is offended and of supplication for the conversion of sinners?"[5]

At a time when the human family was ready to sacrifice all that was most sacred on the altar of the petty and selfish interests of nations, races, ideologies, groups, and individuals, our Blessed Mother came from heaven, offering to implant in the hearts of all those who trust in her the Love of God burning in her own heart. At that time, it was only to three children, yet the example of their lives spread and multiplied, especially as a result of the travels of the Pilgrim Virgin, in countless groups throughout the world dedicated to the cause of fraternal solidarity. May the seven years which separate us from the centenary of the apparitions hasten the fulfilment of the prophecy of the triumph of the Immaculate Heart of Mary, to the glory of the Most Holy Trinity.

5. *Memoirs of Sister Lúcia*, I, 162.

MARIAN SOLEMNITIES AND FEASTS

ASSUMPTION

23. *God Is Victorious*

From the Homily of His Holiness Pope Benedict XVI, Solemnity of the Assumption of the Blessed Virgin Mary, Parish Church of St. Thomas of Villanova, Castel Gandolfo, Tuesday, 15 August 2006

In the Magnificat, the great hymn of Our Lady that we have just heard in the Gospel, we find some surprising words. Mary says: "Henceforth all generations will call me blessed" (Lk 1:48). The Mother of the Lord prophesies the Marian praises of the Church for all of the future, the Marian devotion of the People of God until the end of time. In praising Mary, the Church did not invent something "adjacent" to Scripture: she responded to this prophecy which Mary made at that moment of grace.

And Mary's words were not only personal, perhaps arbitrary words. Elizabeth, filled with the Holy Spirit as St. Luke said, exclaimed with a loud cry: "Blessed is she who believed. . ." (Lk 1:45). And Mary, also filled with the Holy Spirit, continues and completes what Elizabeth said, affirming: "all generations will call me blessed." It is a real prophecy, inspired by the Holy Spirit, and in venerating Mary, the Church responds to a command of the Holy Spirit; she does what she has to do.

We do not praise God sufficiently by keeping silent about his saints, especially Mary, "the Holy One" who became his dwelling place on earth. The simple and multiform light of God appears to us exactly in its variety and richness only in the countenance of the saints, who are the true mirrors of his light. And it is precisely by looking at Mary's face that we can see more clearly than in any other way the beauty, goodness, and mercy of God. In her face we can truly perceive the divine light. "All generations will call me blessed." We can praise Mary, we can venerate Mary for she is "blessed," she is blessed forever. And this is the subject of this Feast. She is blessed because she is united to God, she lives with God and in God. On the eve of his Passion, taking leave of his disciples, the Lord said: "In my Father's house are many rooms. . . . I go to prepare a place for you" (Jn 14:1–3). By saying, "I am the handmaid of the Lord; let it be done to me according to your word" (Lk 1:38), Mary prepared God's dwelling here on earth; with her body and soul, she became his dwelling place and thereby opened the earth to heaven.

In the Gospel we have just heard, St. Luke, with various allusions, makes us understand that Mary is the true Ark of the Covenant, that the mystery of the Temple—God's dwelling place here on earth—is fulfilled in Mary. God, who became present here on earth, truly dwells in Mary. Mary becomes his tent. What all the cultures desire—that God dwell among us—is brought about here. St. Augustine says: "Before conceiving the Lord in her body she had already conceived him in her soul."[1] She had made room for the Lord in her soul and thus really became the true Temple where God made himself incarnate, where he became present on this earth. Thus, being God's dwelling place on earth, in her the eternal dwelling place has already been prepared, it has already been prepared for ever. And this constitutes the whole content

1. St. Augustine, *Discourses*, 215, 4.

of the Dogma of the Assumption of Mary, body and soul, into heavenly glory, expressed here in these words. Mary is "blessed" because—totally, in body and soul and forever—she became the Lord's dwelling place. If this is true, Mary does not merely invite our admiration and veneration, but she guides us, shows us the way of life, shows us how we can become blessed, how to find the path of happiness.

Let us listen once again to Elizabeth's words fulfilled in Mary's Magnificat: "Blessed is she who believed." The first and fundamental act in order to become a dwelling place of God and thus find definitive happiness is to believe: it is faith, faith in God, in that God who showed himself in Jesus Christ and makes himself heard in the divine Word of Holy Scripture. Believing is not adding one opinion to others. And the conviction, the belief, that God exists is not information like any other. Regarding most information, it makes no difference to us whether it is true or false; it does not change our lives. But if God does not exist, life is empty, the future is empty. And if God exists, everything changes, life is light, our future is light, and we have guidance for how to live. Therefore, believing constitutes the fundamental orientation of our life. To believe, to say: "Yes, I believe that you are God, I believe that you are present among us in the Incarnate Son," gives my life a direction, impels me to be attached to God, to unite with God and so to find my dwelling place, and the way to live. To believe is not only a way of thinking or an idea; as has already been mentioned, it is a way of acting, a manner of living. To believe means to follow the trail indicated to us by the Word of God. In addition to this fundamental act of faith, which is an existential act, a position taken for the whole of life, Mary adds another word: "His mercy is on those who fear him" (Lk 1:50).

Together with the whole of Scripture, she is speaking of "fear of God." Perhaps this is a phrase with which we are not very familiar or do not like very much. But "fear of God" is not anguish; it is something quite different. As children, we are not anxious about the Father but we have fear of God, the concern not to destroy the love on which our life is based. Fear of God is that sense of responsibility that we are bound to possess, responsibility for the portion of the world that has been entrusted to us in our lives. It is responsibility for the good administration of this portion of the world and of history, and one thus helps the just building of the world, contributing to the victory of goodness and peace. "All generations will call you blessed" (Lk 1:48): this means that the future, what is to come, belongs to God, it is in God's hands, that it is God who conquers. Nor does he conquer the mighty dragon of which today's first reading speaks, the dragon that represents all the powers of violence in the world. They seem invincible but Mary tells us that they are not invincible.

The Woman—as the first reading and the Gospel show us—is stronger, because God is stronger. Of course, in comparison with the dragon, so heavily armed, this Woman who is Mary, who is the Church, seems vulnerable or defenseless. And truly God is vulnerable in the world, because he is Love and love is vulnerable. Yet he holds the future in his hands: it is love, not hatred, that triumphs; it is peace that is victorious in the end. This is the great consolation contained in the Dogma of Mary's Assumption, body and soul, into heavenly glory. Let us thank the Lord for this consolation, but let us also see it as a commitment for us to take the side of good and peace. And let us pray to Mary, Queen of Peace, to help peace to be victorious today: "Queen of Peace, pray for us!" Amen!

24. *God Is Heaven*

From the Homily of His Holiness Pope Benedict XVI, Solemnity of the Assumption of the Blessed Virgin Mary, Parish Church of St. Thomas of Villanova, Castel Gandolfo, Friday, 15 August 2008

The Solemnity of the Assumption of the Blessed Virgin Mary, the oldest Marian Feast, returns every year in the heart of summer. It is an opportunity to rise with Mary to the heights of the spirit where one breathes the pure air of supernatural life and contemplates the most authentic beauty, the beauty of holiness. The atmosphere of today's celebration is steeped in paschal joy. "Today," the antiphon of the Magnificat says, "the Virgin Mary was taken up to Heaven. Rejoice, for she reigns with Christ forever. Alleluia." This proclamation speaks to us of an event that is utterly unique and extraordinary, yet destined to fill the heart of every human being with hope and happiness. Mary is indeed the first fruit of the new humanity, the creature in whom the mystery of Christ—his Incarnation, death, Resurrection, and Ascension into Heaven—has already fully taken effect, redeeming her from death and conveying her, body and soul, to the Kingdom of immortal life. For this reason, as the Second Vatican Council recalls, the Virgin Mary is a sign of certain hope and comfort to us.[2] Today's feast impels us to lift our gaze to Heaven; not to a heaven consisting of abstract ideas or even an imaginary heaven created by art, but the Heaven

2. Second Vatican Council, *Lumen Gentium*, no. 68.

of true reality which is God himself. God is Heaven. He is our destination, the destination and the eternal dwelling place from which we come and for which we are striving.

St. Germanus, Bishop of Constantinople in the eighth century, in a homily given on the Feast of the Assumption, addressing the heavenly Mother of God, said: "You are the One who through your immaculate flesh reunited the Christian people with Christ. . . . Just as all who thirst hasten to the fountain, so every soul hastens to you, the Fountain of love, and as every man aspires to live, to see the light that never fades, so every Christian longs to enter the light of the Most Blessed Trinity where you already are."[3] It is these same sentiments that inspire us today as we contemplate Mary in God's glory. In fact, when she fell asleep in this world to reawaken in Heaven, she simply followed her Son Jesus for the last time, on his longest and most crucial journey, his passage "from this world to the Father" (Jn 13:1).

Like him, together with him, she departed this world to return "to the Father's House" (cf. Jn 14:2). And all this is not remote from us as it might seem at first sight, because we are all children of the Father, God; we are all brothers and sisters of Jesus and we are all also children of Mary, our Mother. And we all aspire to happiness. And the happiness to which we all aspire is God, so we are all journeying on toward this happiness we call Heaven, which in reality is God. And Mary helps us, she encourages us to ensure that every moment of our life is a step forward on this exodus, on this journey toward God. May she help us in this way to make the reality of heaven, God's greatness, also present in the life of our

3. St. Germanus of Constantinople, *In Sanctae Dei Genetricis Dormitionem*, Sermo I.

world. Is this not basically the paschal dynamism of the human being, of every person who wants to become heavenly, perfectly happy, by virtue of Christ's Resurrection? And might this not be the beginning and anticipation of a movement that involves every human being and the entire cosmos? She, from whom God took his flesh and whose soul was pierced by a sword on Calvary, was associated first and uniquely in the mystery of this transformation for which we, also often pierced by the sword of suffering in this world, are all striving.

The new Eve followed the new Adam in suffering, in the Passion, and so too in definitive joy. Christ is the first fruits, but his risen flesh is inseparable from that of his earthly Mother, Mary. In Mary, all humanity is involved in the Assumption to God, and together with her all creation, whose groans and sufferings, St. Paul tells us, are the birth-pangs of the new humanity. Thus are born the new Heaven and the new earth in which death shall be no more, neither shall there be mourning nor crying nor pain any more (cf. Rv 21:1–4).

What a great mystery of love is presented to us once again today for our contemplation! Christ triumphed over death with the omnipotence of his love. Love alone is omnipotent. This love impelled Christ to die for us and thus to overcome death. Yes, love alone gives access to the Kingdom of life! And Mary entered after her Son, associated with his Glory, after being associated with his Passion. She entered it with an uncontainable force, keeping the way behind her open to us all. And for this reason we invoke her today as "Gate of Heaven," "Queen of Angels," and "Refuge of sinners." It is certainly not reasoning that will make us understand this reality which is so sublime, but rather simple, forthright faith and the silence of prayer that puts us in touch with the Mystery that infinitely exceeds us. Prayer helps us speak with God and hear how the Lord speaks to our heart. Let us ask Mary today to make us the gift of her faith, that faith which enables us already to live in the dimension between finite and infinite, that faith which also transforms the sentiment of time and the passing of our existence, that faith in which we are profoundly aware that our life is not retracted by the past but attracted towards the future, towards God, where Christ, and behind him Mary, has preceded us. By looking at Mary's Assumption into Heaven, we understand better that even though our daily life may be marked by trials and difficulties, it flows like a river to the divine ocean, to the fullness of joy and peace. We understand that our death is not the end but rather the entrance into life that knows no death. Our setting on the horizon of this world is our rising at the dawn of the new world, the dawn of the eternal day. "Mary, while you accompany us in the toil of our daily living and dying, keep us constantly oriented to the true homeland of bliss. Help us to do as you did."

Dear brothers and sisters, dear friends who are taking part in this celebration this morning, let us pray this prayer to Mary together. In the face of the sad spectacle of all the false joy and at the same time of all the anguished suffering, which is spreading through the world, we must learn from her to become ourselves signs of hope and comfort; we must proclaim with our own lives Christ's Resurrection. "Help us, Mother, bright Gate of Heaven, Mother of Mercy, source through whom came Jesus Christ, our life and our joy. Amen."

25. *Triumphant in Heaven*

From the Homily of His Holiness Pope Benedict XVI, Solemnity of the Assumption of the Blessed Virgin Mary, Parish Church of St. Thomas of Villanova, Castel Gandolfo, Sunday, 15 August 2010

Today the Church is celebrating one of the most important feasts of the Liturgical Year dedicated to Mary Most Holy: the Assumption. At the end of her earthly life Mary was taken up, body and soul, into Heaven, that is, into the glory of eternal life, into full and perfect communion with God.

It is 60 years since Venerable Pope Pius XII, on 1 November 1950, solemnly defined this Dogma and, although it is somewhat complicated, I would like to read the formula of dogmatization. The Pope says: "Hence the revered Mother of God, from all eternity joined in a hidden way with Jesus Christ in one and the same decree of predestination, immaculate in her conception, a most perfect virgin in her divine motherhood, the noble associate of the divine Redeemer who has won a complete triumph over sin and its consequences, finally obtained, as the supreme culmination of her privileges, that she should be preserved free from the corruption of the tomb and that, like her own Son, having overcome death, she might be taken up body and soul to the glory of Heaven where, as Queen, she sits in splendor at the right hand of her Son, the immortal King of the Ages."[4]

This then is the nucleus of our faith in the Assumption: we believe that Mary, like Christ her Son, overcame death and is already

4. Pope Pius XII, Apostolic Constitution *Munificentissimus Deus* (November 1, 1950), no. 40.

triumphant in heavenly glory, in the totality of her being, "in body and soul." In today's second reading, St. Paul helps us to shed a little more light on this mystery, starting from the central event of human history and of our faith: that is, the event of Christ's Resurrection which is "the first fruits of those who have fallen asleep." Immersed in his Paschal Mystery, we are enabled to share in his victory over sin and death. Here lies the startling secret and key reality of the whole human saga. St. Paul tells us that we are "incorporated" Adam, the first man and the old man, that we all possess the same human heritage to which belong suffering, death, and sin. But every day adds something new to this reality that we can all see and live: not only are we part of this heritage of the one human being that began with Adam but we are also "incorporated" in the new man, in the Risen Christ, and thus the life of the Resurrection is already present in us. Therefore, this first biological "incorporation" is incorporation into death, it is an incorporation that generates death. The second, new "incorporation," that is given to us in Baptism is an "incorporation" that gives life. Again, I cite today's second reading: St. Paul says: "For as by a man came death, by a man has come also the resurrection of the dead. For as in Adam all die, so also in Christ shall all be made alive. But each in his own order: Christ, the first fruits, then at his coming, those who belong to Christ" (1 Cor 15:21–24).

Now, what St. Paul says of all human beings, the Church in her infallible Magisterium says of Mary in a precise and clear manner: The Mother of God is so deeply integrated into Christ's Mystery that at the end of her earthly life she already participates with her whole self in her Son's Resurrection. She lives what we await at the end of time when the "last enemy," death, will have been destroyed (cf. 1 Cor 15:26); she already lives what we proclaim in the Creed: "We look for the Resurrection of the dead, and the life of the world to come."

We can then ask ourselves: what are the roots of this victory over death wonderfully anticipated in Mary? Its roots are in the faith of the Virgin of Nazareth, as the Gospel passage we have heard testifies (Lk 1:39–56): a faith that is obedience to the word of God and total abandonment to the divine action and initiative, in accordance with what the Archangel announced to her. Faith, therefore, is Mary's greatness, as Elizabeth joyfully proclaims: Mary is "blessed among women" and "blessed is the fruit of [her] womb," for she is "Mother of the Lord" because she believed and lived uniquely the "first" of the Beatitudes, the Beatitude of faith. Elizabeth confesses it in her joy and in that of her child, who leaps in her womb: "And blessed is she who believed that there would be a fulfilment of what was spoken to her from the Lord" (Lk 1:45). Dear friends, let us not limit ourselves to admiring Mary in her destiny of glory, as a person very remote from us. No! We are called to look at all that the Lord, in his love, wanted to do for us, too, for our final destiny: to live through faith in a perfect communion of love with him and hence to live truly.

In this regard, I would like to reflect on an aspect of the affirmation of the dogma where assumption into heavenly glory is mentioned. All of us today are well aware that by the term "Heaven" we are not referring to somewhere in the universe, to a star or such like, no. We mean something far greater and far more difficult to define with our limited human conceptions. With this term "Heaven" we wish to say that God, the God who made himself close to us, does not abandon us in or after death but keeps a place for us and gives us eternity. We mean that in God there is room for us. To understand this reality a little better, let us look at our own lives. We all experience that when people die they continue to exist, in a certain way, in the memory and heart of those who knew and loved them. We might say that a part of the person lives on in them, but it resembles a "shadow" because this survival in the heart of their loved ones is destined to end. God, on the contrary, never passes away and we all exist by virtue of his love. We exist because he loves us, because he conceived of us and called us to life. We exist in God's thoughts and in God's love. We exist in the whole of our reality, not only in our "shadow." Our serenity, our hope, and our peace are based precisely on this: in God, in his thoughts and in his love, it is not merely a "shadow" of ourselves that survives but rather we are preserved and ushered into eternity with the whole of our being in him, in his creator love. It is his Love that triumphs over death and gives us eternity and it is this love that we call "Heaven": God is so great that he also makes room for us. And Jesus the man, who at the same time is God, is the guarantee for us that the being-man and the being-God can exist and live, the one within the other, for eternity.

This means that not only a part of each one of us will continue to exist, as it were pulled to safety, while other parts fall into ruin; on the contrary, it means that God knows and loves the whole of the human being, what we are. And God welcomes into his eternity what is developing and becoming now, in our life made up of suffering and love, of hope, joy, and sorrow. The whole of man, the whole of his life, is taken by God and, purified in him, receives eternity. Dear Friends! I think this is a truth that should fill us with deep joy. Christianity does not proclaim merely some salvation of the soul in a vague afterlife in which all that is precious and dear to us in this world would be eliminated, but promises eternal life, "the life of the world to come." Nothing that is precious and dear to us will fall into ruin; rather, it will find fullness in God. Every hair of our head is counted, Jesus said one day (cf. Mt 10:30). The definitive world will also be the fulfilment of this earth, as St. Paul says: "Creation itself will be set free from its bondage to decay and obtain the glorious liberty of the children of God" (Rom 8:21). Then we understand that Christianity imparts a strong hope in a bright future and paves the way to the realization of this future. We are called, precisely as Christians, to build this new world, to work so that, one day, it may become the "world of God," a world that will surpass all that we ourselves have been able to build. In Mary taken up into Heaven, who fully shares in the Resurrection of the Son, we contemplate the fulfilment of the human creature in accordance with "God's world."

Let us pray the Lord that he will enable us to understand how precious in his eyes is the whole of our life; may he strengthen our faith in eternal life; make us people of hope who work to build a world open to God, people full of joy who can glimpse the beauty of the future world amidst the worries of daily life and in this certainty live, believe, and hope. Amen!

26. *God Comes Closer to Us*

From the Homily of His Holiness Pope Benedict XVI, Solemnity of the Assumption of the Blessed Virgin Mary, Parish Church of St. Thomas of Villanova, Castel Gandolfo, Wednesday, 15 August 2012

On 1 November 1950, Venerable Pope Pius XII proclaimed as Dogma that the Virgin Mary "having completed the course of her earthly life, was assumed body and soul into heavenly glory."[5] This truth of faith was known by Tradition, was affirmed by the Fathers of the Church, and was a particularly important aspect in the veneration of the Mother of Christ. Precisely this devotional element, so to speak, was the driving force behind the formulation of this Dogma. The Dogma appears as an act of praise and exaltation of the Holy Virgin. It also emerges from the text of the Apostolic Constitution, where it affirms that the Dogma is proclaimed for "the honor of her Son . . . for the increase of the glory of that same august Mother, and for the joy and exultation of the entire Church."[6] What was already celebrated in the veneration and devotion of the People of God as the highest and most permanent glorification of Mary was thus expressed in the form of a dogma; the act of the proclamation of the Assumption was presented almost as a liturgy of faith. And in the Gospel which we have just heard, Mary herself prophetically pronounces a few words that orientate us in this perspective. She says: "For behold, henceforth all generations will call me blessed" (Lk 1:48). It is a prophecy for the whole history of the Church. These words of the Magnificat,

5. Pope Pius XII, *Munificentissimus Deus*, no. 44.

6. Pope Pius XII, *Munificentissimus Deus*, no. 44.

recorded by St. Luke, indicate that praising the Blessed Virgin, Mother of God, intimately united to Christ her Son, regards the Church of all ages and of all places. The fact that the Evangelist noted these words presupposes that the glorification of Mary was already present in the time of St. Luke and he considered it to be a duty and a commitment of the Christian community for all generations. Mary's words tell us that it is a duty of the Church to remember the greatness of Our Lady for the faith. This Solemnity is an invitation to praise God, and to look upon the greatness of Our Lady, for we know who God is in the faces of those who belong to him.

But why is Mary glorified by her Assumption into Heaven? St. Luke, as we have heard, sees the roots of the exaltation and praise of Mary in Elizabeth's words: "Blessed is she who believed" (Lk 1:45). And the Magnificat, this canticle to God, alive and active in history, is a hymn of faith and love, which springs from the heart of the Virgin. She lived with exemplary fidelity and kept in the inmost depths of her heart the words of God to his people, the promises he made to Abraham, Isaac, and Jacob, making them the content of her prayer: the Word of God in the Magnificat became the word of Mary, the lamp for her journey, thus preparing her to receive even in her womb the Word of God made flesh. Today's Gospel passage recalls this presence of God in history and in the unfolding of events; in particular, there is a reference to the Second Book of Samuel, chapter 6 (2 Sam 6:1–15), in which David moves the Holy Ark of the Covenant. The comparison is clear to the Evangelist: Mary expecting the birth of her Son Jesus is the Holy Ark that contains the presence of God, a presence that is a source of consolation, of total joy. John, in fact, leaps in Elizabeth's womb, just as David danced before the Ark. Mary is the "visit" of God that creates joy. Zechariah, in his song of praise, says explicitly: "Blessed be the Lord God of Israel, for he has visited and redeemed his people" (Lk 1:68). The house of Zechariah experienced the visit of God by the unexpected birth of John the Baptist, but above all by the presence of Mary, who bore within her womb the Son of God.

But now let us ask ourselves: how does the Assumption of Mary help our journey? The first answer is: in the Assumption, we see that in God there is room for man, God himself is the house with many rooms of which Jesus speaks (cf. Jn 14:2); God is man's home, in God there is God's space. And Mary, by uniting herself, united to God, does not distance herself from us. She does not go to an unknown galaxy, but whoever approaches God comes closer, for God is close to us all; and Mary, united to God, shares in the presence of God, is so close to us, to each one of us.

There is a beautiful passage from St. Gregory the Great on St. Benedict that we can apply to Mary, too. St. Gregory the Great says that the heart of St. Benedict expanded so much that all creation could enter it. This is even truer of Mary: Mary, totally united to God, has a heart so big that all creation can enter this heart, and the ex-votos in every part of the earth show it. Mary is close, she can hear us, she can help us, she is close to every one of us. In God there is room for man and God is close, and Mary, united to God, is very close; she has a heart as great as the heart of God.

But there is also another aspect: in God not only is there room for man; in man there is room for God. This too we see in Mary, the Holy Ark who bears the presence of God. In us there is space for God and this presence of God in us, so important for bringing light to the world with all its sadness, with its problems. This presence is realized in the faith: in the faith we open the doors of our existence so that God may enter us, so that God can be the power that gives life and a path to our existence. In us there is room, let us open ourselves like Mary opened herself, saying: "Let your will be done, I am the servant of the Lord." By opening ourselves to God, we lose nothing. On the contrary, our life becomes rich and great.

And so, faith and hope and love are combined. Today there is much discussion on a better world to be awaited: it would be our hope. If and when this better world comes, we do not know, I do not know. What is certain is that a world which distances itself from God does not become better but worse. Only God's presence can guarantee a good world. Let us leave it at that. One thing, one hope is certain: God expects us, waits for us, we do not go out into a void, we are expected. God is expecting us, and on going to that other world we find the goodness of the Mother, we find our loved ones, we find eternal Love. God is waiting for us: this is our great joy and the great hope that is born from this Feast. Mary visits us, and she is the joy of our life and joy is hope.

What is there to say then? A great heart, the presence of God in the world, room for God within us and room for us in God, hope, being expected: this is the symphony of this Feast, the instruction that meditating on this Solemnity gives us. Mary is the dawn and the splendor of the Church triumphant; she is the consolation and the hope of people still on the journey, it says in today's Preface.[7] Let us entrust ourselves to her Motherly intercession, that she may obtain that he strengthen our faith in eternal life; may she help us to live the best way the time that God has given us with hope.

7. "Preface: The Glory of Mary Assumed into Heaven," in *The Roman Missal*, 929.

May it be a Christian hope, that is not only nostalgia for Heaven, but a living and active desire for God who is here in the world, a desire for God that makes us tireless pilgrims, nourishing in us the courage and the power of faith, which at the same time is the courage and the power of love. Amen.

MARIAN SOLEMNITIES AND FEASTS

IMMACULATE CONCEPTION

27. *True Freedom*

From the Homily of His Holiness Pope Benedict XVI, Solemnity of the Immaculate Conception, of the Blessed Virgin Mary
St. Peter's Basilica, Thursday, 8 December 2005

Pope Paul VI solemnly concluded the Second Vatican Council in the square in front of St. Peter's Basilica 40 years ago, on 8 December 1965. It had been inaugurated, in accordance with John XXIII's wishes, on 11 October 1962, which was then the Feast of Mary's Motherhood, and ended on the day of the Immaculate Conception. The Council took place in a Marian setting. It was actually far more than a setting: it was the orientation of its entire process. It refers us, as it referred the Council Fathers at that time, to the image of the Virgin who listens and lives in the Word of God, who cherishes in her heart the words that God addresses to her and, piecing them together like a mosaic, learns to understand them (cf. Lk 2:19, 51). It refers us to the great Believer who, full of faith, put herself in God's hands, abandoning herself to his will; it refers us to the humble Mother who, when the Son's mission so required, became part of it, and at the same time, to the courageous woman who stood beneath the Cross while the disciples fled.

In his Discourse on the occasion of the promulgation of the Dogmatic Constitution on the Church, Paul VI described Mary as "*tutrix huius Concilii*"— "Patroness of this Council" and, with an unmistakable allusion to the account of Pentecost transmitted by Luke (Acts 1:12–14), said that the Fathers were gathered in the Council Hall *"cum Maria, Matre Iesu"* and would also have left it in her name.[1] Indelibly printed in my memory is the moment when, hearing his words: *"Mariam Sanctissimam declaramus Matrem Ecclesiae"*—"We declare Mary the Most Holy Mother of the Church," the Fathers spontaneously rose at once and paid homage to the Mother of God, to our Mother, to the Mother of the Church, with a standing ovation. Indeed, with this title, the Pope summed up the Marian teaching of the Council and provided the key to understanding it. Not only does Mary have a unique relationship with Christ, the Son of God who, as man, chose to become her Son. Since she was totally united to Christ, she also totally belongs to us. Yes, we can say that Mary is close to us as no other human being is, because Christ becomes man for all men and women and his entire being is "being here for us." Christ, the Fathers said, as the Head, is inseparable from his Body which is the Church, forming with her, so to speak, a single living subject. The Mother of the Head is also the Mother of all the Church; she is, so to speak, totally emptied of herself; she has given herself entirely to Christ and with him is given as a gift to us all. Indeed, the more the human person gives himself, the more he finds himself.

The Council intended to tell us this: Mary is so interwoven in the great mystery of the Church that she and the Church are inseparable, just as she and Christ are inseparable. Mary mirrors the Church, anticipates the Church in her person, and in all the turbulence that affects the suffering, struggling Church she always remains the Star of salvation. In her lies the true center in which

1. Cf. *Oecumenicum Concilium Vaticanum II*, Constitutiones Decreta Declarationes, Vatican City, 1966, p. 983, 985.

we trust, even if its peripheries very often weigh on our soul. In the context of the promulgation of the Constitution on the Church, Paul VI shed light on all this through a new title deeply rooted in Tradition, precisely with the intention of illuminating the inner structure of the Church's teaching, which was developed at the Council. The Second Vatican Council had to pronounce on the institutional components of the Church: on the Bishops and on the Pontiff, on the priests, lay people and Religious, in their communion and in their relations; it had to describe the Church journeying on, "clasping sinners to her bosom, at once holy and always in need of purification. . . ."[2] This "Petrine" aspect of the Church, however, is included in that "Marian" aspect. In Mary, the Immaculate, we find the essence of the Church without distortion. We ourselves must learn from her to become "ecclesial souls," as the Fathers said, so that we too may be able, in accordance with St. Paul's words, to present ourselves "blameless" in the sight of the Lord, as he wanted us from the very beginning (cf. Col 1:21; Eph 1:4).

But now we must ask ourselves: What does "Mary, the Immaculate" mean? Does this title have something to tell us? Today, the liturgy illuminates the content of these words for us in two great images. First of all comes the marvelous narrative of the annunciation of the Messiah's coming to Mary, the Virgin of Nazareth. The Angel's greeting is interwoven with threads from the Old Testament, especially from the Prophet Zephaniah. He shows that Mary, the humble provincial woman who comes from a priestly race and bears within her the great priestly patrimony of Israel, is "the holy remnant" of Israel to which the prophets referred in all

2. Second Vatican Council, *Lumen Gentium*, no. 8.

the periods of trial and darkness. In her is present the true Zion, the pure, living dwelling-place of God. In her the Lord dwells, in her he finds the place of his repose. She is the living house of God, who does not dwell in buildings of stone but in the heart of living man. She is the shoot which sprouts from the stump of David in the dark winter night of history. In her, the words of the Psalm are fulfilled: "The earth has yielded its fruits" (Ps 67:7). She is the offshoot from which grew the tree of redemption and of the redeemed. God has not failed, as it might have seemed formerly at the beginning of history with Adam and Eve or during the period of the Babylonian Exile, and as it seemed anew in Mary's time when Israel had become a people with no importance in an occupied region and with very few recognizable signs of its holiness. God did not fail. In the humility of the house in Nazareth lived holy Israel, the pure remnant. God saved and saves his people. From the felled tree trunk Israel's history shone out anew, becoming a living force that guides and pervades the world. Mary is holy Israel: she says "yes" to the Lord, she puts herself totally at his disposal and thus becomes the living temple of God.

The second image is much more difficult and obscure. This metaphor from the Book of Genesis speaks to us from a great historical distance and can only be explained with difficulty; only in the course of history has it been possible to develop a deeper understanding of what it refers to. It was foretold that the struggle between humanity and the serpent, that is, between man and the forces of evil and death, would continue throughout history. It was also foretold, however, that the "offspring" of a woman would one day triumph and would crush the head of the serpent to death; it was foretold that the offspring of the woman—and in this offspring the woman and the mother herself—would be victorious and that thus, through man, God would triumph. If we set ourselves with the believing and praying Church to listen to this text, then we can begin to understand what original sin, inherited sin, is and also what the protection against this inherited sin is, what redemption is. What picture does this passage show us? The human being does not trust God. Tempted by the serpent, he harbors the suspicion that in the end, God takes something away from his life, that God is a rival who curtails our freedom and that we will be fully human only when we have cast him aside; in brief, that only in this way can we fully achieve our freedom. The human being lives in the suspicion that God's love creates a dependence and that he must rid himself of this dependency if he is to be fully himself. Man does not want to receive his existence and the fullness of his life from God. He himself wants to obtain from the tree of knowledge the power to shape the world, to make himself a god, raising himself to God's level, and to overcome death and darkness with his own efforts. He does not want to rely on love that to him seems untrustworthy; he relies solely on his own knowledge, since it confers power upon him. Rather than on love, he sets his sights on power, with which he desires to take his own life autonomously in hand. And in doing so, he trusts in deceit rather than in truth and thereby sinks with his life into emptiness, into death.

Love is not dependence but a gift that makes us live. The freedom of a human being is the freedom of a limited being, and therefore is itself limited. We can possess it only as a shared freedom, in the communion of freedom: only if we live in the right way, with one another and for one another, can freedom develop. We live in the right way if we live in accordance with the truth of our being, and that is, in accordance with God's will. For God's will is not a law for the human being imposed from the outside and that constrains him, but the intrinsic measure of his nature, a measure that is engraved within him and makes him the image of God, hence, a free creature. If we live in opposition to love and against the truth—in opposition to God—then we destroy one another and destroy the world. Then we do not find life but act in the interests of death. All this is recounted with immortal images in the history of the original fall of man and the expulsion of man from the earthly Paradise.

Dear brothers and sisters, if we sincerely reflect about ourselves and our history, we have to say that with this narrative is described not only the history of the beginning but the history of all times, and that we all carry within us a drop of the poison of that way of thinking, illustrated by the images in the Book of Genesis. We call this drop of poison "original sin." Precisely on the Feast of the Immaculate Conception, we have a lurking suspicion that a person who does not sin must really be basically boring and that something is missing from his life: the dramatic dimension of being autonomous; that the freedom to say no, to descend into the shadows of sin and to want to do things on one's own is part of being truly human; that only then can we make the most of all the vastness and depth of our being men and women, of being truly ourselves; that we should put this freedom to the test, even in opposition to God, in order to become, in reality, fully ourselves. In a word, we think that evil is basically good, we think that we need it, at least a little, in order to experience the fullness of being. We think that Mephistopheles—the tempter—is right when he says he is the power "that always wants evil and always does good."[3] We think that a little bargaining with evil, keeping for oneself a little freedom against God, is basically a good thing, perhaps even necessary. If we look, however, at the world that surrounds us, we can see that this is not so; in other words, that evil is always poisonous, does not uplift human beings but degrades and humiliates them. It does not make them any greater, purer, or wealthier, but harms and belittles them. This is something we should indeed learn on the day of the Immaculate Conception: the person who abandons himself totally in God's hands does not become God's puppet, a boring "yes man"; he does not lose his freedom. Only the person who entrusts himself totally to God finds true freedom, the great, creative immensity of the freedom of good.

The person who turns to God does not become smaller but greater, for through God and with God he becomes great, he becomes divine, he becomes truly himself. The person who puts himself in God's hands does not distance himself from others, withdrawing into his private salvation; on the contrary, it is only then that his heart truly awakens and he becomes a sensitive, hence, benevolent and open person. The closer a person is to God, the closer he is to people. We see this in Mary. The fact that she is totally with God is the reason why she is so close to human beings. For this reason, she can be the Mother of every consolation and every help, a Mother whom anyone can dare to address in any kind of need, in weakness and in sin, for she has understanding for everything and is for everyone the open power of creative goodness. In her, God

3. J. W. von Goethe, *Faust*, trans. and with an introduction and notes by David Constantine (Penguin Books Limited, 2006), I, 3. This edition's translation is slightly different from the Vatican's.

has impressed his own image, the image of the One who follows the lost sheep even up into the mountains and among the briars and thornbushes of the sins of this world, letting himself be spiked by the crown of thorns of these sins in order to take the sheep on his shoulders and bring it home. As a merciful Mother, Mary is the anticipated figure and everlasting portrait of the Son. Thus, we see that the image of the Sorrowful Virgin, of the Mother who shares her suffering and her love, is also a true image of the Immaculate Conception. Her heart was enlarged by being and feeling together with God. In her, God's goodness came very close to us. Mary thus stands before us as a sign of comfort, encouragement, and hope. She turns to us, saying: "Have the courage to dare with God! Try it! Do not be afraid of him! Have the courage to risk with faith! Have the courage to risk with goodness! Have the courage to risk with a pure heart! Commit yourselves to God, then you will see that it is precisely by doing so that your life will become broad and light, not boring but filled with infinite surprises, for God's infinite goodness is never depleted!"

On this Feast Day, let us thank the Lord for the great sign of his goodness which he has given us in Mary, his Mother and the Mother of the Church. Let us pray to him to put Mary on our path like a light that also helps us to become a light and to carry this light into the nights of history. Amen.

MARIAN SOLEMNITIES AND FEASTS

OUR LADY OF GUADALUPE

28. *She Always Leads Us to Her Divine Son*

From the Homily of His Holiness Pope Benedict XVI, Solemnity of the Blessed Virgin Mary of Guadalupe, On the Bicentenary of Independence of Countries in Latin America and the Caribbean
Saint Peter's Basilica, Monday, 12 December 2011

"The earth has yielded its increase" (Ps 67 [66]:6). The Fathers of the Church recognized in this image, taken from the Psalm we just heard and which invites all the peoples and nations to praise the Lord with joy, the Virgin Mary and Christ, her Son: "The earth is Mary Most Holy, who comes from our earth, our lineage, from this clay, from this mud, from Adam. The earth has yielded its fruit: it first produced a flower . . . this flower then became a fruit so that we might eat it so that we might eat its flesh. Would you like to know what this fruit is? It is the Virgin Son who proceeds from the Virgin Mother; the Lord from the handmaid; God from man; the Son from the Mother; the fruit from the earth."[1] Today, exulting over the fruit of this earth, we too are saying: "Let the peoples praise thee, O God" (Ps 67 [66]:4). We proclaim the gift of redemption gained by Christ and, in Christ, we acknowledge his power and divine majesty.

Moved by these sentiments, I greet fraternally the Cardinals and Bishops who are with us, the various diplomatic representatives, the priests and men and women religious, as well as the

1. St. Jerome, *Breviarum in Psalm*, PL 66, 1010–11.

faithful gathered here in St. Peter's Basilica to celebrate with joy the Solemnity of Our Lady of Guadalupe, Mother and Star of the Evangelization of America. I also remember all those who have joined us in spirit and are praying to God with us for the countries of Latin America and the Caribbean, many of whom are celebrating the bicentenary of their independence at this time and, going beyond the historical, social, and political aspects of these events, are expressing anew to the Most High their gratitude for the great gift of faith they received, a faith that proclaims the redemptive mystery of the death and Resurrection of Jesus Christ, so that all the peoples of the earth may have life in Him. The Successor of Peter could not let this occasion pass without expressing the Church's joy in the many gifts which God, in his infinite kindness, has in these years poured out upon these beloved nations, who so affectionately invoke Mary Most Holy.

The venerated image of the Black Madonna of Tepeyac, with her sweet and peaceful countenance, imprinted on the tilma of the Indio St. Juan Diego, shows her as "the ever-Virgin Mary, Mother of the True God from whom she lives."[2] She reminds us of the "woman clothed with the sun, with the moon under her feet, and on her head a crown of twelve stars; she was with child" (Rev 12:1–2). She signals the presence of the Savior to the indigenous and mestizo population. She always leads us to her divine Son, who is revealed as the foundation of the dignity of every human being, as a love that is stronger than the powers of evil and death, and the fountain of joy, filial trust, consolation, and hope.

2. From the Office of Readings of December 12, *Nicán Mopohua*, 12th ed. (Mexico City, D. F., 1971), 3–19.

The Magnificat that we proclaimed in the Gospel "is the song both of the Mother of God and of the Church; the song of the Daughter of Zion and of the new People of God; the song of thanksgiving for the fullness of graces poured out in the economy of salvation and the song of the 'poor' whose hope is met by the fulfillment of the promises made to our ancestors."[3] In an act of gratitude to her Lord and of the humility of his handmaid, the Virgin Mary praises God for all that he is doing on behalf of his people Israel. God is the One who deserves all honor and glory, the Mighty One who does marvels for his faithful servant and today continues to show his love to all men and women, especially those who are facing difficult trials.

"Lo, your king comes to you; triumphant and victorious is he, humble and riding on an ass" (Zech 9:9), we heard in the first reading. Since the Incarnation of the Word, the divine Mystery is revealed in Jesus Christ, who is the contemporary of every human person in every time and place through the Church, whose Mother and model is Mary. Therefore, today we can continue praising God for the wonders he has worked in the life of the people of Latin America and the whole world, revealing his presence in the Son and the outpouring of his Spirit as the newness of personal and community life. God has hidden these things from the "wise and learned," letting them be known to the humble and simple of heart (cf. Mt 11:25).

By her "yes" to God's call, the Virgin Mary manifested divine love among men. In this sense she, with her simplicity and maternal heart, continues to indicate the one Light and the one Truth: her

3. *Catechism of the Catholic Church*, no. 2619.

Son, Jesus Christ, who is "the definitive answer to the question of the meaning of life, and to those fundamental questions which still trouble so many men and women on the American continent."[4] Similarly, "by her manifold intercession [she] continues to bring us the gifts of eternal salvation. By her maternal charity, she cares for the brethren of her Son, who still journey on earth surrounded by dangers and difficulties, until they are led into their blessed home."[5]

At this time, as various parts of Latin America are commemorating the bicentenary of their Independence, the process of integration in this beloved continent is progressing, while at the same time it is playing a new role on the world scene. In these circumstances, it is important that its diverse people can safeguard the rich treasure of faith and their historical-cultural dynamism, always being the defenders of human life from conception to natural end and promoters of peace; they must likewise care for the family in this genuine nature and mission, at the same time intensifying a vast grass-roots educational campaign that correctly prepares individuals and makes them aware of their capacities in such a way that they can face their destiny with responsibility and dignity. They are likewise called to foster ever more proven initiatives and effective programs that promote reconciliation and fraternity, increase solidarity, and care for the environment, at the same time intensifying efforts to overcome poverty, illiteracy, and corruption, and to eradicate every form of injustice, violence, criminality, civic unrest, drug trafficking, and extortion.

4. Pope John Paul II, Post-Synodal Apostolic Exhortation *Ecclesia in America* (January 22, 1999), no. 10.

5. Second Vatican Council, *Lumen Gentium*, no. 62.

When the Church was preparing to recall the fifth centenary of the planting of the Cross of Christ in the good soil of the American Continent, on that same soil Bl. John Paul II formulated for the first time a program for a new evangelization, new "in its ardor, in its methods, in its expression."[6] Because of my responsibility of confirming in the faith, I also want to encourage the apostolic zeal that is now motivating and driving the "continental mission" promoted in Aparecida, so that "Christian faith may become more deeply rooted in the heart of Latin American individuals and peoples as founding event and living encounter with Christ."[7] Thus there will be a multiplication of genuine disciples and missionaries of the Lord and a renewal of Latin America and the Caribbean's vocation to hope. May the light of God shine more and more on the face of each of the sons and daughters of this beloved land and may his redemptive grace guide their decisions so that they may continue progressing untiringly in the building of a society founded upon the development of the good, the triumph of love, and the spread of justice. With these fervent desires and sustained by the help of Divine Providence, I intend to undertake an Apostolic Journey to Mexico and Cuba before Easter, to proclaim there the Word of Christ and support the conviction that this is a precious time to evangelize with a true faith, a living hope, and an ardent charity.

I commend to the loving mediation of Our Lady of Guadalupe, our heavenly Mother, all these intentions and the present situation of the Latin American and Caribbean nations and their progress

6. Pope John Paul II, *Address to the CELAM Assembly*, March 9, 1983, III: AAS 75, 1983, 778.

7. Fifth General Conference of the Council of the Bishops of Latin America and the Caribbean, Final Document, n. 13.

towards a better future. I likewise invoke upon them the intercession of the many saints and blessed that the Spirit has raised up throughout the length and breadth of the history of this continent, offering heroic models of Christian virtue in diverse states of life and social milieu, that their example may promote more and more a new evangelization under the gaze of Christ, Savior of man and strength of our soul. Amen.

SAINTS

ST. JOSEPH

29. *Remember to Keep the Sabbath*

From the Homily of His Holiness Pope Benedict XVI
Feast of St. Joseph Eucharistic Celebration for all Workers
St. Peter's Basilica, Sunday, 19 March 2006

We have listened together to a famous and beautiful passage from the Book of Exodus, in which the sacred author tells of God's presentation of the Decalogue to Israel. One detail makes an immediate impression: the announcement of the Ten Commandments is introduced by a significant reference to the liberation of the People of Israel. The text says: "I am the Lord your God, who brought you out of the land of Egypt, out of the house of bondage" (Ex 20:2). Thus, the Decalogue is intended as a confirmation of the freedom gained. Indeed, at a closer look, the Commandments are the means that the Lord gives us to protect our freedom, both from the internal conditioning of passions and from the external abuse of those with evil intentions. The "nos" of the Commandments are as many "yeses" to the growth of true freedom.

There is a second dimension of the Decalogue that should also be emphasized: by the Law which he gave through Moses, the Lord revealed that he wanted to make a covenant with Israel. The Law, therefore, is a gift more than an imposition. Rather than commanding what the human being ought to do, its intention is to reveal to all the choice of God: He takes the side of the Chosen

People; he set them free from slavery and surrounds them with his merciful goodness. The Decalogue is a proof of his special love.

Today's liturgy offers us a second message: The Mosaic Law was totally fulfilled in Jesus, who revealed God's wisdom and love through the mystery of the Cross, "a stumbling block to Jews and an absurdity to Gentiles; but to those who are called, Jews and Greeks alike, Christ is the power of God and the wisdom of God" (1 Cor 1:23–24). The Gospel just proclaimed refers precisely to this: Jesus drove the merchants and moneychangers out of the temple. Through the verse of a Psalm: "Zeal for your house has consumed me" (cf. Ps 69[68]:10), the Evangelist provides a key for the interpretation of this significant episode. And Jesus was "consumed" by this "zeal" for the "house of God," which was being used for purposes other than those for which it was intended. To the amazement of everyone present, he responded to the request of the religious leaders who demand evidence of his authority by saying: "Destroy this temple, and in three days I will raise it up" (Jn 2:19). These are mysterious words that were incomprehensible at the time; John, however, paraphrased them for his Christian readers, saying: "Actually, he was talking about the temple of his body" (Jn 2:21). His enemies were to destroy that "temple," but after three days he would rebuild it through the Resurrection. The distressful "stumbling block" of Christ's death was to be crowned by the triumph of his glorious Resurrection. In this Lenten season, while we are preparing to relive this central event of our salvation in the Easter triduum, we are already looking at the Crucified One, seeing in him the brightness of the Risen One.

Dear brothers and sisters, today's Eucharistic Celebration, which combines the commemoration of St. Joseph with meditation on the liturgical texts of the Third Sunday of Lent, gives us the opportunity to consider in the light of the Paschal Mystery another important aspect of human life. I am referring to the reality of work, which exists today in the midst of rapid and complex changes. In many passages, the Bible shows that work is one of the original conditions of the human being. When the Creator shaped man in his image and likeness, he asked him to till the land (cf. Gn 2:5–6). It was because of the sin of our first parents that work became a burden and an affliction (cf. Gn 3:6–8), but in the divine plan it retains its value, unaltered. The Son of God, by making himself like us in all things, dedicated himself for many years to manual activities, so that he was known as "the carpenter's son" (cf. Mt 13:55). The Church has always, but especially in the last century, shown attention and concern for this social context, as the many social interventions of the Magisterium testify and the action of many associations of Christian inspiration show; some of them are gathered here today and represent the whole world of workers.

I am pleased to welcome you, dear friends, and I address my cordial greeting to each one of you. A special thought goes to Bishop Arrigo Miglio of Ivrea and President of the Italian Episcopal Commission for Social Problems and Work, Justice, and Peace, who has interpreted your common sentiments and addressed courteous good wishes to me for my name day. I am deeply grateful to him. Work is of fundamental importance to the fulfilment of the human being and to the development of society. Thus, it must always be organized and carried out with full respect for human dignity and must always serve the common good. At the same time, it is indispensable that people do not allow themselves to be enslaved by work or idolize it, claiming to find in it the ultimate and definitive meaning of life. The invitation contained in the first reading is appropriate in this regard: "Remember to keep holy the Sabbath day. Six days you may labor and do all your work, but the seventh day is the Sabbath of the Lord, your God" (Ex 20:8–9). The Sabbath is a holy day, that is, a day consecrated to God on which man understands better the meaning of his life and his work. It can therefore be said that the biblical teaching on work is crowned by the commandment of rest.

The Compendium of the Social Doctrine of the Church speaks opportunely of this: "For man, bound as he is to the necessity of work, this rest opens to the prospect of a fuller freedom, that of the eternal Sabbath (cf. Heb 4:9–10). Rest gives men and women the possibility to remember and experience anew God's work from Creation to Redemption, in order to recognize themselves as his work (cf. Eph 2:10), and to give thanks for their lives and for their subsistence to him who is their author."[1] Work must serve the true good of humanity, permitting "men as individuals and as members of society to pursue and fulfil their total vocation."[2] For this to happen, technical and professional qualifications, although necessary, do not suffice; nor does the creation of a just social order, attentive to the common good. It is necessary to live a spirituality that helps believers to sanctify themselves through their work, imitating St. Joseph, who had to provide with his own hands for the daily needs of the Holy Family and whom, consequently, the Church holds up as patron of workers. His witness shows that man is the subject and protagonist of work.

1. *Compendium of the Social Doctrine of the Church*, no. 258.
2. Second Vatican Council, *Gaudium et Spes*, no. 35.

I would like to entrust to St. Joseph those young people who are finding integration into the working world difficult, the unemployed and everyone who is suffering hardship due to the widespread employment crisis. Together with Mary, his Spouse, may St. Joseph watch over all workers and obtain serenity and peace for families and for the whole of humanity. May Christians, looking at this great Saint, learn to witness in every working environment to the love of Christ, the source of true solidarity and lasting peace. Amen!

30. *Trust in God*

From the Homily of His Holiness Pope Benedict XVI
Apostolic Journey to Cameroon and Angola
Amadou Ahidjo Stadium of Yaoundé, Thursday, 19 March 2009

Praised be Jesus Christ who has gathered us in this stadium today that we may enter more deeply into his life! Jesus Christ brings us together on this day when the Church, here in Cameroon and throughout the world, celebrates the Feast of Saint Joseph, Husband of the Virgin Mary. I begin by wishing a very happy feast day to all those who, like myself, have received the grace of bearing this beautiful name, and I ask Saint Joseph to grant them his special protection in guiding them towards the Lord Jesus Christ all the days of their life. I also extend cordial best wishes to all the parishes, schools, colleges, and institutions named after Saint Joseph. I thank Archbishop Tonyé-Bakot of Yaoundé for his kind words, and I warmly greet the representatives of the African Episcopal Conferences who have come to Yaoundé for the promulgation of the *Instrumentum Laboris* of the Second Special Assembly for

Africa of the Synod of Bishops. How can we enter into the specific grace of this day? In a little while, at the end of Mass, the liturgy will remind us of the focal point of our meditation when it has us pray: "Lord, today you nourish us at this altar as we celebrate the feast of Saint Joseph. Protect your Church always, and in your love watch over the gifts you have given us."[3] We are asking the Lord to protect the Church always—and he does!—just as Joseph protected his family and kept watch over the child Jesus during his early years.

Our Gospel reading recalls this for us. The angel said to Joseph: "Do not be afraid to take Mary your wife into your home" (Mt 1:20), and that is precisely what he did: "he did as the angel of the Lord had commanded him" (Mt 1:24). Why was Saint Matthew so keen to note Joseph's trust in the words received from the messenger of God, if not to invite us to imitate this same loving trust? Although the first reading which we have just heard does not speak explicitly of Saint Joseph, it does teach us a good deal about him. The prophet Nathan, in obedience to God's command, tells David: "I will raise up your heir after you, sprung from your loins" (2 Sam 7:12). David must accept that he will die before seeing the fulfilment of this promise, which will come to pass "when [his] time comes" and he will rest "with [his] ancestors." We thus come to realize that one of mankind's most cherished desires—seeing the fruits of one's labors—is not always granted by God. I think of those among you who are mothers and fathers of families. Parents quite rightly desire to give the best of themselves to their children, and they want to see them achieve success. Yet make no mistake

3. "Prayer after Communion," Solemnity of St. Joseph, in *The Roman Missal*, 838.

about what this "success" entails: what God asks David to do is to place his trust in him. David himself will not see his heir who will have a throne "firm forever" (2 Sam 7:16), for this heir, announced under the veil of prophecy, is Jesus. David puts his trust in God. In the same way, Joseph trusts God when he hears his messenger, the Angel, say to him: "Joseph, son of David, do not be afraid to take Mary your wife into your home. For it is through the Holy Spirit that this child has been conceived in her" (Mt 1:20). Throughout all of history, Joseph is the man who gives God the greatest display of trust, even in the face of such astonishing news.

Dear fathers and mothers here today, do you have trust in God who has called you to be the fathers and mothers of his adopted children? Do you accept that he is counting on you to pass on to your children the human and spiritual values that you yourselves have received and which will prepare them to live with love and respect for his holy name? At a time when so many people have no qualms about trying to impose the tyranny of materialism, with scant concern for the most deprived, you must be very careful. Africa in general, and Cameroon in particular, place themselves at risk if they do not recognize the True Author of Life! Brothers and sisters in Cameroon and throughout Africa, you who have received from God so many human virtues, take care of your souls! Do not let yourselves be captivated by selfish illusions and false ideals! Believe—yes!—continue to believe in God—Father, Son, and Holy Spirit—he alone truly loves you in the way you yearn to be loved, he alone can satisfy you, can bring stability to your lives. Only Christ is the way of Life. God alone could grant Joseph the strength to trust the Angel. God alone will give you, dear married couples, the strength to raise your family as he wants. Ask it of him!

God loves to be asked for what he wishes to give. Ask him for the grace of a true and ever more faithful love patterned after his own. As the Psalm magnificently puts it: his "love is established forever, his loyalty will stand as long as the heavens" (Ps 88:3).

Just as on other continents, the family today—in your country and across Africa—is experiencing a difficult time; but fidelity to God will help see it through. Certain values of the traditional life have been overturned. Relationships between different generations have evolved in a way that no longer favors the transmission of accumulated knowledge and inherited wisdom. Too often we witness a rural exodus not unlike that known in many other periods of human history. The quality of family ties is deeply affected by this. Uprooted and fragile members of the younger generation who often—sadly—are without gainful employment, seek to cure their pain by living in ephemeral and man-made paradises which we know will never guarantee the human being a deep, abiding happiness. Sometimes the African people too are constrained to flee from themselves and abandon everything that once made up their interior richness. Confronted with the phenomenon of rapid urbanization, they leave the land, physically and morally: not as Abraham had done in response to the Lord's call, but as a kind of interior exile which alienates them from their very being, from their brothers and sisters, and from God himself.

Is this an irreversible, inevitable development? By no means! More than ever, we must "hope against all hope" (Rom 4:18). Here I wish to acknowledge with appreciation and gratitude the remarkable work done by countless associations that promote the life of faith and the practice of charity. May they be warmly thanked! May they find in the word of God renewed strength to carry out their projects for the integral development of the human person in Africa, especially in Cameroon!

The first priority will consist in restoring a sense of the acceptance of life as a gift from God. According to both Sacred Scripture and the wisest traditions of your continent, the arrival of a child is always a gift, a blessing from God. Today it is high time to place greater emphasis on this: every human being, every tiny human person, however weak, is created "in the image and likeness of God" (Gen 1:27). Every person must live! Death must not prevail over life! Death will never have the last word!

Sons and daughters of Africa, do not be afraid to believe, to hope, and to love; do not be afraid to say that Jesus is the Way, the Truth, and the Life, and that we can be saved by him alone. Saint Paul is indeed an inspired author given to the Church by the Holy Spirit as a "teacher of nations" (1 Tim 2:7) when he tells us that Abraham, "hoping against hope, believed that he should become the father of many nations; as he had been told, 'So shall your descendants be'" (Rom 4:18).

"Hoping against hope": is this not a magnificent description of a Christian? Africa is called to hope through you and in you! With Jesus Christ, who trod the African soil, Africa can become the continent of hope! We are all members of the peoples that God gave to Abraham as his descendants. Each and every one of us was thought, willed, and loved by God. Each and every one of us has a role to play in the plan of God: Father, Son, and Holy Spirit. If discouragement overwhelms you, think of the faith of Joseph; if anxiety has its grip on you, think of the hope of Joseph, that descendant of Abraham who hoped against hope; if exasperation or hatred seizes you, think of the love of Joseph, who was the first man to set eyes on the human face of God in the person of the Infant conceived by the Holy Spirit in the womb of the Virgin Mary. Let us praise and thank Christ for having drawn so close to us, and for giving us Joseph as an example and model of love for him.

Dear brothers and sisters, I want to say to you once more from the bottom of my heart: like Joseph, do not be afraid to take Mary into your home—that is to say, do not be afraid to love the Church. Mary, Mother of the Church, will teach you to follow your Pastors, to love your bishops, your priests, your deacons, and your catechists; to heed what they teach you and to pray for their intentions. Husbands, look upon the love of Joseph for Mary and Jesus; those preparing for marriage, treat your future spouse as Joseph did; those of you who have given yourselves to God in celibacy, reflect upon the teaching of the Church, our Mother: "Virginity or celibacy for the sake of the Kingdom of God not only does not contradict the dignity of marriage but presupposes and confirms it. Marriage and virginity are two ways of expressing and living the one mystery of the Covenant of God with his people."[4]

Once more, I wish to extend a particular word of encouragement to fathers so that they may take Saint Joseph as their model. He who kept watch over the Son of Man is able to teach them the deepest meaning of their own fatherhood. In the same way, each father receives his children from God, and they are created in God's own image and likeness. Saint Joseph was the spouse of Mary. In the same way, each father sees himself entrusted with the mystery of womanhood through his own wife. Dear fathers, like Saint Joseph, respect and love your spouse; and by your love and your

4. Pope John Paul II, Apostolic Exhortation *Redemptoris Custos* (August 15, 1989), no. 20.

wise presence, lead your children to God where they must be (cf. Lk 2:49). Finally, to all the young people present, I offer words of friendship and encouragement: as you face the challenges of life, take courage! Your life is priceless in the eyes of God! Let Christ take hold of you, agree to pledge your love to him, and—why not?—maybe even do so in the priesthood or in the consecrated life! This is the supreme service. To the children who no longer have a father, or who live abandoned in the poverty of the streets, to those forcibly separated from their parents, to the maltreated and abused, to those constrained to join paramilitary forces that are terrorizing some countries, I would like to say: God loves you, he has not forgotten you, and Saint Joseph protects you! Invoke him with confidence.

May God bless you and watch over you! May he give you the grace to keep advancing towards him with fidelity! May he give stability to your lives so that you may reap the fruits he awaits from you! May he make you witnesses of his love here in Cameroon and to the ends of the earth! I fervently beg him to give you a taste of the joy of belonging to him, now and forever. Amen.

SAINTS

STS. PETER AND PAUL

31. *Unconditional Belonging to the Lord*

From the Homily of His Holiness Pope Benedict XVI, Solemnity of the Holy Apostles Peter and Paul, Celebration of the First Vespers Basilica of St. Paul Outside-the-Walls, Thursday, 28 June 2007

At this First Vespers of the Solemnity of Sts. Peter and Paul, let us commemorate with gratitude these two Apostles whose blood with that of so many other Gospel witnesses made the Church of Rome fruitful. On their memorial, I am glad to greet you all, dear brothers and sisters, starting with the Cardinal Archpriest and the other Cardinals and Bishops present, Father Abbot and the Benedictine Community to which this Basilica is entrusted, the clerics, the women and men religious and lay faithful gathered here. I address a special greeting to the Delegation of the Ecumenical Patriarchate of Constantinople, which is reciprocating the presence of the Holy See's Delegation in Istanbul for the Feast of St. Andrew. As I had an opportunity to say a few days ago, these meetings and initiatives are not merely an exchange of courtesies between churches but are intended to express the common commitment to do everything possible to hasten the time of full communion between the Christian East and West. I address with these sentiments Metropolitan Emmanuel and Metropolitan Gennadios, sent by my beloved Brother Bartholomew I, to whom I express a grateful and cordial thought. This Basilica, which has hosted profoundly significant ecumenical events, reminds us how important it is to pray together to implore the gift of unity, that unity for which St. Peter and St. Paul spent their lives, to the point of making the supreme sacrifice of their blood.

A very ancient tradition which dates back to apostolic times claims that their last meeting before their martyrdom actually took place not far from here: the two are supposed to have embraced and blessed each other. And on the main portal of this Basilica, they are depicted together, with scenes of both martyrdoms. Thus, from the outset, Christian tradition has considered Peter and Paul to have been inseparable, even if each had a different mission to accomplish. Peter professed his faith in Christ first; Paul obtained as a gift the ability to deepen its riches. Peter founded the first community of Christians who came from the Chosen People; Paul became the Apostle to the Gentiles. With different charisms they worked for one and the same cause: the building of Christ's Church. In the Office of Readings, the liturgy offers us for meditation this well-known text of St. Augustine: "One day is assigned for the celebration of the martyrdom of the two Apostles. But those two were one. Although their martyrdom occurred on different days, they were one. Peter went first, Paul followed. We celebrate this feast day which is made sacred for us by the blood of these Apostles."[5] And St. Leo the Great comments: "About their merits and virtues, which surpass all power of speech, we must not make distinctions, because they were equal in their election, alike in their toils, undivided in their death."[6] In Rome, since the earliest centuries, the bond that unites Peter and Paul in their mission has acquired a very specific significance. Like Romulus and Remus, the

5. St. Augustine, *Sermon* 295, 7, 8.

6. St. Leo the Great, *In Natali Apostolorum Petri et Pauli*, 69, 7.

two mythical brothers who are said to have given birth to the City, so Peter and Paul were held to be the founders of the Church of Rome. Speaking to the City on this topic, St. Leo the Great said: "These are your holy Fathers and true shepherds, who gave you claims to be numbered among the heavenly kingdoms, and built you under much better and happier auspices than they, by whose zeal the first foundations of your walls were laid."[7]

However humanly different they may have been from each other and despite the tensions that existed in their relationship, Peter and Paul appear as the founders of a new City, the expression of a new and authentic way of being brothers which was made possible by the Gospel of Jesus Christ. For this reason, it can be said that the Church of Rome is celebrating her birthday today, since it was these two Apostles who laid her foundations. Furthermore, Rome in our day perceives with greater awareness both her mission and her greatness. St. John Chrysostom wrote: "Not so bright is the heaven, when the sun sends forth his rays, as is the City of Rome, sending out these two lights (Peter and Paul) into all parts of the world. . . . Therefore, I admire the City . . . for these pillars of the Church."[8] We will commemorate St. Peter specifically tomorrow, celebrating the Divine Sacrifice in the Vatican Basilica, built on the site of his martyrdom. This evening we turn our gaze to St. Paul, whose relics are preserved with deep veneration in this Basilica.

At the beginning of the Letter to the Romans, as we have just heard, St. Paul greeted the community of Rome, introducing himself as "a servant of Jesus Christ, called to be an apostle" (Rom 1:1). He uses the term "servant," in Greek, *doulos*, to indicate a

7. St. Leo the Great, *Sermon* 82, 7.

8. St. John Chrysostom, *Homily on St. Paul's Epistle to the Romans*, 32, 24.

relationship of total and unconditional belonging to the Lord Jesus; moreover, it is a translation of the Hebrew, *'ebed*, thus alluding to the great servants whom God chose and called for an important and specific mission. Paul knew he was "called to be an apostle," that is, that he had not presented himself as a candidate, nor was his a human appointment, but solely by a divine call and election. The Apostle to the Gentiles repeats several times in his letters that his whole life is a fruit of God's freely given and merciful grace (cf. 1 Cor 15:9–10; 2 Cor 4:1; Gal 1:15). He was chosen to proclaim "the Gospel of God" (Rom 1:1), to disseminate the announcement of divine Grace which in Christ reconciles man with God, himself, and others. From his letters, we know that Paul was far from being a good speaker; on the contrary, he shared with Moses and Jeremiah a lack of oratory skill. "His bodily presence is weak, and his speech of no account" (2 Cor 10:10), his adversaries said of him. The extraordinary apostolic results that he was able to achieve cannot, therefore, be attributed to brilliant rhetoric or refined apologetic and missionary strategies. The success of his apostolate depended above all on his personal involvement in proclaiming the Gospel with total dedication to Christ; a dedication that feared neither risk, difficulty, nor persecution. "Neither death, nor life," he wrote to the Romans, "nor angels, nor principalities, nor things present, nor things to come, nor powers, nor height, nor depth, nor anything else in all creation, will be able to separate us from the love of God in Christ Jesus our Lord" (Rom 8:38–39). From this we can draw a particularly important lesson for every Christian. The Church's action is credible and effective only to the extent to which those who belong to her are prepared to pay in person for their fidelity to Christ in every circumstance. When this readiness is lacking, the crucial argument of truth on which the Church herself depends is also absent.

Dear brothers and sisters, as in early times, today too Christ needs apostles ready to sacrifice themselves. He needs witnesses and martyrs like St. Paul. Paul, a former violent persecutor of Christians, when he fell to the ground dazzled by the divine light on the road to Damascus, did not hesitate to change sides to the Crucified One and followed him without second thoughts. He lived and worked for Christ, for him he suffered and died. How timely his example is today! And for this very reason I am pleased to announce officially that we shall be dedicating a special Jubilee Year to the Apostle Paul from 28 June 2008 to 29 June 2009, on the occasion of the bimillennium of his birth, which historians have placed between the years 7 and 10 AD. It will be possible to celebrate this "Pauline Year" in a privileged way in Rome, where the sarcophagus which, by the unanimous opinion of experts and an undisputed tradition, preserves the remains of the Apostle Paul, has been preserved beneath the Papal Altar of this Basilica for 20 centuries. It will thus be possible to have a series of liturgical, cultural, and ecumenical events taking place at the Papal Basilica and at the adjacent Benedictine Abbey, as well as various pastoral and social initiatives, all inspired by Pauline spirituality. In addition, special attention will be given to penitential pilgrimages that will be organized to the Apostle's tomb to find in it spiritual benefit. Study conventions and special publications on Pauline texts will also be promoted in order to make ever more widely known the immense wealth of the teaching they contain, a true patrimony of humanity redeemed by Christ. Furthermore, in every part of the world, similar initiatives will be implemented in the dioceses, shrines, and places of worship, by Religious and by the educational institutions and social assistance centers which are named after St. Paul or inspired by him and his teaching.

Lastly, there is one particular aspect to which special attention must be paid during the celebration of the various moments of the 2,000th Pauline anniversary: I am referring to the ecumenical dimension. The Apostle to the Gentiles, who was especially committed to taking the Good News to all peoples, left no stones unturned for unity and harmony among all Christians. May he deign to guide and protect us in this bimillennial celebration, helping us to progress in the humble and sincere search for the full unity of all the members of Christ's Mystical Body. Amen.

32. *You Are the Rock*

From the Homily of His Holiness Pope Benedict XVI
Solemnity of the Holy Apostles Peter and Paul
St. Peter's Basilica, Friday, 29 June 2007

Yesterday afternoon, I went to the Basilica of St. Paul Outside-the-Walls, where I celebrated First Vespers for today's Solemnity of the Holy Apostles Peter and Paul. Beside the sepulcher of the Apostle to the Gentiles I paid homage to his memory and announced the Pauline Year which, on the occasion of the bimillennium of his birth, will be celebrated from 28 June 2008 until 29 June 2009. This morning, we have gathered round the sepulcher of St. Peter in accordance with tradition. Present here to receive the pallium are the Metropolitan Archbishops appointed during the past year, to whom I extend my special greeting. Also present, sent by the

Ecumenical Patriarch of Constantinople, Bartholomew I, is an eminent Delegation; I welcome it with cordial gratitude, thinking back to last 30 November when I was in Istanbul-Constantinople for the Feast of St. Andrew. I greet the Greek Orthodox Metropolitan Emmanuel of France, Metropolitan Gennadios of Sassima and the Deacon Andreas. Welcome, dear brothers! The visits we pay each other every year are a sign that the search for full communion is always present and desired by the Ecumenical Patriarch and the Bishop of Rome.

Today's Feast offers me the opportunity to meditate once again on Peter's confession, the decisive moment in the journey of the disciples with Jesus. The Synoptic Gospels have it take place in the district of Caesarea Philippi (cf. Mt 16:13–20; Mk 8:27–30; Lk 9:18–22). John, for his part, keeps for us another important confession by Peter, after the miracle of the multiplication of the loaves and Jesus's Address in the Synagogue of Capernaum (cf. Jn 6:66–70). Matthew, in the text just proclaimed, recalls Jesus's attribution of the nickname Cephas, "Rock," to Simon. Jesus said that he desired to build his Church "on this rock" and with this in view, conferred on Peter the power of the keys (cf. Mt 16:17–19). It clearly emerges from these accounts that Peter's confession is inseparable from his pastoral duty to Christ's flock which was entrusted to him. According to all the Evangelists, Simon's confession takes place at a crucial moment in Jesus's life when, after preaching in Galilee, he resolutely set out for Jerusalem in order to bring his saving mission to completion with his death on the Cross and his Resurrection. The disciples were involved in this decision: Jesus invited them to make a choice that would bring them to distinguish themselves from the crowd so as to become the community of those who believed in him, his "family," the beginning of the Church.

In fact, there are two ways of "seeing" and "knowing" Jesus: one—that of the crowd—is more superficial; the other—that of the disciples—more penetrating and genuine. With his twofold question: "What do the people say?" and "who do you say that I am?" Jesus invited the disciples to become aware of this different perspective. The people thought that Jesus was a prophet. This was not wrong, but it does not suffice; it is inadequate. In fact, it was a matter of delving deep, of recognizing the uniqueness of the person of Jesus of Nazareth and his newness. This is how it still is today: many people draw near to Jesus, as it were, from the outside. Great scholars recognize his spiritual and moral stature and his influence on human history, comparing him to Buddha, Confucius, Socrates, and other wise and important historical figures. Yet they do not manage to recognize him in his uniqueness. What Jesus said to Philip at the Last Supper springs to mind: "Have I been with you so long, and yet you do not know me, Philip?" (Jn 14:9). Jesus is often also considered as one of the great founders of a religion from which everyone may take something in order to form his or her own conviction. Today too, "people" have different opinions about Jesus, just as they did then. And as he did then, Jesus also repeats his question to us, his disciples today: "And who do you say that I am?" Let us make Peter's answer our own. According to the Gospel of Mark he said: "You are the Christ" (8:29); in Luke, the affirmation is: "The Christ of God" (Lk 9:20); in Matthew resounds, "You are the Christ, the Son of the living God" (16:16); finally, in John: "You are the Holy One of God." These are all correct answers which are also right for us.

Let us reflect on Matthew's text in particular, quoted by today's liturgy. According to certain experts, the formula which appears there presupposes the post-Resurrection context and might even be connected with a personal appearance of the Risen Jesus to Peter, an appearance similar to that which Paul experienced on the road to Damascus. In fact, the responsibility conferred on Peter by the Lord was rooted in the personal relationship which the Jesus of history had with Simon the fisherman, from his first meeting with him when he said to him, "'So you are Simon. . . . You shall be called Cephas' (which means Peter)" (Jn 1:42). The Evangelist John emphasizes it, he who was also a fisherman and an associate, together with his brother James, of the two brothers, Simon and Andrew. The Jesus who called Saul after the Resurrection is the same Jesus who—still immersed in history—after his baptism in the Jordan approached the four brother fishermen who were then disciples of the Baptist (cf. Jn 1:35–42). He sought them out on the shores of Lake Galilee and called them to follow him, to become "fishers of men" (cf. Mk 1:16–20). He then entrusted Peter with a specific task, thereby recognizing in him a special gift of faith from the heavenly Father. Of course, all this was then illumined by the Paschal experience, but always remaining firmly anchored in the historical events prior to Easter. The parallel between Peter and Paul cannot diminish the importance of Simon's historical journey with his Master and Lord, who from the outset attributed to him the characteristic of the "rock" on which he intended to build his new community, the Church.

In the Synoptic Gospels, Peter's confession is always followed by Jesus's announcement of his imminent Passion. Peter reacted to this announcement because he was not yet able to understand.

Nonetheless, this was a fundamental element on which Jesus strongly insisted. Indeed, the titles attributed to him by Peter—you are "the Christ," "the Christ of God," "the Son of the living God"—can only be properly understood in light of the mystery of his death and Resurrection. And the opposite is also true: the event of the Cross reveals its full meaning only if "this man" who suffered and died on the Cross "truly was the Son of God," to use the words uttered by the centurion as he stood before the Crucified Christ (cf. Mk 15:39). These texts clearly say that the integrity of the Christian faith stems from the confession of Peter, illumined by the teaching of Jesus on his "way" toward glory, that is, on his absolutely unique way, being the Messiah and the Son of God. It was a narrow "way," a shocking "manner" for the disciples of every age, who are inevitably led to think according to men rather than according to God (cf. Mt 16:23).

Today too, as in Jesus's day, it does not suffice to possess the proper confession of faith: it is always necessary to learn anew from the Lord the actual way in which he is Savior and the path on which we must follow him. Indeed, we have to recognize that even for believers, the Cross is always hard to accept. Instinct impels one to avoid it and the tempter leads one to believe that it is wiser to be concerned with saving oneself rather than losing one's life through faithfulness to love, faithfulness to the Son of God made man. Who do you say I am? What was it that the people to whom Jesus was speaking found hard to accept? What continues to be hard for many people also in our time? It is difficult to accept that he claimed not only to be one of the prophets but the Son of God, and that he claimed God's own authority for himself. Listening to him preaching, seeing him heal the sick, evangelize the lowly and the poor, and reconcile sinners, little by little the disciples came to realize that he was the Messiah in the most exalted sense of the word, that is, not only a man sent by God, but God himself made man. Clearly, all this was far beyond them, it exceeded their capacity for understanding. They were able to express their faith with the titles of the Judaic tradition: "Christ," "Son of God," "Lord." However, to adhere truly to reality, these titles had in some way to be rediscovered in their most profound truth: Jesus himself revealed their true meaning with his life, ever surprising, even paradoxical considering the customary concepts. And the faith of the disciples itself had to progressively adapt. It presents itself as a pilgrimage which begins in the experience of the historical Jesus, finds its foundation in the Paschal Mystery, but must then advance further thanks to the working of the Holy Spirit. This was also the faith of the Church in the course of history, this is also our faith as Christians of today. Firmly resting on the "rock" of Peter, it is a pilgrimage toward the fullness of that truth which the Fisherman of Galilee professed with passionate conviction: "You are the Christ, the Son of the Living God" (Mt 16:16).

In Peter's profession of faith, dear brothers and sisters, we can feel that we are all one, despite the divisions that have wounded the Church's unity down the centuries and whose consequences are still being felt. Today, in the name of Sts. Peter and Paul, let us renew, together with our brothers who have come from Constantinople—whom I thank once again for their presence at our celebration—our commitment to accept to the very end the desire of Christ, who wants us to be fully united. With the concelebrating Archbishops, let us accept the gift and responsibility of communion between the See of Peter and the Metropolitan churches entrusted to their pastoral care. May the Holy Mother of God always guide us and accompany us with her intercession: may her unswerving faith, which sustained the faith of Peter and of the other Apostles, continue to sustain that of the Christian generations, our own faith: Queen of Apostles, pray for us! Amen.

33. *I Live by Faith*

From the Homily of His Holiness Pope Benedict XVI
Solemnity of the Holy Apostles Peter and Paul, Celebration of the First Vespers, Basilica of St. Paul Outside-the-Walls, Saturday, 28 June 2008

We have gathered near the tomb of St. Paul, who was born 2,000 years ago at Tarsus in Cilicia, in present-day Turkey. Who was St. Paul? In the temple of Jerusalem, faced with the frenzied crowd that wanted to kill him, he presented himself with these words: "I am a Jew, born at Tarsus in Cilicia, but brought up in this city [Jerusalem] at the feet of Gamaliel, educated according to the strict manner of the law of our fathers, being zealous for God. . ." (Acts 22:3). At the end of his journey he was to say of himself: "For this I was appointed a preacher and apostle . . . a teacher of the Gentiles in faith and truth" (1 Tm 2:7; cf. 2 Tm 1:11). A teacher of the Gentiles, an apostle and a herald of Jesus Christ, this is how he described himself, looking back over the path of his life. But this glance does not look only to the past. "A teacher of the Gentiles"—these words open to the future, to all peoples and all generations. For us Paul is not a figure of the past whom we remember with veneration. He is also our teacher, an Apostle and herald of Jesus Christ for us too.

Thus we are not gathered to reflect on past history, irrevocably behind us. Paul wants to speak to us—today. That is why I chose to establish this special "Pauline Year": in order to listen to him and learn today from him, as our teacher, "the faith and the truth" in which the reasons for unity among Christ's disciples are rooted. In this perspective, for this 2,000th anniversary of the Apostle's birth I wished to light a special "Pauline Flame" that will remain lit throughout the year in a special brazier placed in the Basilica's four-sided portico. To solemnize this event, I have also inaugurated the so called "Pauline Door," through which I entered the Basilica, accompanied by the Patriarch of Constantinople, by the Cardinal Archpriest and by other religious Authorities. It is a cause of deep joy to me that the opening of the Pauline Year has acquired a special ecumenical character through the presence of numerous delegates and representatives of other churches and ecclesial communities, whom I welcome with an open heart. I greet first of all His Holiness Patriarch Bartholomew I and the members of the delegation that accompany him, as well as the large group of lay people who have come to Rome from various parts of the world to experience with him and with all of us these moments of prayer and reflection. I greet the fraternal delegates of the churches which have special ties with the Apostle Paul—Jerusalem, Antioch, Cyprus, Greece—and which form the geographical environment of the Apostle's life before his arrival in Rome. I cordially greet the Brethren of the various churches and ecclesial communities of the East and the West, together with all of you who have desired to take part in this solemn initiation of the "Year" dedicated to the Apostle to the Gentiles.

Thus, we are gathered here to question ourselves on the great Apostle to the Gentiles. Let us not ask ourselves only: who was Paul? Let us ask ourselves above all: who is Paul? What does he say to me? At this moment, at the beginning of the "Pauline Year" that we are inaugurating, I would like to choose, from the rich testimony of the New Testament, three texts in which his inner features, his specific character, appear. In the Letter to the Galatians, St. Paul gives a very personal profession of faith in which he opens his heart to readers of all times and reveals what was the most intimate drive of his life. "I live by faith in the Son of God who loved me and gave himself for me" (Gal 2:20). All Paul's actions begin from this center. His faith is the experience of being loved by Jesus Christ in a very personal way. It is awareness of the fact that Christ did not face death for something anonymous but rather for love of him—of Paul—and that, as the Risen One, he still loves him; in other words, Christ gave himself for him. Paul's faith is being struck by the love of Jesus Christ, a love that overwhelms him to his depths and transforms him. His faith is not a theory, an opinion about God and the world. His faith is the impact of God's love in his heart. Thus, this same faith was love for Jesus Christ.

Paul is presented by many as a pugnacious man who was well able to wield the sword of his words. Indeed, there was no lack of disputes on his journey as an Apostle. He did not seek a superficial harmony. In the first of his letters, addressed to the Thessalonians, he himself says: "We had courage . . . to proclaim to you the Gospel of God in the face of great opposition. . . . In fact, we never spoke words of adulation, as you know" (1 Thes 2:2, 5). The truth was too great for him to be willing to sacrifice it with a view to external success. For him, the truth that he experienced in his encounter with the Risen One was well worth the fight, persecution, and suffering. But what most deeply motivated him was being loved by Jesus Christ and the desire to communicate this love to others. Paul was a man capable of loving, and all of his actions and suffering can only be explained on the basis of this core sentiment. It is only on this basis that we can understand the concepts on which his proclamation was founded. Let us take another key word of his: freedom. The experience of being loved to the very end by Christ had opened his eyes to the truth and to the way of human existence. It was an experience that embraced everything. Paul was free as a man loved by God, who, by virtue of God, was able to love together with him. This love then became the "law" of his life and in this very way, the freedom of his life. He speaks and acts motivated by the responsibility of love. Here freedom and responsibility are indivisibly united. Since Paul lives in the responsibility of love, he is free; since he is one who loves, he lives his life totally in the responsibility of this love and does not take freedom as a pretext to act arbitrarily and egoistically. In the same spirit, Augustine formulated the phrase that later became famous: *Dilige et quod vis fac*—"love and do what you please."[9] The one who loves Christ as Paul loved him can truly do as he pleases because his love is united to Christ's will and thus with God's will; because his will is anchored to the truth and because his will is no longer merely his own, arbitrary to the autonomous self, but is integrated into God's freedom from which he receives the path to take.

9. St. Augustine, *In Epistolam Joannis ad Parthos*, Tractatus 7, sect. 8.

In the search for the inner features of St. Paul, I would like, secondly, to recall the words that the Risen Christ addressed to him on the road to Damascus. First the Lord asked him: "Saul, Saul, why do you persecute me?" To the question: "Who are you, Lord?" Saul is given the answer: "I am Jesus, whom you are persecuting" (Acts 9:4f.). In persecuting the Church, Paul was persecuting Jesus himself. "You persecute me." Jesus identifies with the Church in a single subject. This exclamation of the Risen One, which transformed Saul's life, in summary already contains the entire doctrine on the Church as the Body of Christ. Christ did not withdraw himself into Heaven, leaving ranks of followers to carry out "his cause" on earth. The Church is not an association that desires to promote a specific cause. In her there is no question of a cause. In her it is a matter of the person of Jesus Christ, who, also as the Risen One, remained "flesh." He has "flesh and bones" (Lk 24:39), the Risen One says, in Luke's Gospel, to the disciples who thought he was a ghost. He has a Body. He is personally present in his Church; "Head and Body" form one being, Augustine would come to say. "Do you not know that your bodies are members of Christ?" Paul wrote to the Corinthians (1 Cor 6:15). And he added: just as, according to the book of Genesis, man and woman become one flesh, thus Christ and his followers become one spirit, that is, one in the new world of the Resurrection (cf. 1 Cor 6:16ff.). In all of this the Eucharistic mystery appears, in which Christ continually gives his Body and makes of us his Body: "The bread that we break, is it not a participation in the body of Christ? Because there is one bread, we who are many are one body, for we all partake of the one bread" (1 Cor 10:16f.). With these words, at this moment, not only Paul addresses us but also the Lord himself: how could you pierce my body? Before the Face of Christ, these words become at the same time an urgent plea: Bring us together from all our divisions. Grant that this may once again become reality today: there is one bread, therefore we, although we are many, are one body. For Paul, the words about the Church as the body of Christ are not just any comparison. They go far beyond a comparison. "Why do you persecute me?" Christ ceaselessly draws us into his body, building his Body from the Eucharistic center that for Paul is the center of Christian existence by virtue of which everyone, as also every individual, can experience in a totally personal way: he has loved me and given himself for me.

I would like to conclude with words St. Paul spoke near the end of his life. It is an exhortation to Timothy from prison while he was facing death, "with the strength that comes from God bear your share of hardship which the Gospel entails," the Apostle said to his disciple (2 Tm 1:8). These words, which mark the end of the Apostle's life as a testament, refer back to the beginning of his mission. When, after his encounter with the Risen One, while Paul lay blind in his dwelling at Damascus, Ananias was charged to visit the feared persecutor and to lay his hands upon him so that he might regain his sight. Ananias's objection that this Saul was a dangerous persecutor of Christians, was met with the response: this man must carry my name before the Gentiles and kings: "I will show him how much he must suffer for the sake of my name" (Acts 9:15f.). The task of proclamation and the call to suffer for Christ's sake are inseparable. The call to become the teacher of the Gentiles is, at the same time and intrinsically, a call to suffering in communion with Christ who redeemed us through his Passion. In a world in which falsehood is powerful, the truth is paid for with suffering. The one who desires to avoid suffering, to keep it at bay, keeps life itself and its greatness at bay; he cannot be a servant of truth and thus a servant of faith. There is no love without suffering—without the suffering of renouncing oneself, of the transformation and purification of self for true freedom. Where there is nothing worth suffering for, even life loses its value. The Eucharist—the center of our Christian being—is founded on Jesus's sacrifice for us; it is born from the suffering of love which culminated in the Cross. We live by this love that gives itself. It gives us the courage and strength to suffer with Christ and for him in this world, knowing that in this very way our life becomes great and mature and true. In the light of all St. Paul's letters, we see how the prophecy made to Ananias at the time of Paul's call came true in the process of teaching the Gentiles: "I will show him how much he must suffer for the sake of my name." His suffering made him credible as a teacher of truth who did not seek his own advantage, his own glory, or his personal satisfaction but applied himself for the sake of the One who loved us and has given himself for us all. Let us now thank the Lord for having called Paul, making him the light to the Gentiles and the teacher of us all, and let us pray to him: "Give us even today witnesses of the Resurrection, struck by the impact of your love and able to bring the light of the Gospel in our time." St. Paul, pray for us! Amen.

34. *Bishop of Souls*

From the Homily of His Holiness Pope Benedict XVI
Solemnity of the Holy Apostles Peter and Paul
St. Peter's Basilica, Monday, 29 June 2009

I address my cordial greeting to you all with the words of the Apostle by whose tomb we stand: "May grace and peace be multiplied to you" (1 Pt 1:2). I greet in particular the Members of the Delegation of the Ecumenical Patriarchate of Constantinople and the numerous Metropolitans who will receive the pallium today. In the opening prayer of this solemn day, we ask the Lord that the Church may always follow the teaching of the Apostles from whom she first received the announcement of the faith. The request we address to God at the same time calls us into question: are we following the teaching of the great founder Apostles? Do we really know them? In the Pauline Year that ended yesterday, we endeavored to listen anew to him, the "teacher of the Gentiles," hence to learn anew the alphabet of faith. We endeavored to recognize Christ with Paul and through Paul, and thus to find the way to an upright Christian life. In the Canon of the New Testament, in addition to the letters of St. Paul, there are also two other letters under the name of St. Peter. The first ends with an explicit greeting from Rome, which, however, appears under the apocalyptic pseudonym of Babylon: "She who is at Babylon, who is likewise chosen, sends you greetings" (1 Pt 5:13). By calling the Church of Rome "likewise chosen," he sets her within the great community of all the local churches in the community of all those whom God has gathered, so that in the "Babylon" of this world's time they might build up his people and introduce God into history.

St. Peter's First Letter is a greeting addressed from Rome to the Christendom of all epochs. It invites us to listen to "the teaching of the Apostles," which shows us the way to life. This letter is a very rich text that wells up from the heart and touches the heart. Its center is (and how could it be otherwise?) the figure of Christ who is illustrated as the One who suffers and loves, as Crucified and Risen: "When he was reviled, he did not revile in return; when he suffered, he did not threaten. . . . By his wounds you have been healed" (1 Pt 2:23f.). Then starting from the center that is Christ, the letter is also an introduction to the fundamental Christian Sacraments of Baptism and the Eucharist and a discourse addressed to priests in which Peter describes himself as a fellow priest with them. He speaks to Pastors of all generations as one who was personally made responsible by the Lord for tending his sheep and has thus received a specific priestly mandate.

So what does St. Peter tell us precisely in the Year for Priests about the priest's task? First of all he understands the priestly ministry as being based totally on Christ. He calls Christ the "Shepherd and Guardian of . . . souls" (1 Pt 2:25). Where the Italian [and the English] translation speak of "Guardian," the Greek text uses the word *episcopos* (bishop). A little further on, Christ is described as the chief Shepherd: *archipoimen* (1 Pt 5:4). It is surprising that Peter should call Christ himself a Bishop, Bishop of souls. What did he mean by this? The Greek term *episcopos* contains the verb "to see"; for this reason it is translated as "guardian," in other words "supervisor." Yet external supervision, as might befit a prison guard, is certainly not what is meant here. Rather it means watching over from above, seeing from the lofty position of God. Seeing from God's perspective is seeing with love that wants to serve the other, wants to help him to become truly himself. Christ is the "Bishop of souls," Peter tells us. This means: he sees us from the perspective of God. In seeing from God's viewpoint, one has an overall vision, one sees the dangers as well as the hopes and possibilities. From God's perspective one sees the essential, one sees the inner man. If Christ is the Bishop of souls, the objective is to prevent the human soul from becoming impoverished and to ensure that the human being does not lose his essence, the capacity for truth and love; to ensure that he becomes acquainted with God; that he does not get lost in blind alleys; that he does not end in loneliness but remains altogether open. Jesus, the "Bishop of souls," is the prototype of every episcopal and presbyteral ministry. To be a Bishop, to be a priest, means in this perspective to assume the position of Christ. It means thinking, seeing, and acting from his exalted vantage point. It means starting from Christ in order to be available to human beings so that they find life. Thus the word "Bishop" is very close to the term "Shepherd"; indeed, the two concepts become interchangeable. It is the shepherd's task to feed and tend his flock and take it to the right pastures. Grazing the flock means taking care that the sheep find the right nourishment, that their hunger is satisfied and their thirst quenched. The metaphor apart, this means: the word of God is the nourishment that the human being needs. Making God's word ever present and new and thereby giving nourishment to people is the task of the righteous Pastor. And he must also know how to resist the enemies, the wolves. He must go first, point out the way, preserve the unity of the flock.

Peter, in his discourse to priests, highlights another very important thing. It is not enough to speak. Pastors must make themselves "examples to the flock" (1 Pt. 5:3). When it is lived, the word of God is brought from the past into the present. It is marvelous to see how in saints the word of God becomes a word addressed to our time. In such figures as Francis and then again, as Padre Pio and many others, Christ truly became a contemporary of their generation, he emerged from the past to enter the present. This is what being a Pastor means: a model for the flock, living the word now, in the great community of holy Church. Very briefly, I would like to call your attention further to two other affirmations in the First Letter of St. Peter which concern us in a special way in our time. There is first of all the sentence, today discovered anew, on the basis of which medieval theologians understood their task, the task of the theologian: "in your hearts reverence Christ as Lord. Always be prepared to make a defense to anyone who calls you to account for the hope that is in you" (1 Pt 3:15). Christian faith is hope. It paves the way to the future. And it is a hope that possesses reasonableness, a hope whose reason we can and must explain. Faith comes from the eternal Reason that entered our world and showed us the true God. Faith surpasses the capacity of our reason, just as love sees more than mere intelligence. But faith speaks to reason and in the dialectic confrontation can be a match for reason. It does not contradict it but keeps up with it and goes beyond it to introduce us into the greater Reason of God. As Pastors of our time, it is our task to be the first to understand the reason of faith. It is our task not to let it remain merely a tradition but to recognize it as a response to our questions. Faith demands our rational participation, which is deepened and purified in a sharing of love. It is one of our duties as Pastors to penetrate faith with thought, to be able to show the reason for our hope within the debates of our time. Yet although it is so necessary, thought alone does not suffice. Just as speaking alone does not suffice. In his baptismal and Eucharistic catechesis in chapter 2 of his letter, Peter alludes to the Psalm used by the ancient Church in the context of communion, that is, to the verse which says: "O taste and see that the Lord is good!" (Ps 34[33]:8; 1 Pt 2:3). Tasting alone leads to seeing. Let us think of the disciples of Emmaus: it was only in convivial communion with Jesus, only in the breaking of the bread, that their eyes were opened. Only in truly experienced communion with the Lord were they able to see. This applies to us all; over and above thinking and speaking, we need the experience of faith, the vital relationship with Jesus Christ.

Faith must not remain theory: it must be life. If we encounter the Lord in the Sacrament, if we speak to him in prayer, if in the decisions of daily life we adhere to Christ, then "we see" more and more how good he is; then we experience how good it is to be with him. Moreover, the capacity to communicate faith to others in a credible way stems from this certainty lived. The Curé d'Ars was not a great thinker; but he "tasted" the Lord. He lived with him even in the details of daily life, as well as in the great demands of his pastoral ministry. In this way he became "one who sees." He had tasted, so he knew that the Lord is good. Let us pray the Lord that he may grant us this ability to taste, and that we may thus become credible witnesses of the hope that is in us.

Lastly, I would like to point out another small but important statement of St. Peter. Right at the beginning of his letter he tells us that the goal of our faith is the salvation of souls (cf. 1:9). In the world of language and thought of the Christianity of today this is a strange, and for some, perhaps even shocking assertion. The word "soul" had fallen into discredit. It is said that this could lead to a division of man into spiritual and physical, body and soul, whereas in reality he would be an indivisible unit. In addition, "the salvation of souls" as a goal of faith seems to indicate an individualistic Christianity, a loss of responsibility for the world overall, in its corporeity and in its materiality. Yet none of this is found in St. Peter's letter. Zeal for the witness in favor of hope and responsibility for others characterizes the entire text. To understand what he says on the salvation of souls as a destination of faith, we must start from another angle. It remains true that the lack of care for souls, the impoverishment of the inner man, not only destroys the individual but threatens the destiny of humanity overall. Without the healing of souls, without the healing of man from within, there can be no salvation for humanity. To our surprise, St. Peter describes the true ailment of souls as ignorance, that is, not knowing God. Those who are not acquainted with God, or at least do not seek him sincerely, are left outside true life (cf. 1 Pt 1:14). Yet another word from the letter could be useful to understand better the formula "salvation of souls." "Purify your souls by obedience to the truth" (1:22). It is obedience to the truth that purifies the soul and it is coexistence with falsehood that pollutes it. Obedience to the truth begins with the small truths of daily life that can often be demanding and painful. This obedience then extends to obedience without reservations before the Truth itself that is Christ. This obedience not only purifies us but above all also frees us for service to Christ and thus for the salvation of the world, which nevertheless always begins with the obedient purification of one's own soul through the truth. We may point out the way towards the truth only if by obedience and patience we let ourselves be purified by the truth.

And now I address you, dear brothers in the Episcopate, who will shortly receive the pallium from my hands. It was woven from the wool of lambs which the Pope blesses on the Feast of St. Agnes. In this way it also recalls the lambs and sheep of Christ, which the Risen Lord entrusted to Peter with the task of tending them (cf. Jn 21:15–18). The pallium recalls the flock of Jesus Christ which you, dear brothers, must tend in communion with Peter. It reminds us of Christ himself, who, as the Good Shepherd, took the lost sheep, humanity, on his shoulders to bring it home. It reminds us that he, the supreme Pastor, wanted to make himself the Lamb, to take upon himself from within the destiny of us all; to carry us and to heal us from within. Let us pray the Lord that he will grant us to be just Pastors following in his footsteps, "not under compulsion but willingly, as God would have you do it . . . eagerly . . . examples to the flock" (1 Pt 5:2f). Amen.

35. *The Mission of the Church*

From the Homily of His Holiness Pope Benedict XVI, Solemnity of the Holy Apostles Peter and Paul, Celebration of the First Vespers
Basilica of St. Paul Outside-the-Walls, Monday, 28 June 2010

With the celebration of First Vespers, we enter the Solemnity of Sts. Peter and Paul. We have the grace to do so gathered in prayer by the tomb of the Apostle to the Gentiles, in the Papal Basilica named after him. For this reason, I wish to focus my brief reflection on the perspective of the Church's missionary vocation.

The third Antiphon of the Psalter, which we have prayed in addition to the biblical reading, is oriented in this direction. The first two Antiphons are dedicated to St. Peter and the third to St. Paul, and it says: "You are the chosen instrument of God, St. Paul, Apostle, the preacher of truth in all the world." And in the brief reading, taken from the opening address of the Letter to the Romans, Paul introduces himself as "apostle by God's call, set apart for the service of the Gospel" (cf. Rom 1:1). The figure of Paul, his person and his ministry, the whole of his life and his hard work for the Kingdom of God is entirely dedicated to the service of the Gospel. In these texts one notices a sense of movement, where the protagonist is not man, but God, the breath of the Holy Spirit, that impels the Apostle on the highways of the world to bring the Good News to everyone: the promises of the Prophets are fulfilled in Jesus, the Christ, the Son of God, who died for our sins and was raised for our justification. Saul is no longer, instead there is Paul, indeed there is Christ who lives in him (cf. Gal 2:20) and wants to reach out to all people. Although the Feast of the Holy Patrons of Rome thus calls to mind the twofold aspiration to unity and to universality that is characteristic of this Church, the context in which we are gathered this evening calls us to give priority to the latter, letting ourselves, so to speak, be "drawn" by St. Paul and his extraordinary vocation.

When, during the Second Vatican Council, the Servant of God Giovanni Battista Montini was elected Successor of Peter, he chose to take the name of the Apostle to the Gentiles. Paul VI included in his program for the implementation of the Council the convocation, in 1974, of the Assembly of the Synod of Bishops on the theme of evangelization in the modern world. About a year later, he published the Apostolic Exhortation *Evangelii Nuntiandi*, which begins with these words: "There is no doubt that the effort to proclaim the Gospel to the people of today, who are buoyed up by hope but at the same time often oppressed by fear and distress, is a service rendered to the Christian community and also to the whole of humanity."[10] The timeliness of these words is striking. Paul VI's special missionary sensitivity can be perceived in them and, through his voice, the Council's deep yearning for the evangelization of the contemporary world. This yearning culminates in the Decree *Ad Gentes* but runs through all the documents of the Second Vatican Council and, even earlier, inspired the thoughts and work of the Council Fathers, convoked to represent, in an unprecedented, tangible way, the dissemination throughout the world achieved by the Church.

Words are useless to explain how Venerable John Paul II, in his long Pontificate, developed this missionary outreach that it should always be remembered corresponded with the very nature of the Church which, with St. Paul, can and must always repeat: "If I preach the Gospel, that gives me no ground for boasting. For necessity is laid upon me. Woe to me if I do not preach the Gospel!" (1 Cor 9:16). Pope John Paul II represented the Church's missionary nature "in the flesh" with his Apostolic Journeys and with the insistence of his Magisterium on the urgent need for a "new evangelization": "new" not in its content but in its inner thrust, open to the grace of the Holy Spirit which constitutes the force of the new law of the Gospel that always renews the Church; "new" in ways that correspond with the power of the Holy Spirit and which are suited to the times and situations; "new" because

10. Pope Paul VI, Apostolic Exhortation *Evangelii Nuntiandi* (December 8, 1975), no. 1.

of being necessary even in countries that have already received the proclamation of the Gospel. It is evident to all that my Predecessor gave the Church's mission an extraordinary impetus, not only, I repeat, because of the distances he covered but above all because of the genuine missionary spirit that motivated him and that he left as a legacy at the dawn of the third millennium.

In receiving this legacy, I was able to state, at the beginning of my Petrine ministry, that the Church is young and open to the future. And I repeat this today, close to the tomb of St. Paul. The Church is an immense force for renewal in the world. This is not, of course, because of her own strength but because of the power of the Gospel in which the Holy Spirit of God breathes, God Creator and Redeemer of the world. The challenges of the present time, the historical and social and, especially, the spiritual challenges, are certainly beyond the human capacity. It sometimes seems to us Pastors of the Church that we are reliving the experience of the Apostles when thousands of needy people followed Jesus and he asked them: what can we do for all these people? They were then aware of their powerlessness. Yet Jesus himself had shown them that with faith in God nothing is impossible and that a few loaves and fish, blessed and shared, could satisfy the hunger of all. However, there was not and there is not hunger solely for material food: there is a deeper hunger that only God can satisfy. Human beings of the third millennium want an authentic, full life; they need truth, profound freedom, love freely given. Even in the deserts of the secularized world, man's soul thirsts for God, for the living God. It was for this reason that John Paul II wrote: "The mission of Christ the Redeemer, which is entrusted to the Church, is still very far from completion," and he added: "an overall view of the human race shows that this mission is still only beginning and that we must commit ourselves wholeheartedly to its service."[11] There are regions of the world that are still awaiting a first evangelization; others that have received it, but need a deeper intervention; yet others in which the Gospel put down roots a long time ago, giving rise to a true Christian tradition but in which, in recent centuries with complex dynamics, the secularization process has produced a serious crisis of the meaning of the Christian faith and of belonging to the Church.

From this perspective, I have decided to create a new body, in the form of a "Pontifical Council," whose principal task will be to promote a renewed evangelization in the countries where the first proclamation of the faith has already resonated and where churches with an ancient foundation exist but are experiencing the progressive secularization of society and a sort of "eclipse of the sense of God," which constitute a challenge to finding adequate means to re-propose the perennial truth of the Gospel of Christ.

Dear brothers and sisters, the challenge of the new evangelization calls into question the universal Church and asks us to continue with commitment our search for full Christian unity. An eloquent sign of hope in this regard is the custom of reciprocal visits between the Church of Rome and that of Constantinople for the Feast day of their respective Holy Patrons. Today, therefore, we welcome with renewed joy and gratitude the Delegation sent by Patriarch Bartholomaios I, to whom we address our most cordial greeting. May the intercession of Sts. Peter and Paul obtain for the entire Church ardent faith and apostolic courage, to proclaim to the

11. Pope John Paul II, Encyclical Letter *Redemptoris Missio* (December 7, 1990), no. 1.

world the truth we all need, the truth that is God, the beginning and end of the universe and of history, the merciful and faithful Father, hope of eternal life. Amen.

36. *The Church's Freedom*

From the Homily of His Holiness Pope Benedict XVI
Solemnity of the Holy Apostles Peter and Paul
St. Peter's Basilica, Tuesday, 29 June 2010

In their great wealth, the biblical texts of this Eucharistic Liturgy on the Solemnity of the Holy Apostles Peter and Paul highlight a theme that could be summed up in these words: God is close to his faithful servants and delivers them from all evil and delivers the Church from negative powers. It is the theme of the Church's freedom, that presents an historical aspect and another that is more profoundly spiritual.

This theme runs through the whole of today's Liturgy of the Word. The first and second readings speak respectively of St. Peter and St. Paul, stressing God's liberating action in their regard. The text of the Acts of the Apostles especially describes with an abundance of detail the intervention of the Angel of the Lord who sets Peter free from his chains and leads him out of the prison of Jerusalem in which Herod the King had had him locked up and placed under strict surveillance (cf. Acts 12:1–11). Paul, on the other hand, in writing to Timothy when he felt he was approaching the end of his earthly life, makes a concise summary of it from which emerges the fact that the Lord has always been close to him, has delivered him from many dangers and will free him again, introducing him into his eternal Kingdom (cf. 2 Tim 4:6–8, 17–18). The theme is reinforced by the Responsorial Psalm (Ps 34[33]) and is also given a special development in the Gospel passage of Peter's profession where Christ promises that the powers of death shall not prevail over the Church (cf. Mt 16:18).

A close look at this theme reveals a certain progression. In the first reading a specific episode is recounted that shows the Lord's intervention to release Peter from prison. In the second reading Paul, on the basis of his extraordinary apostolic experience, says that he is convinced that the Lord, who has already rescued him "from the lion's mouth," will rescue him "from every evil," opening the gates of Heaven to him; on the other hand, in the Gospel nothing further is said of the individual apostles but it speaks rather of the Church as a whole and of her indemnity from the forces of evil, meant in the full and profound sense. Thus we see that Jesus's promise "the powers of death shall not prevail against" the Church does indeed include the historical experiences of persecution that Peter and Paul and other Gospel witnesses suffered, but goes beyond them, with the intention of assuring protection, especially from threats of a spiritual kind; in accordance with what Paul himself writes in his Letter to the Ephesians: "for we are not contending against flesh and blood, but against the principalities, against the powers, against the world rulers of this present world of darkness, against the evil spirits in the heavens" (Eph 6:12).

Indeed, if we think of the two millenniums of the Church's history, we may note as the Lord Jesus had foretold (cf. Mt 10:16–33) that trials for Christians have never been lacking and in certain periods and places have assumed the character of true and proper persecution. Yet, despite the suffering they cause, they do not constitute the gravest danger for the Church. Indeed, she is subjected to the greatest danger by what pollutes the faith and Christian life of her members and communities, corroding the integrity of the Mystical Body, weakening her capacity for prophecy and witness, and marring the beauty of her face. The Pauline letters already testified to this reality. The First Letter to the Corinthians, for example, responds precisely to certain problems of division, inconsistence, and infidelity to the Gospel that seriously threaten the Church. However, the Second Letter to Timothy, a passage to which we listened, also speaks of the perils of the "last days," identifying them with negative attitudes that belong to the world and can contaminate the Christian community: selfishness, vanity, pride, the attachment to money, etc. (cf. 2 Tim 3:1–5). The Apostle's conclusion is reassuring: men who do evil, he writes, "will not get very far, for their folly will be plain to all" (2 Tim 3:9). Therefore a guarantee exists of the freedom that God assures the Church, freedom both from material ties that seek to prevent or to coerce her mission and from spiritual and moral evils that can tarnish her authenticity and credibility.

The subject of the Church's freedom, which Christ guaranteed to Peter, is also specifically relevant to the rite of the conferral of the pallium, which today we renew for 38 Metropolitan Archbishops, to whom I address my most cordial greeting, which I extend with affection to all who have wished to accompany them on this pilgrimage. Communion with Peter and with his Successors is in fact a guarantee of freedom for the Church's Pastors and for the communities entrusted to them. It has been highlighted at both levels in the previous reflections. At the historical level, union with the Apostolic See guarantees the particular churches and the bishops' conferences freedom from local, national, or supranational powers that in some cases can hinder the Church's mission. In addition, and more essentially, the Petrine ministry is a guarantee of freedom in the sense of full adherence to the truth, to the authentic tradition, so that the People of God may be preserved from errors concerning faith and morals. Therefore the fact that new Metropolitans come to Rome every year to receive the pallium from the Pope's hands as a gesture of communion should be understood in its true sense, and the subject of the Church's freedom gives us a particularly important key to its interpretation. This appears obvious in the case of Churches marked by persecution or subjected to political interference or other harsh trials. However, this is equally important in the case of communities that suffer the influence of misleading doctrines or ideological trends and practices contrary to the Gospel. In this sense, therefore, the pallium becomes a pledge of freedom, comparable to the "yoke" of Jesus which he invites each person to take upon his or her shoulders (cf. Mt 11:29–30). Just as Christ's commandment, although exacting, is "easy and light" and, instead of weighing on those who carry it uplifts them, so the bond with the Apostolic See, although demanding, sustains the Pastor and the portion of the Church entrusted to his care, making them freer and stronger.

I would like to draw one last instruction from the word of God, and in particular from Christ's promise that the powers of death will not prevail over his Church. These words can also have an ecumenical meaning since, as I mentioned just now, one of the typical effects of the action of the Evil One is, precisely, the internal division of the ecclesial community. Ruptures are in fact symptoms of the power of sin that continues to act in members of the Church even after the redemption. However, Christ's word is clear: "*Non praevalebunt*"—"They shall not prevail" (Mt 16:18). The unity of the Church is rooted in her union with Christ, and the cause of full Christian unity that must ever be sought and renewed, from generation to generation, is also sustained by his prayer and his promise. In the struggle against the spirit of evil, God gave us, in Jesus, the "Advocate" defender, and after his Pasch, "another Counsellor" (cf. Jn 14:16), the Holy Spirit, who stays with us always and leads the Church towards the fullness of the truth (cf. Jn 14:16; 16:13) that is also the fullness of love and of unity. With these sentiments of trusting hope, I am glad to greet the Delegation of the Patriarchate of Constantinople which, in accordance with the beautiful custom of reciprocal visits, is taking part in the celebrations for the Holy Patrons of Rome. Let us thank God together for the progress in ecumenical relations between Catholic and Orthodox, and let us renew our commitment to respond generously to God's grace that is leading us to full communion.

Dear friends, I cordially greet each one of you, Your Eminences, my brothers in the Episcopate, the Ambassadors and the Civil Authorities and, in particular, the Mayor of Rome, the priests, religious, and lay faithful. Thank you for coming. May the Holy Apostles Peter and Paul obtain that you increase in love for the Holy Church, Mystical Body of Christ and Messenger of Unity and Peace for all mankind. May they also obtain that you joyfully offer for her holiness and her missionary efforts your endeavors and suffering, borne out of faithfulness to the Gospel. May the Virgin Mary, Queen of Apostles and Mother of the Church, always watch over you and in particular over the ministry of the Metropolitan

Archbishops. With her heavenly help may you always live and act in that freedom which Christ won for us. Amen.

37. He Calls Me Friend

From the Homily of His Holiness Pope Benedict XVI
Solemnity of the Holy Apostles Peter and Paul
St. Peter's Basilica, Wednesday, 29 June 2011

"Non iam dicam servos, sed amicos"— "I no longer call you servants, but friends" (cf. Jn 15:15). Sixty years on from the day of my priestly ordination, I hear once again deep within me these words of Jesus that were addressed to us new priests at the end of the ordination ceremony by the Archbishop, Cardinal Faulhaber, in his slightly frail yet firm voice. According to the liturgical practice of that time, these words conferred on the newly-ordained priests the authority to forgive sins. "No longer servants, but friends": at that moment I knew deep down that these words were no mere formality, nor were they simply a quotation from Scripture. I knew that, at that moment, the Lord himself was speaking to me in a very personal way. In baptism and confirmation he had already drawn us close to him, he had already received us into God's family. But what was taking place now was something greater still. He calls me his friend. He welcomes me into the circle of those he had spoken to in the Upper Room, into the circle of those whom he knows in a very special way, and who thereby come to know him in a very special way. He grants me the almost frightening faculty to do what only he, the Son of God, can legitimately say and do: I forgive you your sins. He wants me—with his authority—to be

able to speak, in his name ("I" forgive), words that are not merely words, but an action, changing something at the deepest level of being. I know that behind these words lies his suffering for us and on account of us. I know that forgiveness comes at a price: in his Passion he went deep down into the sordid darkness of our sins. He went down into the night of our guilt, for only thus can it be transformed. And by giving me authority to forgive sins, he lets me look down into the abyss of man, into the immensity of his suffering for us men, and this enables me to sense the immensity of his love. He confides in me: "No longer servants, but friends." He entrusts to me the words of consecration in the Eucharist. He trusts me to proclaim his word, to explain it aright and to bring it to the people of today. He entrusts himself to me. "You are no longer servants, but friends": these words bring great inner joy, but at the same time, they are so awe-inspiring that one can feel daunted as the decades go by amid so many experiences of one's own frailty and his inexhaustible goodness.

"No longer servants, but friends": this saying contains within itself the entire program of a priestly life. What is friendship? *Idem velle, idem nolle*—wanting the same things, rejecting the same things: this was how it was expressed in antiquity. Friendship is a communion of thinking and willing. The Lord says the same thing to us most insistently: "I know my own and my own know me" (Jn 10:14). The Shepherd calls his own by name (cf. Jn 10:3). He knows me by name. I am not just some nameless being in the infinity of the universe. He knows me personally. Do I know him? The friendship that he bestows upon me can only mean that I too try to know him better; that in the Scriptures, in the Sacraments, in prayer, in the communion of saints, in the people who come to me, sent by him,

I try to come to know the Lord himself more and more. Friendship is not just about knowing someone, it is above all a communion of the will. It means that my will grows into ever greater conformity with his will. For his will is not something external and foreign to me, something to which I more or less willingly submit or else refuse to submit. No, in friendship, my will grows together with his will, and his will becomes mine: this is how I become truly myself. Over and above communion of thinking and willing, the Lord mentions a third, new element: he gives his life for us (cf. Jn 15:13; 10:15). Lord, help me to come to know you more and more. Help me to be ever more at one with your will. Help me to live my life not for myself, but in union with you to live it for others. Help me to become ever more your friend.

Jesus's words on friendship should be seen in the context of the discourse on the vine. The Lord associates the image of the vine with a commission to the disciples: "I appointed you that you should go out and bear fruit, and that your fruit should abide" (Jn 15:16). The first commission to the disciples, to his friends, is that of setting out—appointed to go out, stepping outside oneself and towards others. Here we hear an echo of the words of the risen Lord to his disciples at the end of Matthew's Gospel: "Go therefore and make disciples of all nations . . ." (cf. Mt 28:19f.). The Lord challenges us to move beyond the boundaries of our own world and to bring the Gospel to the world of others, so that it pervades everything and hence the world is opened up for God's kingdom. We are reminded that even God stepped outside himself, he set his glory aside in order to seek us, in order to bring us his light and his love. We want to follow the God who sets out in this way, we want to move beyond the inertia of self-centeredness, so that he himself can enter our world.

After the reference to setting out, Jesus continues: bear fruit, fruit that abides. What fruit does he expect from us? What is this fruit that abides? Now, the fruit of the vine is the grape, and it is from the grape that wine is made. Let us reflect for a moment on this image. For good grapes to ripen, sun is needed, but so too is rain, day and night. For noble wine to mature, the grapes need to be pressed, patience is needed while the juice ferments, watchful care is needed to assist the processes of maturation. Noble wine is marked not only by sweetness, but by rich and subtle flavors, the manifold aroma that develops during the processes of maturation and fermentation. Is this not already an image of human life, and especially of our lives as priests? We need both sun and rain, festivity and adversity, times of purification and testing, as well as times of joyful journeying with the Gospel. In hindsight, we can thank God for both: for the challenges and the joys, for the dark times and the glad times. In both, we can recognize the constant presence of his love, which unfailingly supports and sustains us.

Yet now we must ask: what sort of fruit does the Lord expect from us? Wine is an image of love: this is the true fruit that abides, the fruit that God wants from us. But let us not forget that in the Old Testament the wine expected from noble grapes is above all an image of justice, which arises from a life lived in accordance with God's law. And this is not to be dismissed as an Old Testament view that has been surpassed—no, it still remains true. The true content of the Law, its summa, is love for God and for one's neighbor. But this twofold love is not simply saccharine. It bears within itself the precious cargo of patience, humility, and growth in the conforming of our will to God's will, to the will of Jesus Christ, our friend. Only in this way, as the whole of our being takes on the qualities of truth and righteousness, is love also true, only thus is it ripe fruit. Its inner demand—faithfulness to Christ and to his Church—seeks a fulfilment that always includes suffering. This is the way that true joy grows. At a deep level, the essence of love, the essence of genuine fruit, coincides with the idea of setting out, going towards: it means self-abandonment, self-giving, it bears within itself the sign of the Cross. Gregory the Great once said in this regard: if you are striving for God, take care not to go to him by yourselves alone—a saying that we priests need to keep before us every day.[12]

Dear friends, perhaps I have dwelt for too long on my inner recollections of sixty years of priestly ministry. Now it is time to turn our attention to the particular task that is to be performed today. On the feast of Saints Peter and Paul, my most cordial greeting goes first of all to the Ecumenical Patriarch Bartholomaios I and to the Delegation he has sent, to whom I express sincere thanks for their most welcome visit on the happy occasion of this feast of the holy Apostles who are Rome's patrons. I also greet the Cardinals, my brother bishops, the ambassadors and civil authorities as well as the priests, the confrères of my first Mass, religious, and lay faithful. I thank all of you for your presence and your prayers.

The metropolitan archbishops appointed since the feast of Saints Peter and Paul last year are now going to receive the pallium. What does this mean? It may remind us in the first instance of Christ's easy yoke that is laid upon us (cf. Mt 11:29f.). Christ's

12. Cf. St. Gregory the Great, *Homiliae in Evangelia*, PL 76, 1097f.

yoke is identical with his friendship. It is a yoke of friendship and therefore "a sweet yoke," but as such it is also a demanding yoke, one that forms us. It is the yoke of his will, which is a will of truth and love. For us, then, it is first and foremost the yoke of leading others to friendship with Christ and being available to others, caring for them as shepherds. This brings us to a further meaning of the pallium: it is woven from the wool of lambs blessed on the feast of Saint Agnes. Thus, it reminds us of the Shepherd who himself became a lamb, out of love for us. It reminds us of Christ, who set out through the mountains and the deserts, in which his lamb, humanity, had strayed. It reminds us of him who took the lamb—humanity—me—upon his shoulders, in order to carry me home. It thus reminds us that we too, as shepherds in his service, are to carry others with us, taking them as it were upon our shoulders and bringing them to Christ. It reminds us that we are called to be shepherds of his flock, which always remains his and does not become ours. Finally, the pallium also means quite concretely the communion of the shepherds of the Church with Peter and with his successors—it means that we must be shepherds for unity and in unity, and that it is only in the unity represented by Peter that we truly lead people to Christ.

Sixty years of priestly ministry—dear friends, perhaps I have spoken for too long about this. But I felt prompted at this moment to look back upon the things that have left their mark on the last six decades. I felt prompted to address to you, to all priests and bishops and to the faithful of the Church, a word of hope and encouragement; a word that has matured in long experience of how good the Lord is. Above all, though, it is a time of thanksgiving: thanks to the Lord for the friendship that he has bestowed upon me and that he wishes to bestow upon us all. Thanks to the people who have formed and accompanied me. And all this includes the prayer that the Lord will one day welcome us in his goodness and invite us to contemplate his joy.

38. *Open to God's Action*

From the Homily of His Holiness Pope Benedict XVI
Solemnity of the Holy Apostles Peter and Paul
St. Peter's Basilica, Friday, 29 June 2012

We are gathered around the altar for our solemn celebration of Saints Peter and Paul, the principal patrons of the Church of Rome. Present with us today are the metropolitan archbishops appointed during the past year, who have just received the pallium, and to them I extend a particular and affectionate greeting. Also present is an eminent delegation from the Ecumenical Patriarchate of Constantinople, sent by His Holiness Bartholomaios I, and I welcome them with fraternal and heartfelt gratitude. In an ecumenical spirit, I am also pleased to greet and to thank the Choir of Westminster Abbey, who are providing the music for this liturgy alongside the Cappella Sistina. I also greet the ambassadors and civil authorities present. I am grateful to all of you for your presence and your prayers.

In front of Saint Peter's Basilica, as is well known, there are two imposing statues of Saint Peter and Saint Paul, easily recognizable by their respective attributes: the keys in the hand of Peter and the sword held by Paul. Likewise, at the main entrance to the Basilica of Saint Paul Outside-the-Walls, there are depictions of scenes from the life and the martyrdom of these two pillars of the Church. Christian tradition has always considered Saint Peter and Saint Paul to be inseparable: indeed, together, they represent the whole Gospel of Christ. In Rome, their bond as brothers in the faith came to acquire a particular significance. Indeed, the Christian community of this City considered them a kind of counterbalance to the mythical Romulus and Remus, the two brothers held to be the founders of Rome. A further parallel comes to mind, still on the theme of brothers: whereas the first biblical pair of brothers demonstrate the effects of sin, as Cain kills Abel, yet Peter and Paul, much as they differ from one another in human terms and notwithstanding the conflicts that arose in their relationship, illustrate a new way of being brothers, lived according to the Gospel, an authentic way made possible by the grace of Christ's Gospel working within them. Only by following Jesus does one arrive at this new brotherhood: this is the first and fundamental message that today's solemnity presents to each one of us, the importance of which is mirrored in the pursuit of full communion, so earnestly desired by the ecumenical Patriarch and the Bishop of Rome, as indeed by all Christians.

In the passage from Saint Matthew's Gospel that we have just heard, Peter makes his own confession of faith in Jesus, acknowledging him as Messiah and Son of God. He does so in the name of the other Apostles too. In reply, the Lord reveals to him the mission that he intends to assign to him, that of being the "rock," the visible foundation on which the entire spiritual edifice of the Church is built (cf. Mt 16:16–19). But in what sense is Peter the rock? How is he to exercise this prerogative, which naturally he did not receive for his own sake? The account given by the evangelist Matthew tells us first of all that the acknowledgment of Jesus's identity made by Simon in the name of the Twelve did not come "through flesh and blood," that is, through his human capacities, but through a particular revelation from God the Father. By contrast, immediately afterwards, as Jesus foretells his passion, death, and resurrection, Simon Peter reacts on the basis of "flesh and blood": he "began to rebuke him, saying, this shall never happen to you" (Mt 16:22). And Jesus in turn replied: "Get behind me, Satan! You are a hindrance to me . . ." (Mt 16:23). The disciple who, through God's gift, was able to become a solid rock, here shows himself for what he is in his human weakness: a stone along the path, a stone on which men can stumble—in Greek, *skandalon*. Here we see the tension that exists between the gift that comes from the Lord and human capacities; and in this scene between Jesus and Simon Peter we see anticipated in some sense the drama of the history of the papacy itself, characterized by the joint presence of these two elements: on the one hand, because of the light and the strength that come from on high, the papacy constitutes the foundation of the Church during its pilgrimage through history; on the other hand, across the centuries, human weakness is also evident, which can only be transformed through openness to God's action.

And in today's Gospel there emerges powerfully the clear promise made by Jesus: "the gates of the underworld," that is, the forces of evil, will not prevail, *non praevalebunt*. One is reminded of the account of the call of the prophet Jeremiah, to whom the Lord said, when entrusting him with his mission: "Behold, I make you this day a fortified city, an iron pillar, and bronze walls, against the whole land, against the kings of Judah, its princes, its priests, and the people of the land. They will fight against you; but they shall not prevail against you"—*non praevalebunt*—"for I am with you, says the Lord, to deliver you!" (Jer 1:18–19). In truth, the promise that Jesus makes to Peter is even greater than those made to the prophets of old: they, indeed, were threatened only by human enemies, whereas Peter will have to be defended from the "gates of the underworld," from the destructive power of evil. Jeremiah receives a promise that affects him as a person and his prophetic ministry; Peter receives assurances concerning the future of the Church, the new community founded by Jesus Christ, which extends to all of history, far beyond the personal existence of Peter himself.

Let us move on now to the symbol of the keys, which we heard about in the Gospel. It echoes the oracle of the prophet Isaiah concerning the steward Eliakim, of whom it was said: "And I will place on his shoulder the key of the house of David; he shall open, and none shall shut; and he shall shut, and none shall open" (Is 22:22). The key represents authority over the house of David. And in the Gospel there is another saying of Jesus addressed to the scribes and the Pharisees, whom the Lord reproaches for shutting off the kingdom of heaven from people (cf. Mt 23:13). This saying also helps us to understand the promise made to Peter: to him, inasmuch as he is the faithful steward of Christ's message, it belongs to open the gate of the Kingdom of Heaven, and to judge whether to admit or to refuse (cf. Rev 3:7). Hence the two images—that of the keys and that of binding and loosing—express similar meanings which reinforce one another. The expression "binding and loosing" forms part of rabbinical language and refers on the one hand to doctrinal decisions, and on the other hand to disciplinary power, that is, the faculty to impose and to lift excommunication. The parallelism "on earth . . . in the heavens" guarantees that Peter's decisions in the exercise of this ecclesial function are valid in the eyes of God.

In chapter 18 of Matthew's Gospel, dedicated to the life of the ecclesial community, we find another saying of Jesus addressed to the disciples: "Truly I say to you, whatever you bind on earth shall be bound in heaven, and whatever you loose on earth shall be loosed in heaven" (Mt 18:18). Saint John, in his account of the appearance of the risen Christ in the midst of the Apostles on Easter evening, recounts these words of the Lord: "Receive the Holy Spirit. If you forgive the sins of any, they are forgiven: if you retain the sins of any, they are retained" (Jn 20:22–23). In the light of these parallels, it appears clearly that the authority of loosing and binding consists in the power to remit sins. And this grace, which defuses the powers of chaos and evil, is at the heart of the Church's mystery and ministry. The Church is not a community of the perfect, but a community of sinners, obliged to recognize their need for God's love, their need to be purified through the Cross of Jesus Christ. Jesus's sayings concerning the authority of Peter and the Apostles make it clear that God's power is love, the love that shines forth from Calvary. Hence we can also understand why, in the Gospel account, Peter's confession of faith is immediately followed by the first prediction of the Passion: through his death, Jesus conquered the powers of the underworld, with his blood he poured out over the world an immense flood of mercy, which cleanses the whole of humanity in its healing waters.

Dear brothers and sisters, as I mentioned at the beginning, the iconographic tradition represents Saint Paul with a sword, and we know that this was the instrument with which he was killed. Yet as we read the writings of the Apostle of the Gentiles, we discover that the image of the sword refers to his entire mission of evangelization. For example, when he felt death approaching, he wrote to Timothy: "I have fought the good fight" (2 Tim 4:7). This was certainly not the battle of a military commander but that of a herald of the Word of God, faithful to Christ and to his Church, to which he gave himself completely. And that is why the Lord gave him the crown of glory and placed him, together with Peter, as a pillar in the spiritual edifice of the Church.

Dear Metropolitan Archbishops, the pallium that I have conferred on you will always remind you that you have been constituted in and for the great mystery of communion that is the Church, the spiritual edifice built upon Christ as the cornerstone, while in its earthly and historical dimension, it is built on the rock of Peter. Inspired by this conviction, we know that together we are all cooperators of the truth, which as we know is one and "symphonic," and requires from each of us and from our communities a constant commitment to conversion to the one Lord in the grace of the one Spirit. May the Holy Mother of God guide and accompany us always along the path of faith and charity. Queen of Apostles, pray for us! Amen.

SAINTS

ST. AUGUSTINE

39. *The Experience of Conversion*

From the Homily of His Holiness Pope Benedict XVI
Pastoral Visit to Vigevano and Pavia
Orti Borromaici, Pavia, Sunday, 22 April 2007

Yesterday afternoon, I met the diocesan Community of Vigevano and the heart of my Pastoral Visit was the Eucharistic concelebration in Piazza Ducale; today, I have the joy of visiting your Diocese and a culminating moment of our encounter is also here at Holy Mass. I greet with affection my brothers who are concelebrating with me: Cardinal Dionigi Tettamanzi, Archbishop of Milan; Bishop Giovanni Giudici, Pastor of your Diocese; Bishop emeritus Giovanni Volta, the retired Pastor; and the other Prelates of Lombardy. I am grateful to the government representatives and local administrations for their presence. I address my cordial greeting to the priests, deacons, Religious, leaders of lay associations, the young people, the sick, and all the faithful, and I extend my thoughts to the entire population of this ancient and noble city, and of the Diocese.

During the Easter Season, the Church presents to us, Sunday after Sunday, some passages from the preaching with which, after Easter, the Apostles, particularly Peter, invited Israel to have faith in Jesus Christ, the Risen One, thereby founding the Church.

In today's reading, the Apostles stand before the Sanhedrin—before that institution which, having sentenced Jesus to death, could not tolerate that this same Jesus was now beginning to be active again through the Apostles' preaching. They could not tolerate that his saving power was once more making itself felt and that his Name was attracting people who believed in him as the promised Redeemer. They accused the Apostles. Their accusation is: "You want to make us responsible for that man's blood" (Acts 5:28). Peter, however, reacted to this accusation with a brief catechesis on the essence of Christian faith: "No, we do not want to make you responsible for his blood. The effect of the death and Resurrection of Jesus is quite different. God has exalted him as 'Head and Savior' of all, and of you, too, his People of Israel." And where will this "Head" lead us? What does this "Savior" bring? He leads us, St. Peter tells us, to conversion—creates for us the leeway and opportunity to mend our ways and repent, begin again (cf. Acts 5:31). And he offers us forgiveness for our sins: he introduces us into the proper relationship with God, hence, into the proper relationship of each individual with himself or herself and with others.

Peter's brief catechesis did not only apply to the Sanhedrin. It speaks to us all, for Jesus, the Risen One, is also alive today. And for all generations, for all men and women, he is the "Head" who shows us the way and the "Savior" who straightens out our lives. The two terms: "conversion" and "forgiveness of sins," which correspond to the titles of Christ "Head," *archegòs* in Greek, and "Savior," are the key words of Peter's catechesis, words intended to move our hearts too, here and now. And what do they mean? The path we must take—the path that Jesus points out to us—is called "conversion." But what is it? What must we do? In every life, conversion has its own form, because every human being is something new and no one is merely a copy of another. But in the course of history, the Lord has sent us models of conversion to whom we can look to find guidance. We could thus look at Peter himself, to whom the Lord said at the Last Supper: "[W]hen you have turned again, strengthen your brethren" (Lk 22:32).

We could look at Paul as a great convert. The city of Pavia speaks of one of the greatest converts in the history of the Church: St. Aurelius Augustine. He died on 28 August in 430 in the port town of Hippo, in Africa, at that time surrounded and besieged by the Vandals. After the considerable turmoil of a turbulent history, the King of the Longobards acquired Augustine's remains for the city of Pavia so that today they belong to this City in a special way, and, in it and from it, have something special to say to all of us, to humanity, but to all of us here in particular. In his book *Confessions*, Augustine touchingly described the development of his conversion which achieved its goal with Baptism, administered to him by Bishop Ambrose in the Cathedral of Milan. Readers of his *Confessions* can share in the journey that Augustine had to make in a long inner struggle to receive at last, at the baptismal font on the night before Easter 387, the Sacrament which marked the great turning point in his life. A careful examination of the course of St. Augustine's life enables one to perceive that his conversion was not an event of a single moment but, precisely, a journey. And one can see that this journey did not end at the baptismal font. Just as prior to his baptism Augustine's life was a journey of conversion, after it too, although differently, his life continued to be a journey of conversion—until his last illness, when he had the penitential Psalms hung on the walls so that he might have them always before his eyes, and when he excluded himself from receiving the Eucharist in order to go back once again over the path of his repentance and receive salvation from Christ's hands as a gift of God's mercy. Thus, we can rightly speak of Augustine's "conversions," which actually consisted of one important conversion in his quest for the Face of Christ and then in the journeying on with him.

I would like to mention briefly three important landmarks in this process of conversion, three "conversions." The first fundamental conversion was the inner march towards Christianity, towards the "yes" of the faith and of Baptism. What was the essential aspect of this journey? On the one hand, Augustine was a son of his time, deeply conditioned by the customs and passions prevalent then as well as by all the questions and problems that beset any young man. He lived like all the others, yet with a difference: he continued to be a person constantly seeking. He was never satisfied with life as it presented itself and as so many people lived it. The question of the truth tormented him ceaselessly. He longed to discover truth. He wanted to succeed in knowing what man is; where we ourselves come from, where we are going and how we can find true life. He desired to find the life that was right and not merely to live blindly, without meaning or purpose. Passion for truth is the true key phrase of his life. Passion for the truth truly guided him. There is a further peculiarity: anything that did not bear Christ's Name did not suffice for him. Love for this Name, he tells us, he had tasted from his mother's milk.[13] And he always believed—sometimes rather vaguely, at other times, more clearly—that God exists and takes care of us.[14] But to truly know this God and to become really familiar with this Jesus Christ and reach the point of saying "yes" to him with all its consequences—this was the great interior struggle

13. Cf. St. Augustine, *Confessions*, 3, 4, 8.

14. Cf. St. Augustine, *Confessions*, 6, 5, 8.

of his youthful years. St. Augustine tells us that through Platonic philosophy he learned and recognized that "in the beginning was the Word"—the Logos, creative reason. But philosophy, which showed him that the beginning of all things was creative reason, did not show him any path on which to reach it; this Logos remained remote and intangible. Only through faith in the Church did he later find the second essential truth: the Word, the Logos, was made flesh. Thus, he touches us and we touch him. The humility of God's Incarnation—this is the important step—must be equalled by the humility of our faith, which lays down its self-important pride and bows upon entering the community of Christ's Body; which lives with the Church and through her alone can enter into concrete and bodily communion with the living God. I do not have to say how deeply all this concerns us: to remain seekers; to refuse to be satisfied with what everyone else says and does; to keep our gaze fixed on the eternal God and on Jesus Christ; to learn the humility of faith in the corporeal Church of Jesus Christ, of the Logos Incarnate.

Augustine described his second conversion at the end of the 10th book of his *Confessions* with the words: "Terrified by my sins and the pile of my misery, I had racked my heart and had meditated, taking flight to live in solitude. But you forbade me and comforted me, saying: 'That is why Christ died for all, so that those who live should not live for themselves, but for him who died for them' (2 Cor 5:15)."[15] What had happened? After his baptism, Augustine had decided to return to Africa and with some of his friends had founded a small monastery there. His life was then to be totally dedicated

15. St. Augustine, *Confessions*, 10, 43, 70.

to conversation with God and reflection on and contemplation of the beauty and truth of his Word. Thus, he spent three happy years in which he believed he had achieved the goal of his life; in that period, a series of valuable philosophical and theological works came into being. In 391, four years after his baptism, he went to the port town of Hippo to meet a friend whom he desired to win over for his monastery. But he was recognized at the Sunday liturgy in the cathedral in which he took part. It was not by chance that the Bishop of the city, a man of Greek origin who was not fluent in Latin and found preaching rather a struggle, said in his homily that he was hoping to find a priest to whom he could entrust the task of preaching. People instantly grabbed hold of Augustine and forced him forward to be ordained a priest to serve the city. Immediately after his forced ordination, Augustine wrote to Bishop Valerius: "I was constrained . . . to accept second place at the helm, when as yet I knew not how to handle an oar. . . . And from this derived the tears which some of my brethren perceived me shedding in the city at the time of my ordination."[16] Augustine's beautiful dream of a contemplative life had vanished. As a result, his life had fundamentally changed. He could now no longer dedicate himself solely to meditation in solitude. He had to live with Christ for everyone. He had to express his sublime knowledge and thoughts in the thoughts and language of the simple people in his city. The great philosophical work of an entire lifetime, of which he had dreamed, was to remain unwritten. Instead, however, we have been given something far more precious: the Gospel translated into the language of everyday life and of his sufferings. These were now part

16. St. Augustine, *Letter 21*, 1ff.

of his daily life, which he described as the following: "reprimanding the undisciplined, comforting the fainthearted, supporting the weak, refuting opponents . . . encouraging the negligent, soothing the quarrelsome, helping the needy, liberating the oppressed, expressing approval to the good, tolerating the wicked and loving all."[17] "Continuously preaching, arguing, rebuking, building God's house, having to manage for everyone—who would not shrink from such a heavy burden?"[18] This was the second conversion which this man, struggling and suffering, was constantly obliged to make: to be available to everyone, time and again, and not for his own perfection; time and again, to lay down his life with Christ so that others might find him, true Life.

Further, there was a third, decisive phase in the journey of conversion of St. Augustine. After his Ordination to the priesthood, he had requested a vacation period to study the Sacred Scriptures in greater detail. His first series of homilies, after this pause for reflection, were on the Sermon on the Mount; he explained the way to an upright life, "the perfect life," pointed out by Christ in a new way. He presented it as a pilgrimage to the holy mountain of the Word of God. In these homilies it is possible to further perceive all the enthusiasm of faith newly discovered and lived; his firm conviction that the baptized, in living totally in accordance with Christ's message, can precisely be "perfect" in accordance with the Sermon on the Mount. Approximately 20 years later, Augustine wrote a book called the *Retractations*, in which he critically reviewed all the works he had thus far written, adding corrections wherever he had in the meantime learned something new. With

17. St. Augustine, *Sermon* 340, 3.

18. St. Augustine, *Sermon* 339, 4.

regard to the ideal of perfection in his homilies on the Sermon on the Mount, he noted: "In the meantime, I have understood that one alone is truly perfect and that the words of the Sermon on the Mount are totally fulfilled in one alone: Jesus Christ himself. The whole Church, on the other hand—all of us, including the Apostles—must pray every day: forgive us our trespasses as we forgive those who trespass against us."[19] Augustine had learned a further degree of humility—not only the humility of integrating his great thought into the humble faith of the Church, not only the humility of translating his great knowledge into the simplicity of announcement, but also the humility of recognizing that he himself and the entire pilgrim Church needed and continually need the merciful goodness of a God who forgives every day. And we, he added, liken ourselves to Christ, the only Perfect One, to the greatest possible extent when we become, like him, people of mercy.

Let us now thank God for the great light that shines out from St. Augustine's wisdom and humility and pray the Lord to give to us all, day after day, the conversion we need, and thus lead us toward true life. Amen.

19. Cf. St. Augustine, *Retractations*, I 19, 1–3.

SAINTS

ST. JOHN HENRY NEWMAN

40. *Heart Speaks Unto Heart*

From the Homily of His Holiness Pope Benedict XVI
Mass with the Beatification of Venerable John Henry Newman
Cofton Park of Rednal, Birmingham, Sunday, 19 September 2010

This day that has brought us together here in Birmingham is a most auspicious one. In the first place, it is the Lord's Day, Sunday, the day when our Lord Jesus Christ rose from the dead and changed the course of human history forever, offering new life and hope to all who live in darkness and in the shadow of death. That is why Christians all over the world come together on this day to give praise and thanks to God for the great marvels he has worked for us. This particular Sunday also marks a significant moment in the life of the British nation, as it is the day chosen to commemorate the seventieth anniversary of the Battle of Britain. For me as one who lived and suffered through the dark days of the Nazi regime in Germany, it is deeply moving to be here with you on this occasion, and to recall how many of your fellow citizens sacrificed their lives, courageously resisting the forces of that evil ideology. My thoughts go in particular to nearby Coventry, which suffered such heavy bombardment and massive loss of life in November 1940. Seventy years later, we recall with shame and horror the dreadful toll of death and destruction that war brings in its wake, and we renew our resolve to work for peace and reconciliation wherever the threat of conflict looms. Yet there is another, more joyful reason why this is an auspicious day for Great Britain, for the Midlands, for Birmingham. It is the day that sees Cardinal John Henry Newman formally raised to the altars and declared Blessed.

I thank Archbishop Bernard Longley for his gracious welcome at the start of Mass this morning. I pay tribute to all who have worked so hard over many years to promote the cause of Cardinal Newman, including the Fathers of the Birmingham Oratory and the members of the Spiritual Family Das Werk. And I greet everyone here from Great Britain, Ireland, and further afield; I thank you for your presence at this celebration, in which we give glory and praise to God for the heroic virtue of a saintly Englishman.

England has a long tradition of martyr saints, whose courageous witness has sustained and inspired the Catholic community here for centuries. Yet it is right and fitting that we should recognize today the holiness of a confessor, a son of this nation who, while not called to shed his blood for the Lord, nevertheless bore eloquent witness to him in the course of a long life devoted to the priestly ministry, and especially to preaching, teaching, and writing. He is worthy to take his place in a long line of saints and scholars from these islands, Saint Bede, Saint Hilda, Saint Aelred, Blessed Duns Scotus, to name but a few. In Blessed John Henry, that tradition of gentle scholarship, deep human wisdom and profound love for the Lord has borne rich fruit, as a sign of the abiding presence of the Holy Spirit deep within the heart of God's people, bringing forth abundant gifts of holiness.

Cardinal Newman's motto, *Cor ad cor loquitur*, or "Heart speaks unto heart," gives us an insight into his understanding of the Christian life as a call to holiness, experienced as the profound desire of the human heart to enter into intimate communion with the Heart of God. He reminds us that faithfulness to prayer gradually transforms us into the divine likeness. As he wrote in one of his many fine sermons, "a habit of prayer, the practice of turning to God and the unseen world in every season, in every place, in every emergency—prayer, I say, has what may be called a natural effect in spiritualizing and elevating the soul. A man is no longer what he was before; gradually . . . he has imbibed a new set of ideas, and become imbued with fresh principles."[20] Today's Gospel tells us that no one can be the servant of two masters (cf. Lk 16:13), and Blessed John Henry's teaching on prayer explains how the faithful Christian is definitively taken into the service of the one true Master, who alone has a claim to our unconditional devotion (cf. Mt 23:10). Newman helps us to understand what this means for our daily lives: he tells us that our divine Master has assigned a specific task to each one of us, a "definite service," committed uniquely to every single person: "I have my mission," he wrote, "I am a link in a chain, a bond of connection between persons. He has not created me for naught. I shall do good, I shall do his work; I shall be an angel of peace, a preacher of truth in my own place . . . if I do but keep his commandments and serve him in my calling."[21]

The definite service to which Blessed John Henry was called involved applying his keen intellect and his prolific pen to many of the most pressing "subjects of the day." His insights into the relationship between faith and reason, into the vital place of revealed

20. St. John Henry Newman, *Parochial and Plain Sermons* (Longmans, Green, and Company, 1909), iv, 230–31.

21. St. John Henry Newman, *Meditations and Devotions* (Longmans, Green, and Company, 1907), 301–2.

religion in civilized society, and into the need for a broadly-based and wide-ranging approach to education were not only of profound importance for Victorian England, but continue today to inspire and enlighten many all over the world. I would like to pay particular tribute to his vision for education, which has done so much to shape the ethos that is the driving force behind Catholic schools and colleges today. Firmly opposed to any reductive or utilitarian approach, he sought to achieve an educational environment in which intellectual training, moral discipline, and religious commitment would come together. The project to found a Catholic University in Ireland provided him with an opportunity to develop his ideas on the subject, and the collection of discourses that he published as *The Idea of a University* holds up an ideal from which all those engaged in academic formation can continue to learn. And indeed, what better goal could teachers of religion set themselves than Blessed John Henry's famous appeal for an intelligent, well-instructed laity: "I want a laity, not arrogant, not rash in speech, not disputatious, but men who know their religion, who enter into it, who know just where they stand, who know what they hold and what they do not, who know their creed so well that they can give an account of it, who know so much of history that they can defend it."[22] On this day when the author of those words is raised to the altars, I pray that, through his intercession and example, all who are engaged in the task of teaching and catechesis will be inspired to greater effort by the vision he so clearly sets before us.

While it is John Henry Newman's intellectual legacy that has understandably received most attention in the vast literature

22. St. John Henry Newman, *The Present Position of Catholics in England* (London: Longmans, Green, and Co., 1899), ix, 390.

devoted to his life and work, I prefer on this occasion to conclude with a brief reflection on his life as a priest, a Pastor of souls. The warmth and humanity underlying his appreciation of the pastoral ministry is beautifully expressed in another of his famous sermons: "Had Angels been your priests, my brethren, they could not have condoled with you, sympathized with you, have had compassion on you, felt tenderly for you, and made allowances for you, as we can; they could not have been your patterns and guides, and have led you on from your old selves into a new life, as they can who come from the midst of you."[23] He lived out that profoundly human vision of priestly ministry in his devoted care for the people of Birmingham during the years that he spent at the Oratory he founded, visiting the sick and the poor, comforting the bereaved, caring for those in prison. No wonder that on his death so many thousands of people lined the local streets as his body was taken to its place of burial not half a mile from here. One hundred and twenty years later, great crowds have assembled once again to rejoice in the Church's solemn recognition of the outstanding holiness of this much-loved father of souls. What better way to express the joy of this moment than by turning to our heavenly Father in heartfelt thanksgiving, praying in the words that Blessed John Henry Newman placed on the lips of the choirs of angels in heaven:

> Praise to the Holiest in the height
> And in the depth be praise;
> In all his words most wonderful,
> Most sure in all his ways![24]

23. St. John Henry Newman, "Men, not Angels: The Priests of the Gospel," in *Discourses to Mixed Congregations*, 3.

24. St. John Henry Newman, *The Dream of Gerontius*, ca. 1865.

SAINTS

ST. JOHN PAUL II

41. *Totus Tuus*

From the Homily of His Holiness Pope Benedict XVI
Mass on the First Anniversary of the Passing of Pope John Paul II
St. Peter's Basilica, Monday, 3 April 2006

In these days, on the first anniversary of his death, the memory of the Servant of God John Paul II is particularly vivid throughout the Church and the world. With the Marian Vigil yesterday evening, we relived the precise moment of his devout passing one year ago, whereas today we are here in this same St. Peter's Square to offer the Eucharistic Sacrifice in suffrage for his chosen soul. Together with the Cardinals, Bishops, priests and Religious, I greet with affection the numerous pilgrims who have arrived from very many places, especially from Poland, to bear witness to their esteem, affection, and deep gratitude. Let us pray for this beloved Pontiff, allowing ourselves to be illuminated by the Word of God we have just heard.

In the first reading from the Book of Wisdom, we were reminded of the eternal destiny that awaits the righteous: a destiny of superabundant happiness, an incomparable reward for the sufferings and trials they faced during their lives. "God tested them and found them worthy of himself; like gold in the furnace he tried them, and like a sacrificial burnt offering he accepted them" (Wis 3:5–6). The term "burnt offering" refers to the sacrifice in which the victim was entirely burned, consumed by the flames; consequently, it was a sign of total offering to God. This biblical expression reminds us of the mission of John Paul II, who made his life a gift to God and to the Church and, especially in the celebration of the Eucharist, lived out the sacrificial dimension of his priesthood. Among the invocations dear to him was one that comes from the "*Litanie di Gesù Cristo Sacerdote e Vittima*" that he chose to place at the end of his book *Gift and Mystery*, published on the occasion of the 50th anniversary of his ordination to the Priesthood.[25] "*Iesu, Pontifex qui tradidisti temetipsum Deo oblationem et hostiam*"—"Jesus, High Priest who gave yourself to God as offering and victim, have mercy on us." How frequently did he repeat this invocation! It expresses clearly the profoundly priestly character of his whole life. He never made a mystery of his desire to become increasingly one with Christ the Priest through the Eucharistic Sacrifice, a source of tireless apostolic dedication.

It was faith, of course, that was at the root of this total offering of himself. In the second reading that we have just heard, St. Peter too uses the image of the gold tested by fire and applies it to faith (cf. 1 Pt 1:7). In fact, in life's difficulties it is especially the quality of the faith of each one of us that is tried and tested: its firmness, its purity, its consistency with life. Well, the late Pontiff, whom God had endowed with multiple human and spiritual gifts, in passing through the crucible of apostolic labors and sickness, appeared more and more as a "rock" of faith. To those who had the opportunity to be close to him, that firm and forthright faith was almost tangible. If it impressed the circle of his collaborators, it did not fail during his long Pontificate to spread its beneficial influence throughout the Church in a crescendo that reached its highest point in the last

25. Cf. St. John Paul II, *Gift and Mystery: On the Fiftieth Anniversary of My Priestly Ordination* (Image, 1999), 113–16.

months and days of his life. It was a convinced, strong, and authentic faith—free of the fears and compromises that have infected the hearts of so many people—thanks partly to his many Apostolic Pilgrimages in every part of the world, and especially thanks to that last "journey," his agony and his death.

The Gospel passage that has just been proclaimed helps us to understand another aspect of his human and religious personality. We might say that among the Apostles, he, the Successor of Peter, supremely imitated John the "beloved disciple," who stood under the Cross with Mary at the moment of the Redeemer's abandonment and death. The evangelist relates that Jesus, when he saw them standing near, entrusted the one to the other: "Woman, behold, your son! . . . Behold, your mother!" (Jn 19:26–27). The dying Lord's words were particularly dear to John Paul II. Like the Apostle and Evangelist, he too wanted to take Mary into his home: *"et ex illa hora accepit eam discipulus in sua"* (Jn 19:27). The expression *"accepit eam in sua"* is singularly compact. It indicates John's decision to make Mary share in his own life, so as to experience that whoever opens his heart to Mary is actually accepted by her and becomes her own. The motto that stands out in the coat of arms of the Pontificate of Pope John Paul II, *Totus Tuus,* sums up this spiritual and mystical experience well, in a life completely oriented to Christ through Mary: *"ad Iesum per Mariam."*

Dear brothers and sisters, this evening our thoughts turn with emotion to the moment of the beloved Pontiff's death, but at the same time our hearts are, as it were, impelled to look ahead. We feel reverberating within them his repeated invitations to advance without fear on the path of fidelity to the Gospel, to be heralds and witnesses of Christ in the third millennium. We cannot but recall his ceaseless exhortations to cooperate generously in creating a more just humanity with greater solidarity, to be peacemakers and builders of hope. May our gaze always remain fixed on Christ, "the same yesterday and today and forever" (Heb 13:8), who firmly guides his Church. We believed in his love and it is the encounter with him that "gives life a new horizon and a decisive direction."[26] May the power of Jesus's Spirit be for you all a source of peace and joy, dear brothers and sisters, as it was for Pope John Paul II. And may the Virgin Mary, Mother of the Church, help us to be in all circumstances, as he was, tireless apostles of his divine Son and prophets of his merciful love. Amen!

42. *Servant of God*

From the Homily of His Holiness Pope Benedict XVI
Mass on the Second Anniversary of the Passing of Pope John Paul II
St. Peter's Basilica, Monday, 2 April 2007

Two years ago, at a slightly later hour than now, beloved Pope John Paul II departed this world for the house of the Father. With this celebration, let us first of all renew our thanksgiving to God for having given him to us for well near 27 years as a father and reliable guide in the faith, a zealous Pastor and courageous prophet of hope, a tireless witness and passionate servant of God's love. As we offer the Eucharistic Sacrifice in suffrage for his chosen soul, we remember the unforgettable devotion with which he celebrated the Holy Mysteries and adored the Sacrament of the Altar, the center of his life and of his untiring mission. I want to express my gratitude to

26. cf. *Deus Caritas Est*, n. 1.

all of you who have wished to take part in this Holy Mass. I address a particular greeting to Cardinal Stanislaw Dziwisz, Archbishop of Kraków, imagining the sentiments that must be filling his heart at this moment. I greet the other Cardinals, Bishops, priests, and men and women Religious present; the pilgrims who have come here expressly from Poland; all the young people whom Pope John Paul II loved with a unique passion and the many members of the faithful from every part of Italy and the world who have gathered here in St. Peter's Square for today's appointment.

The second anniversary of the departure of this beloved Pontiff is taking place in a particularly favorable context for recollection and prayer. Yesterday, in fact, with Palm Sunday, we entered Holy Week, and the Liturgy makes us relive the last days of the Lord Jesus's earthly life. Today, it takes us to Bethany, where, precisely "six days before the Passover," as the Evangelist John notes, Lazarus, Martha, and Mary asked the Teacher to supper. The Gospel account impresses an intense paschal atmosphere on our meditation: the supper at Bethany is a prelude to Jesus's death in the sign of his anointing by Mary, a homage she pays to the Teacher which he accepts as foretelling his burial (cf. Jn 12:7). However, it is also an announcement of the Resurrection through the very presence of Lazarus restored to life, an eloquent witness of Christ's power over death. Not only pregnant with Paschal significance, the narrative of the supper at Bethany is imbued with an anguishing resonance filled with love and devotion, a mist of joy and pain: festive joy at the visit of Jesus and his disciples, at the resurrection of Lazarus and at the Passover now at hand; deep sorrow because this Passover might be the last, as they were led to fear by the scheming of the

Jews who desired the death of Jesus and by the threats to Lazarus whose death they were also planning.

One action in this Gospel passage is drawn to our attention, and which even now speaks to our hearts in a special way: Mary of Bethany, at a certain point, "took a pound of costly ointment of pure nard and anointed the feet of Jesus and wiped his feet with her hair" (Jn 12:3). This is one of those details of Jesus's life which St. John cherished among his dearest memories and which is charged with inexhaustible feeling. He speaks of love for Christ, a superabundant, wondrous love like that "costly" ointment poured over his feet. This event symptomatically shocked Judas Iscariot: the logic of love clashed with the logic of profit. For us, gathered in prayer in memory of my Venerable Predecessor, the gesture of the anointing of Mary of Bethany is full of spiritual echoes and suggestions. It evokes John Paul II's shining witness of love for Christ, unreserved and unstinting. The "house," that is, the entire Church, "was filled with the fragrance" of his love (cf. Jn 12:3). Of course, we who were close to him benefited from it and are grateful to God, but even those who knew him from afar were able to enjoy it because Pope Wojtyła's love for Christ was so strong, so intense, we could say, that it overflowed in every region of the world. Was not the esteem, respect, and affection expressed to him at his death by believers and nonbelievers alike an eloquent witness of this?

St. Augustine wrote, commenting on this passage of John's Gospel: "'The house was filled with the fragrance.' The world is filled with the fame of a good character: for a good character is like a sweet scent. . . . Through the good, the name of the Lord is honored."[27] This is really true; the intense and fruitful pastoral ministry and, even more, the calvary of the agony and serene death of our beloved Pope showed the people of our time that Jesus Christ was truly his "all." The fruitfulness of this witness, as we know, depended on the Cross. In Karol Wojtyła's life, the word "cross" was not merely a word. From his childhood, he was familiar with suffering and death. As priest and Bishop and especially as Supreme Pontiff, he took most seriously the Risen Christ's last call to Simon Peter on the shore of the Lake of Galilee: "Follow me. . . . Follow me!" (Jn 21:19, 22). His whole life, particularly with the slow but implacable advance of the disease which gradually stripped him of everything, became an offering to Christ, a living proclamation of his passion in hope brimming with faith in the resurrection. He lived his Pontificate in the sign of "prodigality," generously spending himself without reserve. What motivated him other than mystical love for Christ, for the One who, on 16 October 1978, had him called with the ceremonial words: "*Magister adest et vocat te*"—"the Teacher is here and is calling you"?

On 2 April 2005, the Teacher called him again, this time without intermediaries, in order to take him home to the house of the Father. And once again he promptly responded with his brave heart in a whisper: "Let me go to the Lord."[28] He had been preparing for a long time for this last encounter with Jesus, as the various drafts of his Testament reveal. During the long periods he spent in his private chapel he spoke to Jesus, abandoning himself totally to his will, and entrusted himself to Mary, repeating the *Totus Tuus*.

27. St. Augustine, *In Joannis Evangelium Tractatus*, 50, 7.

28. Cf. S. Dziwisz, *Una Vita con Karol. Conversazione con Gian Franco Svidercoschi* (BUR, Rizzoli, 2011), 223.

Like his Divine Teacher, he lived his agony in prayer. On the last day of his life, on the eve of Divine Mercy Sunday, he asked that the Gospel of John be read to him. With the help of those who were nursing him, he wanted to take part in all the daily prayers and in the Liturgy of the Hours, he wanted to do adoration and meditation. He died while he was praying. He truly fell asleep in the Lord. "And the house was filled with the fragrance of the ointment" (Jn 12:3). Let us return to this most evocative annotation by the Evangelist John. The Pope's sweet scent of faith, hope, and charity filled his house, filled St. Peter's Square, filled the Church and spread throughout the world. What happened after his death was for believers an effect of that "fragrance" which reached everyone near and far and attracted them to a man whom God had gradually conformed to his Christ. For this reason, we can apply to him the words of the first Song of the Servant of the Lord which we heard in the first reading: "Behold my servant, whom I uphold, my chosen, in whom my soul delights; I have put my Spirit upon him, he will bring forth justice to the nations. . ." (Is 42:1). "Servant of God": this is what he was and this is what we in the Church call him now, while the process of his Beatification continues. This morning, the diocesan investigation into his life, virtues, and fame of sanctity was concluded. "Servant of God," a particularly appropriate title for him. The Lord called him to his service on the path of the priesthood and little by little unfolded before him ever broader horizons: from his own Diocese to the universal Church. This dimension of universality reached its apex at the moment of his death, an event the whole world lived with a participation unprecedented in history.

Dear brothers and sisters, the Responsorial Psalm has placed words full of trust on our lips. In the Communion of Saints, we seem to hear them spoken aloud by our beloved John Paul II, who, from the Father's House, we are sure of it, never ceases to accompany the Church on her way: "Wait for the Lord; be strong, and let your heart take courage; yes, wait for the Lord!" (Ps 27[26]:13–14). Yes, let your heart take courage, dear brothers and sisters, and burn with hope! With this invitation in our hearts let us continue the Eucharistic Celebration, already looking at the light of the Resurrection of Christ that will shine out in the Easter Vigil after the dramatic darkness of Good Friday. May the *Totus Tuus* of the beloved Pontiff encourage us to follow him on the path of the gift of ourselves to Christ through the intercession of Mary, and may she herself, the Virgin Mary, obtain it for us while we entrust to her motherly hands this father, brother, and friend of ours, that he may rest in God and rejoice in peace. Amen.

43. *The Splendor of Divine Mercy*

From the Homily of His Holiness Pope Benedict XVI
Mass on the Third Anniversary of the Passing of Pope John Paul II
St. Peter's Basilica, Wednesday, 2 April 2008

The date 2 April is impressed in the Church's memory as the day of the departure from this world of the Servant of God Pope John Paul II. Let us relive with emotion the hours of that Saturday evening when the news of his death was greeted by a great prayerful crowd that filled St. Peter's Square to overflowing. For several days, the Vatican Basilica and this Square were truly the heart of the world. A never-ending river of pilgrims paid homage to the body of the venerated Pontiff, and his funeral was marked by a further testimony of the esteem and affection he had won in the hearts of multitudes of believers and people who had come from every corner of the earth. Today too, as it did three years ago, 2 April falls shortly after Easter. The heart of the Church is still deeply immersed in the mystery of the Lord's Resurrection. We can truly interpret the whole life of my beloved Predecessor, particularly his Petrine ministry, in the sign of the Risen Christ. He had an extraordinary faith in him and carried on an unusual and uninterrupted conversation with him. Indeed, among his many human and supernatural qualities, he possessed exceptional spiritual and mystic sensibilities. It was enough to see him praying: he literally immersed himself in God and it seemed that in those moments everything else was foreign to him. At liturgical celebrations he was attentive to the mystery-in-action, showing an outstanding ability to grasp the eloquence of God's Word in the development of history, at the profound level of God's plan. As he often said, Holy Mass for him was the center of every day, and every day of his life. The "living and holy" reality of the Eucharist gave him the spiritual energy to guide the People of God on their journey through history.

John Paul II passed away on the eve of the Second Sunday of Easter, at the end of the "day that the Lord has made." His agony took place throughout this "day," in the new space-time which is the "eighth day," desired by the Most Holy Trinity through the work of the Incarnate Word, dead and Risen. In this spiritual dimension Pope John Paul II often demonstrated that during his life he had in a certain way already been steeped in this spiritual dimension, both earlier and especially in the fulfilment of his mission as Supreme Pontiff. His Pontificate as a whole and in a multitude of specific moments appears to us as a sign and testimony of the Resurrection of Christ. The paschal dynamism that made John Paul II's life a total response to the Lord's call could not be expressed without participation in the suffering and death of the Divine Master and Redeemer. "The saying is sure," the Apostle Paul said: "If we have died with him, we shall also live with him; if we endure, we shall also reign with him" (2 Tm 2:11–12). Since his childhood, Karol Wojtyła had experienced the truth of these words, encountering the Cross on his way, in his family and among his people. It was not long before he decided to carry it with Jesus, following in his footsteps. He wanted to be Jesus's faithful servant to the point of accepting the call to the priesthood as a lifelong gift and commitment. He lived with him and wished to die with him, all through the unique mediation of Mary Most Holy, Mother of the Church and Mother of the Redeemer, intimately and effectively associated with the saving mystery of his death and Resurrection.

In this evocative reflection, may we be guided by the biblical readings just proclaimed: "Do not be afraid" (Mt 28:5). The words we have just heard, which the Angel of the Resurrection addressed to the women by the empty tomb, had become a sort of motto that had been on Pope John Paul II's lips since the solemn beginning of his Petrine ministry. He often repeated them to the Church and to humanity on the way towards the Year 2000, and then through that historical goal and beyond, to the dawn of the third millennium. He always spoke them with unbending firmness, first brandishing his crosier crowned with a Crucifix and then, when his physical energy was ebbing away, almost clinging to it until that last Good Friday, when he took part in the Way of the Cross in his private Chapel, gripping the Cross tightly in his arms. We cannot forget his last and silent testimony of love for Jesus. That eloquent scene of human suffering and faith on that last Good Friday also showed believers and the world the secret of the entire Christian life. His "Do not be afraid" was not based on human strength or successes achieved but only on the Word of God, the Cross and the Resurrection of Christ. As John Paul II was gradually emptied of everything, at last even the ability to speak, this entrustment of himself to Christ appeared ever more clearly. As it was for Jesus, so too it was for John Paul II: in the end, words gave way to the extreme sacrifice, to the gift of self. And his death was sealed by a life entirely given to Christ and even physically conformed to him with features of suffering and trusting abandonment in the Heavenly Father's arms. "Let me go to the Father" were his last words, the fulfilment of a life completely spent in striving to know and contemplate the Face of the Lord.

Venerable and dear brothers, I thank you all for joining me at this Holy Mass of suffrage for beloved John Paul II. I address a special thought to the participants of the First World Congress on Divine Mercy, which is opening this very day and which intends to deepen his rich Magisterium on the subject. God's mercy, as he himself said, is a privileged key to the interpretation of his Pontificate. He wanted the message of God's merciful love to be made known to all and urged the faithful to witness to it.[29] This is why he desired to raise to the honor of the altars Sr. Faustina Kowalska, a humble Sister who, through a mysterious divine plan, became a prophetic

29. Cf. Pope John Paul II, *Homily at Kraków-Łagiewniki*, August 17, 2002.

messenger of Divine Mercy. The Servant of God John Paul II had known and personally experienced the terrible tragedies of the twentieth century and for a long time wondered what could stem the tide of evil. The answer could only be found in God's love. In fact, only Divine Mercy is able to impose limitations on evil; only the almighty love of God can defeat the tyranny of the wicked and the destructive power of selfishness and hate. For this reason, during his last Visit to Poland, he said on his return to the land of his birth: "Apart from the mercy of God there is no other source of hope for mankind."[30]

Let us give thanks to the Lord for having given the Church this faithful and courageous servant of his. Let us praise and bless the Blessed Virgin Mary for having watched ceaselessly over his person and ministry, for the benefit of the Christian people and all humanity. And while we offer the redeeming Sacrifice for his chosen soul, let us pray to him to continue to intercede from Heaven for each one of us, especially for me, whom Providence called to take up his priceless spiritual legacy. The Church, following his teaching and example, faithfully continues without compromise in her evangelizing mission and never ceases to spread Christ's merciful love, a source of true peace for the whole world. Amen.

30. Pope John Paul II, *Homily at Kraków-Łagiewniki.*

44. *Champion of Christ*

From the Homily of His Holiness Pope Benedict XVI
Mass on the Fourth Anniversary of the Passing of Pope John Paul II
St. Peter's Basilica, Thursday, 2 April 2009

Four years ago today, my beloved Predecessor, the Servant of God John Paul II, ended his earthly pilgrimage after a period of great suffering that lasted for some time. We are celebrating the Blessed Eucharist in suffrage for his soul, while we thank the Lord for having given him to the Church, for so many years, as a zealous and generous Pastor. We are united this evening by his memory that lives on in the hearts of the people, as is demonstrated by the uninterrupted pilgrimage of the faithful to his tomb in the Vatican Grottos. I therefore preside at this Holy Mass with emotion and joy, while I greet and thank you for your presence, venerable brothers in the Episcopate and in the Priesthood, and you, dear faithful who have come from various parts of the world, especially from Poland, for this important celebration. I would like to greet the Poles and in particular the young Poles. On the fourth anniversary of the death of John Paul II, hear his appeal: "Have no fear of entrusting yourselves to [Christ]! He will guide you, he will grant you the strength to follow him every day and in every situation."[31] I hope that this thought of the Servant of God will guide you on the paths of your life, and will lead you to the happiness of the morning of the Resurrection. I greet the Cardinal Vicar, the Cardinal Archbishop of Kraków dear Cardinal Stanisław, the other Cardinals and Prelates; I greet the priests, and the men and women religious. I greet you in a special way, young people of

31. Pope John Paul II, *Prayer Vigil at Tor Vergata*, August 19, 2000.

Rome, who with this celebration are preparing yourselves for the World Youth Day that we will experience together next Sunday, Palm Sunday. Your presence reminds me of the enthusiasm that John Paul II knew how to instill in the new generations. His memory is an incentive to all of us gathered in this Basilica, in which he celebrated the Eucharist on many occasions, to let ourselves be illuminated and called into question by the word of God that has just been proclaimed.

The Gospel on this Thursday in the fifth week of Lent proposes for our meditation the last part of chapter eight of John, which contains, as we heard, a long discussion on the identity of Jesus. A little earlier he had presented himself as "the light of the world" (Jn 8:12), using at least three times (vv. 24, 28, 58) the expression "I AM," that forcefully recalls God's name as it was revealed to Moses (cf. Ex 3:14). And he added: "If anyone keeps my word, he will never see death" (Jn 8:51), thus declaring that he had been sent by God, who is his Father, to bring men and women the radical freedom from sin and death that is indispensable for entering eternal life. However, his words wounded the pride of those with whom he was conversing and even the reference to the great Patriarch Abraham became a source of conflict. "Truly, truly, I say to you," the Lord said, "before Abraham was, I Am" (Jn 8:58). Without mincing his words, he declared his preexistence, hence his superiority as regards Abraham, provoking understandably a shocked reaction in the Jews. But Jesus cannot be silent about his identity; he knows that in the end the Father himself will account for him, glorifying him through his death and Resurrection because, precisely when he is raised on the Cross, he will be revealed as the Only Begotten Son of God (cf. Jn 8:28; Mk 15:39).

Dear friends, in meditating on this Gospel passage of John it comes naturally to me to consider how difficult it actually is to bear witness to Christ. And my thoughts turn to the beloved Servant of God Karol Wojtyła, John Paul II, who from his youth showed himself to be a daring and ardent champion of Christ: He did not hesitate to expend all his energy in order to spread Christ's light everywhere, he never stooped to compromises when it was a matter of proclaiming and defending his Truth; he never tired of radiating his love. From the beginning of his Pontificate until 2 April 2005, John Paul II was never afraid to proclaim, to everyone and always, that Jesus alone is the Savior and true Liberator of humankind and of the whole human being.

In the first reading we heard the words addressed to Abraham: "I will make you exceedingly fruitful" (Gn 17:6). If witnessing to one's adherence to the Gospel is never easy, the certainty that God makes our commitment fruitful when it is sincere and generous is certainly comforting. From this important viewpoint, too, the spiritual experience of the Servant of God John Paul II is apparent to us. In looking at his life, we see God's promise of fruitfulness to Abraham, as it were, realized and echoed in the first reading from the Book of Genesis. One might say that especially in the years of his long Pontificate, he brought forth to faith many sons and daughters. You are the visible sign of it, dear young people here this evening: you, the young people of Rome and you, young people who have come from Sydney and from Madrid, to represent in spirit the throngs of young men and women who took part in the 23rd World Youth Day in various parts of the world. How many vocations to the priesthood and to the consecrated life, how many young families determined to live the Gospel ideal and to strive for holiness are bound to the witness and preaching of my venerable Predecessor! How many teenagers converted or persevered on their Christian journey thanks to his prayers, his encouragement, his support, and his example!

It is true! John Paul II succeeded in communicating a strong charge of hope founded on faith in Jesus Christ, who "is the same yesterday and today and forever" (Heb 13:8), as the motto for the Great Jubilee of the Year 2000 declared. As an affectionate father and an attentive educator, he pointed out firm and reliable reference points, indispensable to all and especially to the young. And in the hour of his agony and his death, this new generation wished to show him that it had understood his teaching, gathering silently in prayer in St. Peter's Square and in so many other places in the world. The young people felt his death would be a loss: it was "their" Pope, whom they saw as "their father" in the faith, who had died. At the same time they were aware that, as a legacy, he had bequeathed to them his courage and the consistency of his witness. Had he not stressed many a time the need for radical adherence to the Gospel, urging adults and young people to take this common educational responsibility seriously? I too, as you know, have wished to take up his concern, pausing on various occasions to speak of the educational emergency that today concerns families, the Church, society, and especially the new generations. While they are growing up, the young need adults who can suggest principles and values to them. They feel in need of people who can teach by their example, more than by their words, to expend themselves for high ideals.

But where can one find the light and wisdom to bring to completion this mission that involves us all together, in the Church and in society? It is certainly not enough to appeal to human resources;

first of all it is also necessary to trust in divine help. "The Lord is faithful forever": as we have just prayed in the Responsorial Psalm, sure that God never abandons those who stay faithful to him. This is recalled by the theme for the 24th World Youth Day that will be celebrated at the diocesan level next Sunday. It is taken from St. Paul's First Letter to Timothy: "We have set our hope on the living God" (4:10). The Apostle speaks on behalf of the Christian community, on behalf of all who have believed in Christ and are different from "others . . . who have no hope" (1 Thes 4:13). Indeed, it is precisely because they hope, that is, they have trust in the future, a trust that is not based on human ideas or predictions but on God, the "living God."

Dear young people, it is impossible to live without hope. Experience shows that all things, even our life, are at risk; they can collapse for some internal or external reason at any moment. It is normal: all that is human, hence therefore also hope, has no basis in itself but needs a "rock" to which to be anchored. This is why Paul writes that Christians are called to base human hope on the "Living God." In him alone does it become safe and dependable. Actually, only God, who revealed the fullness of his love to us in Jesus Christ, can be our firm hope. Indeed, in him, our hope, we have been saved (cf. Rm 8:24).

However, be careful: in times like these, given the cultural and social context in which we are living, there may be a greater risk of reducing Christian hope to an ideology, to a group slogan or to outward appearances. Nothing is more contrary to Jesus's message! He does not want his disciples to "recite" a part, even that of hope. He wants them "to be" hope and they can only be hope if they remain united to him! He wishes each one of you, dear young friends, to be a small source of hope for your neighbor and, all together, to become an oasis of hope for the society in which you are integrated. Now this is possible on one condition: that you live of him and in him, through prayer and the sacraments, as I wrote in my Message this year.

If Christ's words remain in us we can spread the flame of love that he kindled on earth; we can bear aloft the torch of faith and hope with which we advance towards him while we await his glorious return at the end of time. It is the torch that Pope John Paul handed on to us. He presented it to me, as his Successor; and this evening I shall present it once again, in spirit, in a special way to you, young people of Rome, so that you may continue to be dawn watchmen, alert and joyful in this dawn of the third millennium. Respond generously to Christ's call! In particular, during the Year for Priests which will begin next 19 June, make yourselves promptly available if Jesus calls you, to follow him on the path of the priesthood or the consecrated life.

"Now is the favorable time. This is the day of salvation!" At the Gospel Acclamation the liturgy urged us to renew now—and every moment is a "favorable moment"—our decisive will to follow Christ, certain that he is our salvation. This is basically the message that John Paul II repeats to us this evening. While we entrust his elect soul to the maternal intercession of the Virgin Mary, whom he always loved tenderly, let us fervently hope that he will never cease to guide us and to intercede for us from Heaven. May he help each one of us to live, as he did, repeating day after day to God, through Mary with full trust: *Totus Tuus*. Amen.

45. *In the Lord's Footsteps*

From the Homily of His Holiness Pope Benedict XVI
Mass on the Fifth Anniversary of the passing of Pope John Paul II
St. Peter's Basilica, Thursday, 29 March 2010

We are gathered round the altar, near the tomb of the Apostle Peter, to offer the Eucharistic sacrifice in suffrage for the chosen soul of Venerable John Paul II, on the fifth anniversary of his departure. We are doing so a few days early, because this year 2 April falls on Good Friday. All the same, we are in Holy Week, a particularly favorable time for recollection and prayer, in which the Liturgy makes us relive the last days of Jesus's earthly life more intensely. I would like to express my gratitude to all of you who are taking part in this Holy Mass. I cordially greet the Cardinals, especially Archbishop Stanislaw Dziwisz, the Bishops, priests, and men and women religious; as well as the pilgrims who have come specially from Poland, the many young people and the numerous faithful who did not want to miss this Celebration.

In the first reading from the Bible that has been proclaimed, the Prophet Isaiah presents the figure of a "Servant of God" who at the same time is his chosen one, in whom he is well pleased. The Servant was to act with steadfast firmness, with an energy that was never lacking until he had completed the task assigned to him. Yet he appeared not to have at his disposal those human means that seemed indispensable for the implementation of so grandiose a plan. He was to present himself with the power of conviction, and the Spirit whom God had placed within him was to give him the ability to act with gentleness and force, assuring him of ultimate success. What the inspired prophet says of the Servant we may apply to beloved John Paul II: the Lord called him to his service and, in entrusting to him tasks of ever greater responsibility, also accompanied him with his grace and ceaseless assistance. During his long Pontificate, John Paul II did his utmost to proclaim the law with firmness, without weaknesses or indecision, especially when he had to contend with resistance, hostility, or rejection. He knew that the Lord had taken him by the hand and this enabled him to exercise a very fruitful ministry, for which, once again, we give fervent thanks to God.

The Gospel just proclaimed takes us to Bethany, where, as the Evangelist notes, Lazarus, Martha, and Mary were giving a supper for the Teacher (Jn 12:1). This banquet in the house of Jesus's three friends was marked by presentiments of his imminent death: the six days before Easter; the suggestion of Judas, the traitor; Jesus's answer that calls to mind one of the devout burial rites, anticipated by Mary; the hint that they would not always have him with them; and the attempt to put Lazarus to death that mirrors the desire to kill Jesus. In this Gospel account there is one gesture to which I would like to draw attention. Mary of Bethany "took 300 grams [a pound] of costly ointment of pure nard and anointed the feet of Jesus and wiped his feet with her hair" (12:3). Mary's gesture is the expression of great faith and love for the Lord; it is not enough for her to wash the Teacher's feet with water; she sprinkles on them a great quantity of the precious perfume which, as Judas protested, it would have been possible to sell for 300 denarii. She did not anoint his head, as was the custom, but his feet: Mary offers Jesus the most precious thing she has and with a gesture of deep devotion. Love does not calculate, does not measure, does not worry about expense, does not set up barriers, but can give joyfully; it seeks only the good of the other, surmounts meanness, pettiness, resentment, and the narrow-mindedness that human beings sometimes harbor in their hearts.

Mary stood at the feet of Jesus in a humble attitude of service, the same attitude that the Teacher himself was to assume at the Last Supper, when, the fourth Gospel tells us, he "rose from supper, laid aside his garments, and girded himself with a towel. Then he poured water into a basin, and began to wash the disciples' feet" (Jn 13:4–5), so that, he said, "you also should do as I have done to you" (v. 15): the rule of the community of Jesus is that of love which knows how to serve to the point of offering one's life. And the scent spread: "the house," the Evangelist remarks, "was filled with the fragrance of the ointment" (Jn 12:3). The meaning of Mary's action, which is a response to God's infinite Love, spreads among all the guests; no gesture of charity and authentic devotion to Christ remains a personal event or concerns solely the relationship between the individual and the Lord. Rather, it concerns the whole Body of the Church, it is contagious: it instils love, joy, and light.

"He came to his own home, and his own people received him not" (Jn 1:11). Mary's action is in contrast to the attitude and words of Judas who, under the pretext of the aid to be given to the poor, conceals the selfishness and falsehood of a person closed into himself, shackled by the greed for possession and who does not let the good fragrance of divine love envelop him. Judas calculates what one cannot calculate, he enters with a mean mindset the space which is one of love, of giving, of total dedication. And Jesus, who had remained silent until that moment, intervenes defending Mary's gesture: "Let her alone, let her keep it for the day of my burial" (Jn 12:7). Jesus understands that Mary has intuited God's love and points out that his "hour" is now approaching, the "hour" in which Love will find its supreme expression on the wood of the Cross: the Son of God gives himself so that many may have life, he descends to the abysses of death to bring man to the heights of God, who is not afraid to humble himself, to make himself "obedient, unto death, even death on a cross" (Phil 2:8). In the Sermon in which he comments on this Gospel passage, St. Augustine addresses each one of us, with insistent words, the invitation to enter this circuit of love by imitating Mary's gesture and really placing ourselves in the sequela of Christ. Augustine writes: "Whatever soul of you wishes to be truly faithful, anoint like Mary the feet of the Lord with precious ointment. . . . Anoint the feet of Jesus: follow by a good life the Lord's footsteps. Wipe them with your hair: what you have of superfluity, give to the poor, and you have wiped the feet of the Lord."[32]

Dear brothers and sisters, the entire life of Venerable John Paul II was lived under the sign of this love, this capacity to give himself generously, without reserve, without measure, without counting the cost. What motivated him was love for Christ, to whom he consecrated his life, a superabundant and unconditional love. And precisely because he drew ever closer to God in love, he could become a travelling companion for people today, sprinkling in the world the scent of God's Love. Those who had the joy of knowing him and seeing him regularly could appreciate how alive was his certainty that he would "see the goodness of the Lord in the land of the living," as we heard in the Responsorial Psalm (Ps 27[26]:13); a certainty that accompanied him throughout his life

32. St. Augustine, *In Joannis Evangelium Tractatus*, 50, 6.

and that was manifest in a special way during the last period of his pilgrimage on this earth: his increasing physical weakness did not corrode his unshakable faith, his luminous hope, his fervent charity. He let himself be consumed for Christ, for the Church, for the whole world: his was a state of suffering lived to the end for love and with love.

In his Homily for the 25th anniversary of his Pontificate, he confided that he had felt echoing in his soul, at the moment of his election, Jesus's question to Peter: "Do you love me? Do you love me more than these?" (Jn 21:15–16); and he added: "Every day that same dialogue between Jesus and Peter takes place in my heart. In spirit, I focus on the benevolent gaze of the Risen Christ. Although he knows of my human frailty, he encourages me to answer confidently, like Peter: 'Lord, you know everything; you know that I love you' (Jn 21:17). And then he invites me to take on the responsibilities that he himself has entrusted to me."[33] These words are laden with faith and love, the love of God, that conquers everything!

Lastly, I would like to greet the Poles present. Many of you have gathered round the tomb of the Venerable Servant of God with a special feeling as sons and daughters of the same country, who grew up in the same culture and spiritual tradition. The life and work of John Paul II, a great Pole, may be a cause of pride for you. However, you must remember that this is also a great call to be faithful witnesses to faith, hope, and love, as he himself continuously taught. Through the intercession of John Paul II, may the Lord's Blessing sustain you always. As we continue the

33. Pope John Paul II, *Homily of His Holiness John Paul II, XXV Anniversary of His Pontificate* (October 16, 2003).

Eucharistic Celebration, preparing to live the glorious days of the Passion, Death, and Resurrection of the Lord, let us entrust ourselves confidently after the example of Venerable John Paul II to the Blessed Virgin Mary, Mother of the Church, so that she may sustain us in our commitment to being, on every occasion, unflagging apostles of her divine Son and of his merciful Love. Amen!

46. *Do Not Be Afraid!*

From the Homily of His Holiness Pope Benedict XVI
Mass on the Occasion of the Beatification of the Servant of God
Pope John Paul II, St. Peter's Basilica, Sunday, 1 May 2011

Six years ago we gathered in this Square to celebrate the funeral of Pope John Paul II. Our grief at his loss was deep, but even greater was our sense of an immense grace which embraced Rome and the whole world: a grace which was in some way the fruit of my beloved predecessor's entire life, and especially of his witness in suffering. Even then we perceived the fragrance of his sanctity, and in any number of ways God's People showed their veneration for him. For this reason, with all due respect for the Church's canonical norms, I wanted his cause of beatification to move forward with reasonable haste. And now the longed-for day has come; it came quickly because this is what was pleasing to the Lord: John Paul II is blessed!

I would like to offer a cordial greeting to all of you who on this happy occasion have come in such great numbers to Rome from all over the world—cardinals, patriarchs of the Eastern Catholic

Churches, brother bishops and priests, official delegations, ambassadors and civil authorities, consecrated men and women, and lay faithful, and I extend that greeting to all those who join us by radio and television. Today is the Second Sunday of Easter, which Blessed John Paul II entitled Divine Mercy Sunday. The date was chosen for today's celebration because, in God's providence, my predecessor died on the vigil of this feast. Today is also the first day of May, Mary's month, and the liturgical memorial of Saint Joseph the Worker. All these elements serve to enrich our prayer; they help us in our pilgrimage through time and space; but in heaven a very different celebration is taking place among the angels and saints! Even so, God is but one, and one too is Christ the Lord, who like a bridge joins earth to heaven. At this moment we feel closer than ever, sharing as it were in the liturgy of heaven.

"Blessed are those who have not seen and yet have come to believe" (Jn 20:29). In today's Gospel, Jesus proclaims this beatitude: the beatitude of faith. For us, it is particularly striking because we are gathered to celebrate a beatification, but even more so because today the one proclaimed blessed is a Pope, a Successor of Peter, one who was called to confirm his brethren in the faith. John Paul II is blessed because of his faith, a strong, generous, and apostolic faith. We think at once of another beatitude: "Blessed are you, Simon, son of Jonah! For flesh and blood has not revealed this to you, but my Father in heaven" (Mt 16:17). What did our heavenly Father reveal to Simon? That Jesus is the Christ, the Son of the living God. Because of this faith, Simon becomes Peter, the rock on which Jesus can build his Church. The eternal beatitude of John Paul II, which today the Church rejoices to proclaim, is wholly contained in these sayings of Jesus: "Blessed are you, Simon" and "Blessed are those who have not seen and yet have come to believe!" It is the beatitude of faith, which John Paul II also received as a gift from God the Father for the building up of Christ's Church.

Our thoughts turn to yet another beatitude, one which appears in the Gospel before all others. It is the beatitude of the Virgin Mary, the Mother of the Redeemer. Mary, who had just conceived Jesus, was told by Saint Elizabeth: "Blessed is she who believed that there would be a fulfilment of what was spoken to her by the Lord" (Lk 1:45). The beatitude of faith has its model in Mary, and all of us rejoice that the beatification of John Paul II takes place on this first day of the month of Mary, beneath the maternal gaze of the one who by her faith sustained the faith of the Apostles and constantly sustains the faith of their successors, especially those called to occupy the Chair of Peter. Mary does not appear in the accounts of Christ's resurrection, yet hers is, as it were, a continual, hidden presence: she is the Mother to whom Jesus entrusted each of his disciples and the entire community. In particular, we can see how Saint John and Saint Luke record the powerful, maternal presence of Mary in the passages preceding those read in today's Gospel and first reading. In the account of Jesus's death, Mary appears at the foot of the Cross (Jn 19:25), and at the beginning of the Acts of the Apostles she is seen in the midst of the disciples gathered in prayer in the Upper Room (Acts 1:14).

Today's second reading also speaks to us of faith. Saint Peter himself, filled with spiritual enthusiasm, points out to the newly-baptized the reason for their hope and their joy. I like to think how in this passage, at the beginning of his First Letter, Peter does not use language of exhortation; instead, he states a fact. He writes: "you rejoice," and he adds: "you love him; and even though you do not see him now, you believe in him and rejoice with an indescribable and glorious joy, for you are receiving the outcome of your faith, the salvation of your souls" (1 Pet 1:6, 8–9). All these verbs are in the indicative, because a new reality has come about in Christ's resurrection, a reality to which faith opens the door. "This is the Lord's doing," says the Psalm (118:23), and "it is marvelous in our eyes," the eyes of faith.

Dear brothers and sisters, today our eyes behold, in the full spiritual light of the risen Christ, the beloved and revered figure of John Paul II. Today his name is added to the host of those whom he proclaimed saints and blessed during the almost twenty-seven years of his pontificate, thereby forcefully emphasizing the universal vocation to the heights of the Christian life, to holiness, taught by the conciliar Constitution on the Church *Lumen Gentium*. All of us, as members of the people of God—bishops, priests, deacons, laity, men and women religious—are making our pilgrim way to the heavenly homeland where the Virgin Mary has preceded us, associated as she was in a unique and perfect way to the mystery of Christ and the Church. Karol Wojtyła took part in the Second Vatican Council, first as an auxiliary Bishop and then as Archbishop of Kraków. He was fully aware that the Council's decision to devote the last chapter of its Constitution on the Church to Mary meant that the Mother of the Redeemer is held up as an image and model of holiness for every Christian and for the entire Church. This was the theological vision which Blessed John Paul II discovered as a young man and subsequently maintained and deepened throughout his life. A vision which is expressed in the scriptural image of the crucified Christ with Mary, his Mother, at his side. This icon from the Gospel of John (19:25–27) was taken up in the episcopal and later the papal coat-of-arms of Karol Wojtyła: a golden cross with the letter "M" on the lower right and the motto "*Totus Tuus,*" drawn from the well-known words of Saint Louis Marie Grignion de Montfort in which Karol Wojtyła found a guiding light for his life: "*Totus tuus ego sum et omnia mea tua sunt. Accipio te in mea omnia. Praebe mihi cor tuum, Maria*"— "I belong entirely to you, and all that I have is yours. I take you for my all. O Mary, give me your heart."[34]

In his Testament, the new Blessed wrote: "When, on 16 October 1978, the Conclave of Cardinals chose John Paul II, the Primate of Poland, Cardinal Stefan Wyszyński, said to me: 'The task of the new Pope will be to lead the Church into the Third Millennium.'" And the Pope added: "I would like once again to express my gratitude to the Holy Spirit for the great gift of the Second Vatican Council, to which, together with the whole Church—and especially with the whole episcopate—I feel indebted. I am convinced that it will long be granted to the new generations to draw from the treasures that this Council of the twentieth century has lavished upon us. As a Bishop who took part in the Council from the first to the last day, I desire to entrust this great patrimony to all who are and will be called in the future to put it into practice. For my part, I thank the Eternal Shepherd, who has enabled me to serve this very great cause in the course of all the years of my Pontificate."[35] And what is this "cause"? It is the same one that John Paul II presented during his first solemn Mass in Saint Peter's Square in the unforgettable words: "Do not be afraid! Open, open wide the doors to Christ!" What the newly-elected Pope asked of everyone, he was himself

34. St. Louis Marie Grignion de Montfort, *Treatise on True Devotion to the Blessed Virgin*, 266.

35. *Testament of the Holy Father John Paul II*, no. 4.

the first to do: society, culture, political and economic systems he opened up to Christ, turning back with the strength of a titan—a strength which came to him from God—a tide which appeared irreversible. By his witness of faith, love and apostolic courage, accompanied by great human charisma, this exemplary son of Poland helped believers throughout the world not to be afraid to be called Christian, to belong to the Church, to speak of the Gospel. In a word: he helped us not to fear the truth, because truth is the guarantee of liberty. To put it even more succinctly: he gave us the strength to believe in Christ, because Christ is *Redemptor hominis*, the Redeemer of man. This was the theme of his first encyclical, and the thread which runs through all the others.

When Karol Wojtyła ascended to the throne of Peter, he brought with him a deep understanding of the difference between Marxism and Christianity, based on their respective visions of man. This was his message: man is the way of the Church, and Christ is the way of man. With this message, which is the great legacy of the Second Vatican Council and of its "helmsman," the Servant of God Pope Paul VI, John Paul II led the People of God across the threshold of the Third Millennium, which thanks to Christ he was able to call "the threshold of hope." Throughout the long journey of preparation for the great Jubilee, he directed Christianity once again to the future, the future of God, which transcends history while nonetheless directly affecting it. He rightly reclaimed for Christianity that impulse of hope which had in some sense faltered before Marxism and the ideology of progress. He restored to Christianity its true face as a religion of hope, to be lived in history in an "Advent" spirit, in a personal and communitarian existence directed to Christ, the fullness of humanity and the fulfillment of all our longings for justice and peace.

Finally, on a more personal note, I would like to thank God for the gift of having worked for many years with Blessed Pope John Paul II. I had known him earlier and had esteemed him, but for twenty-three years, beginning in 1982 after he called me to Rome to be Prefect of the Congregation for the Doctrine of the Faith, I was at his side and came to revere him all the more. My own service was sustained by his spiritual depth and by the richness of his insights. His example of prayer continually impressed and edified me: he remained deeply united to God even amid the many demands of his ministry. Then too, there was his witness in suffering: the Lord gradually stripped him of everything, yet he remained ever a "rock," as Christ desired. His profound humility, grounded in close union with Christ, enabled him to continue to lead the Church and to give to the world a message which became all the more eloquent as his physical strength declined. In this way he lived out in an extraordinary way the vocation of every priest and bishop to become completely one with Jesus, whom he daily receives and offers in the Church.

Blessed are you, beloved Pope John Paul II, because you believed! Continue, we implore you, to sustain from heaven the faith of God's people. You often blessed us in this Square from the Apostolic Palace: Bless us, Holy Father! Amen.

ALL SAINTS

47. *We All Are Called to Holiness*

From the Homily of His Holiness Pope Benedict XVI
Solemnity of All Saints
Saint Peter's Basilica, Wednesday, 1 November 2006

Our Eucharistic celebration began with the exhortation: "Let us all rejoice in the Lord." The liturgy invites us to share in the heavenly jubilation of the Saints, to taste their joy. The Saints are not a small caste of chosen souls but an innumerable crowd to which the liturgy urges us to raise our eyes. This multitude not only includes the officially recognized Saints, but the baptized of every epoch and nation who sought to carry out the divine will faithfully and lovingly. We are unacquainted with the faces and even the names of many of them, but with the eyes of faith we see them shine in God's firmament like glorious stars.

Today, the Church is celebrating her dignity as "Mother of the Saints, an image of the Eternal City,"[1] and displays her beauty as the immaculate Bride of Christ, source and model of all holiness. She certainly does not lack contentious or even rebellious children, but it is in the Saints that she recognizes her characteristic features and precisely in them savors her deepest joy. In the first reading, the author of the Book of Revelation describes them as "a great multitude which no man could number, from every nation, from all tribes and peoples and tongues" (Rv 7:9). This people includes

1. Cf. A. Manzoni, *La Pentecoste* (1817–1822).

the Saints of the Old Testament, starting with the righteous Abel and the faithful Patriarch, Abraham, those of the New Testament, the numerous early Christian Martyrs and the Blessed and Saints of later centuries, to the witnesses of Christ in this epoch of ours. They are all brought together by the common desire to incarnate the Gospel in their lives under the impulse of the Holy Spirit, the life-giving spirit of the People of God. But "why should our praise and glorification, or even the celebration of this Solemnity, mean anything to the Saints?" A famous homily of St. Bernard for All Saints' Day begins with this question. It could equally well be asked today. And the response the Saint offers us is also timely: "The Saints," he says, "have no need of honor from us; neither does our devotion add the slightest thing to what is theirs. . . . But I tell you, when I think of them, I feel myself inflamed by a tremendous yearning."[2] This, then, is the meaning of today's Solemnity: looking at the shining example of the Saints to reawaken within us the great longing to be like them; happy to live near God, in his light, in the great family of God's friends. Being a Saint means living close to God, to live in his family. And this is the vocation of us all, vigorously reaffirmed by the Second Vatican Council and solemnly proposed today for our attention.

But how can we become holy, friends of God? We can first give a negative answer to this question: to be a Saint requires neither extraordinary actions or works nor the possession of exceptional charisms. Then comes the positive reply: it is necessary first of all to listen to Jesus and then to follow him without losing heart when faced by difficulties. "If anyone serves me," he warns us, "he

2. St. Bernard of Clairvaux, *Opera Omnia*, 5, 364ff.

must follow me; and where I am, there shall my servant be also; if anyone serves me, the Father will honor him" (Jn 12:26). Like the grain of wheat buried in the earth, those who trust him and love him sincerely accept dying to themselves. Indeed, he knows that whoever seeks to keep his life for himself loses it, and whoever gives himself, loses himself, and in this very way finds life (cf. Jn 12:24–25). The Church's experience shows that every form of holiness, even if it follows different paths, always passes through the Way of the Cross, the way of self-denial. The Saints' biographies describe men and women who, docile to the divine plan, sometimes faced unspeakable trials and suffering, persecution and martyrdom. They persevered in their commitment: "they . . . have come out of the great tribulation," one reads in Revelation, "they have washed their robes and made them white in the blood of the Lamb" (Rv 7:14). Their names are written in the book of life (cf. Rv 20:12) and Heaven is their eternal dwelling-place. The example of the Saints encourages us to follow in their same footsteps and to experience the joy of those who trust in God, for the one true cause of sorrow and unhappiness for men and women is to live far from him.

Holiness demands a constant effort, but it is possible for everyone because, rather than a human effort, it is first and foremost a gift of God, thrice Holy (cf. Is 6:3). In the second reading, the Apostle John remarks: "See what love the Father has given us, that we should be called children of God; and so we are" (1 Jn 3:1). It is God, therefore, who loved us first and made us his adoptive sons in Jesus. Everything in our lives is a gift of his love: how can we be indifferent before such a great mystery? How can we not respond to the Heavenly Father's love by living as grateful children? In Christ, he gave us the gift of his entire self and calls us to a personal and profound relationship with him. Consequently, the more we imitate Jesus and remain united to him, the more we enter into the mystery of his divine holiness. We discover that he loves us infinitely, and this prompts us in turn to love our brethren. Loving always entails an act of self-denial, "losing ourselves," and it is precisely this that makes us happy. Thus, we have come to the Gospel of this feast, the proclamation of the Beatitudes which we have just heard resound in this Basilica. Jesus says: Blessed are the poor in spirit, blessed those who mourn, the meek; blessed those who hunger and thirst for justice, the merciful; blessed the pure in heart, the peacemakers, the persecuted for the sake of justice (cf. Mt 5:3–10). In truth, the blessed par excellence is only Jesus. He is, in fact, the true poor in spirit, the one afflicted, the meek one, the one hungering and thirsting for justice, the merciful, the pure of heart, the peacemaker. He is the one persecuted for the sake of justice.

The Beatitudes show us the spiritual features of Jesus and thus express his mystery, the mystery of his death and Resurrection, of his passion and of the joy of his Resurrection. This mystery, which is the mystery of true blessedness, invites us to follow Jesus and thus to walk toward it. To the extent that we accept his proposal and set out to follow him—each one in his own circumstances—we too can participate in his blessedness. With him, the impossible becomes possible and even a camel can pass through the eye of a needle (cf. Mk 10:25); with his help, only with his help, can we become perfect as the Heavenly Father is perfect (cf. Mt 5:48).

Dear brothers and sisters, we are now entering the heart of the Eucharistic celebration that encourages and nourishes holiness. In a little while, Christ will make himself present in the most exalted way, Christ the true Vine to whom the faithful on earth and the Saints in Heaven are united like branches. Thus, the communion of the pilgrim Church in the world with the Church triumphant in glory will increase. In the Preface we will proclaim that the Saints are friends and models of life for us. Let us invoke them so that they may help us to imitate them and strive to respond generously, as they did, to the divine call. In particular, let us invoke Mary, Mother of the Lord and mirror of all holiness. May she, the All Holy, make us faithful disciples of her Son Jesus Christ! Amen.

INDEX

INDEX